STRIKES IN POLITICISATION

To Imogen

Strikes in Politicisation

JACQUELINE E. BRIGGS
University of Lincolnshire and Humberside

Ashgate

Aldershot • Brookfield USA • Singapore • Sydney

Published by
Ashgate Publishing Limited
Gower House
Croft Road
Aldershot
Hants GU11 3HR
England

Ashgate Publishing Company
Old Post Road
Brookfield
Vermont 05036
USA

British Library Cataloguing in Publication Data
Briggs, Jacqueline E.
    Strikes in politicisation
    1.Strikes and lockouts - Great Britain - Political aspects
    I.Title
    331.8'92'941

Library of Congress Cataloging-in-Publication Data
Briggs, Jacqueline E.
    Strikes in politicisation / Jacqueline E. Briggs.
        p.   cm.
    Includes bibliographical references.
    ISBN 1-85521-937-9 (hardcover)
    1. Strikes and lockout–Great Britain. 2. Political
socialization–Great Britain. 3. Coal Strike. Great Britain.
1984-1985. I. Title.
HD5365.A6B75   1997
322'.2–dc21   97-30131
                                                                        CIP

ISBN 1 85521 937 9

Printed and bound by Athenaeum Press, Ltd.,
Gateshead, Tyne & Wear.

This book is to be returned on
or before the date stamped below

Table of Contents

Acknowledgements

I would like to express my sincere thanks and deepest gratitude to my former supervisor, Dr Alex Callinicos whose advice, comments and moral support have been very valuable throughout my years of research. Many thanks to my colleagues, Dr Hugh Bochel, Dr Terence Karran and Dr Youcef Bouandel for their help and advice on conducting research.

I am particularly indebted to the Politics Department at the University of York, to the School of Policy Studies at the University of Lincolnshire and Humberside and to my former place of employment, Wakefield District College - especially for the aid and assistance given to me by the librarians at these institutions. Thanks too to Grace Godfrey for help with typing the appendices.

Special thanks undoubtedly goes to the people of Hemsworth without whom this research would not have been possible.

Last, but not least, thanks to the family and friends, who have and who do share my life, for their support and sacrifice.

Introduction

'I joined the Labour Party during the Strike and I'd never been a member before. I'm still a member'.

'Before the Strike I could take 'em or leave 'em [the police]. Now if I saw one drowning I certainly wouldn't pull him out. I hate the establishment. I hate the police, all except one [the local community constable]'.

'During the Strike, I became politicised during the Strike. I almost joined the Revolutionary Communist Party, not because I thought that they were any good but because I used to go picketing, I've never been a miner but I used to go. Some of my mates went to Orgreave. I just had a deep hatred during the Strike and I think that the Revolutionary Communist Party articulated that hatred better than anybody else' [Now a member of the local Green Party].

'Not more involved, no. More aware, you become'.

'I joined the Labour Party during the Miners' Strike'.

(Comments made by people from Hemsworth)

Most, if not all of us, to whom the label 'employee' could be applied have had to consider the possibility of engaging in strike activity at one time or another. The strike is perhaps the ultimate weapon that an employee is able to wield in an attempt to exert any influence or bargaining power *vis-a-vis* their employer. Strike activity is not a new phenomenon; indeed its history parallels the development of industrialised societies. Its usage, whilst representing a last resort, can offer the supreme sanction against the erosion of workers' rights, conditions of employment and even the loss of employment itself.

The strike is, therefore, a powerful political tool which ought to be used sparingly in order to exert maximum effect. Even a one-day strike can lead to a significant loss of pay. Clearly, a strike of any longer duration is likely to exert a substantial financial burden upon the participants. Its impact upon the employer has to be considered but so too does its likely effects upon the employee. The 'costs', not simply financial, of strike action have to be weighed against the likelihood of achieving one's aims. It may be the case that a strike is entered into only after a significant amount of deliberation and discussion has taken place. Conversely, the strikers may feel that they were given no option but to strike for their livelihood. They may feel cornered and subject to a 'Hobson's Choice' scenario of strike or lose out.

Whatever the catalyst for strike activity, one of the most interesting areas of political inquiry is the impact which the strike has upon its participants. Of no small significance is the effect, if any, which strike activity has upon the politicisation process. In particular, it is worthwhile considering whether participation in strikes has any effect upon the political ideas, attitudes and behaviour of those who take part in them. Examination of the politicisation process is complex. It is often hard to substantiate how and why people vote as they do; to explain why some people are fascinated by the political arena and why others, possibly the majority, find not the merest flicker of enthusiasm. Yet clearly there are such discrepancies in terms of interest and activism and the extent to which strikes impact upon this process is worthy of investigation.

The withdrawal of one's labour constitutes a significant political act - regardless of whether the participants recognise it as such. It may be the case, however, that the precise impact of strike activity upon the politicisation process is dependent upon other factors, such as, the duration of the strike, the amount of media coverage that a strike receives; how 'extreme' the strike activity is in terms of the extent of the confrontation between employees and employers; whether the strikers have participated in picket line duties or made a sgnificant contribution to the strike effort; the extent to which violence has played a part in the dispute, whether the striker is fully supportive of the reasoning behind the action or whether they had to be coerced into 'downing their tools'.

It is possibly true to say that one would need to exist in a political vacuum to participate in strike activity and not undergo some sort of politicisation process. The historical study of industrial relations certainly furnishes enough raw data upon which to investigate the basic hypothesis concerning the linkage between strikes and politicisation. It is worthwhile, therefore, pursuing this line further via a brief historical outline of strike action.

Strikes are not a culturally specific phenomenon. They exist and have existed in all industrialised societies. Workers in countries such as France, Germany, the United States of America, Canada, Spain, etc., have all, at some stage or another, participated in strike action. The ease with which they are prepared to resort to a withdrawal of labour may vary between nations; as may the voracity with which the workers are prepared to pursue their aims. On an international level, it is perhaps the image of the French farmers, with their propensity for direct action, that most easily springs to mind. Canadian and American car plant workers provide another classic example of industrial action.

In terms of the history of strikes, the U.K., being the first industrialised nation, has possibly the greatest experience of industrial conflict. An early example of a strike is the 1888 Matchgirls' Strike where, at one stage, 1,400 women and girls at Bryant and May's factory at Bow, East London went on strike because of low pay. The 1926 General Strike is certain to be etched in the memory of those who have researched the history of strikes and also in those octogenarians and their elders who may have actually experienced this event on a first-hand basis. The General Strike lasted from the 4th to the 12th May 1926. It included miners, transport workers, printers, engineers, builders and workers in heavy industries.

The British mining industry, the focal point of this study, has witnessed its fair share of strikes. The 1926 South Wales Lock-Out, the 1972 Strike, the 1974 Strike, the recent protests over the 1992 round of pit closures are prevalent examples. For most observers, however, the over-riding image of a strike within the mining industry has to be the impression left by the year-long 1984/5 Miners' Strike. In essence, this was said to be a qualitatively different strike to those which had preceded it in the mining industry. For this was not simply a strike about extra pay or better working conditions, it centred on the very survival of those jobs and communities themselves. Many of the participants, when questioned, felt that they were fighting for their very existence. From both an international and an historic perspective, the impact of the 1984/5 Miners' Strike should not be under-estimated. It is undoubtedly recorded as one of *the* greatest strikes of all time for a wide variety of reasons. It is certainly an event that necessitated a significant amount of in-depth investigation and analysis.

The summer of 1996 witnessed a number of political protests in the form of strike action. Rail workers, postal workers and London Underground workers are included amongst those who felt the need to engage in industrial action. The Major Government felt compelled to promise legislation that further reduces the workers' capacity to strike. A harrowing thought as far as employees are concerned but a continuing indication that strike activity still has the capacity to cause alarm bells to ring in the corridors of Westminster and Whitehall - and a clear illustration perhaps that strikes still constitute a powerful political weapon.

The central thesis

The basic contention being made in *Strikes in Politicisation* is that the strike can act as an agency of politicisation. The fact that individuals participate in strike activity, bearing in mind that there are degrees of participation, ranging from simply withdrawing one's labour to undertaking duties on the picket line, can have an effect on the politicisation process. Indeed, the central thesis of the book concerns the notion that strikes *do* affect levels of political participation, political awareness and can induce behavioural changes. It is claimed that strikes can make people much more interested in and involved in political activity. Why should this be? A number of explanations are postulated throughout the book but some of these include; increasing levels of class consciousness; more questioning/cynical approach towards media portrayal of strikes given their own knowledge and direct experiences; differing interpretations of police presence and policing of strikes, again based upon their own first-hand experience; the opportunity which a strike may provide for certain sectors of society, for example, women, to participate in politics in ways in which they may, hitherto, have believed unfeasible or simply not considered before.

The emphasis throughout the book is upon the 1984/5 Miners' Strike, given the data which this industrial conflict furnishes in terms of the politicisation process. The methodological approach taken involves the usage of qualitative research - in particular, the usage of the in-depth interview. Sixty interviews were conducted during the course of the research. The case study method is employed and the focus is upon one particular former mining community, Hemsworth in West Yorkshire. The reasons for choosing this particular constituency are explained later in the book.

It is certainly possible to cite alternative factors as potential agencies of politicisation. It may be the case, for example, that the ageing process is a 'natural' factor that affects political participation rates and interest in political activity. Certain social phenomena, such as divorce, may make people have more of an awareness of the political arena. Here, it is necessary to focus upon what is understood by the term politics and the notion of politics with both a small p and a large P is of particular relevance. The feminist slogan of the 'personal is political' is certainly applicable to the discussion. Yet, although other factors may affect politicisation levels, the basic contention of the book is the *significant* effect which strikes have upon this process. In particular, the case study of the 1984/5 Miners' Strike reveals the quite remarkable extent to which this dispute lead to altered levels of political participation, heightened political awareness and quite specific behavioural changes. The linkage between strikes and politicisation is certainly worthy of the investigation that it receives here.

The Structure of the Book

Strikes in Politicisation tries to assess the extent to which the Miners' Strike of 1984/5 had an impact upon levels of politicisation; particular reference is made to a case study of the Hemsworth area. In order to fully investigate this subject, the book is divided into eight chapters.

The first chapter involves a detailed analysis of the links between trade unions and politics. In particular, analysis is made of the way in which trade unions have affected the political process over the last hundred years or so. Specific reference is made to the links between the Labour Party and trade unions - culminating in the recent loosening of those ties and in the abolition of Clause IV from the Labour Party's Constitution.

Chapter Two concentrates upon the theoretical perspectives and maps out the literature in the area of politicisation. It moves on to an assessment of the role of miners, particularly the National Union of Mineworkers, with respect to the political scenario. Discussion centres on a brief history of the N.U.M., looking at specific examples of where the mineworkers union has undertaken political activity and the extent to which it has achieved success in its political campaigning. The sponsorship of certain Labour Members of Parliament is also examined in an attempt to assess the precise impact of miners on politics. The breakaway Union of Democratic Mineworkers is also assessed.

The focus moves on, in Chapter Three, to a more detailed assessment of the impact of the 1984/5 Miners' Strike and the effect, if any, that this event had upon the process of politicisation. The events of 1984/5 are illuminated and then the links between the events of 1984/5 and the extent of politicisation is addressed. A tri-partite definition of politicisation is utilised; namely, political participation, political awareness and behavioural changes.

Chapter Four examines the role of the police; primarily, in relation to the 1984/5 Miners' Strike and its impact upon levels of politicisation of the community at large but also in respect of the post-Strike scenario. Other 'political' disputes, for example, Wapping, anti-poll tax demonstrations, protests against the exportation of live animals, are assessed in order to ascertain the extent to which the policing of disputes affects the politicisation process.

Attention turns, in Chapter Five, to the role fulfilled by the media and the effect that this had upon levels of politicisation. The media portrayal of the 1984/5 Miners' Strike is examined in detail in order to assess whether media coverage affected the perceptions of those involved in the Strike. Analysis is made of the extent to which the media manipulated and shaped events, as opposed to merely reflecting upon the situation. Were those working within the media abiding by a specific agenda, hidden or otherwise?

In Chapter Six, the focus here is upon levels of politicisation amongst women. Specific reference is made to the impact of the 1984/5 Miners' Strike upon the women of mining communities but levels of female political involvement/non-involvement on a wider basis are also examined. Analysis is given as to why it is that women have, in the past at least, appeared to have less political interest than men.

The following chapter is composed of an in-depth case study - a detailed, qualitative, study of one particular community in the aftermath of the 1984/5 Miners' Strike. The long-term outcomes of the impact of the Strike upon levels of politicisation are highlighted. The legacy of an industrial dispute upon the political awareness/participation rates of those who were deeply involved provides a framework for discussion.

The book concludes with an analysis of the overall findings of the research into industrial disputes and levels of politicisation. The key lessons to be learnt from this detailed assessment of miners and politics are illuminated. Assessment is made of this study's wider applicability. Examination is made of events and issues that galvanise particular individuals into political activity. An attempt is made to investigate why some people are more interested in politics than others and the lessons, if any, that politicians and policy-makers may glean from this study.

Breaking new ground

The book, through a combination of theoretical and empirical research, tries to advance beyond the available literature to an understanding of the links between strike activity and the political process. Although its primary focus is on the long-term impact of the 1984/5 Miners' Strike, it discusses other industrial settings and 'political' disputes.

The book is the only attempt to date which explores the impact of industrial disputes upon the political process in a detailed fashion. It links the political socialisation process with strike activity in a refreshing and thought-provoking manner, providing an in-sight into why some people are more interested and involved in political activity in comparison with the population at large.

Strikes in Politicisation will be of interest to a wide range of people. It should make a contribution to research into the politicisation process and debate concerning the effects of industrial disputes. Amongst those with a particular interest in this text will be students and academics working within the following disciplines; Politics, Government, Industrial Relations, Media Studies, Gender Studies and Sociology. It is claimed, with some degree of certainty, that there will not be any problems with respect to reaching a wide and interested readership.

1 Trade Unions and Politics

Introduction

'I joined the Labour Party during the Strike and I'd never been a member before. I'm still a member'[1].

'Before the Strike I could take 'em or leave 'em (the police). Now if I saw one drowning I certainly wouldn't pull him out. I hate the establishment. I hate the police, all except one (the local community constable)'[2].

'During the Strike, I became politicised during the Strike. I almost joined the Revolutionary Communist Party, not because I thought they were any good but because I used to go picketing, I've never been a miner but I used to go. Some of my mates went to Orgreave. I just had a deep hatred during the Strike, and I think the Revolutionary Communist Party articulated that hatred better than anybody else' (Now a member of the local Green Party)[3].

'Not more involved, no. More aware, you become'[4].

'I joined the Labour Party during the Miners' Strike'[5].

Setting the scene

The history of strikes is virtually as long as the history of trade unionism itself. Any historical analysis of industrial protest will no doubt include reference to major events and disputes such as Luddite and Chartist activity, the first General Strike of 1842 and, possibly, various textile worker disputes in Lancashire and Northern England. With respect to the 1842 Strike, it is worth noting that, 'for a time in August 1842 [it] seemed to pose a threat not only to capital and to property but also to the very security of the State as industrial grievances and political radicalism came together to create what many historians have seen as the first general strike'[6]. The historical assessment may have a geographical focus and concentrate upon particular areas of heavy industry noted as the location for industrial unrest, for example, mill towns, mining communities, dock areas, shipyards. The 1889 dock strike (which led to the setting up of the Transport and General Workers Union) and the 1893 coal lock-out are notable flash-points and worthy of further examination by those interested in the historical dimension. Moving on to the Twentieth Century, the General Strike of 1926 is perhaps the most reknown example of strike action. The Strike began on the 3rd May 1926 and lasted nine days. There were those who feared that the 'industrial protest would become overtly political, threatening both the industrial order and the more general stability of British society'[7]. Parallels may be drawn with the 1984/5 Miners' Strike because the 1926 Strike saw the creation of a breakaway union in Nottinghamshire. Dubbed 'Spencerism', the Nottinghamshire and District Miners' Industrial Union was led by the rebel Labour M.P. George Spencer. The similarities with the Union of Democratic Mineworkers, the group that split from the National Union of Mineworkers in 1984 are obvious.

The post-1945 scenario led to a number of key industrial disputes. There were various unofficial dock strikes in the immediate aftermath of the Second World War, the 1950s and 1960s saw industrial unrest at certain car plants, notably Dagenham, Longbridge and Cowley. The 1970s are probably best remembered for the unrest instigated in response to the Heath legislation, especially the 1971 Industrial Relations Act. The latter part of the decade, now under Callaghan's Labour Government, experienced the 1978/79 'winter of discontent'. This infamous spate of strike activity witnessed disputes amongst road hauliers, refuse collectors and grave diggers, to name a few. The ensuant film footage certainly provided electoral capital for the Conservative Party which they (and their advertising agency Saatchi and Saatchi) were able to use to their advantage at the next four consecutive general elections. One notable feature of strikes in the 1980s was the decline in strikes in the private sector and increase in those in the public sector, especially amongst employees in the service industries. This period witnessed, amongst others, strikes in local government, the National Health Service and the education sector.

Clearly, the above can only hope to provide a snap-shot of the history of industrial protest. Indeed, the historical dimension is outwith the scope of this book but it is interesting, nevertheless, to be able to place contemporary political disputes within the wider chronological framework.

The issue of whether Britain is especially strike prone is addressed in the final chapter. It is appropriate to state, at this point, that there are problems with an international comparative approach. It is very difficult to be able to compare like with like. As Charlesworth *et al* state, 'Different countries vary in what they record for strikes: Some excluding "small disputes", which are classified differently in various countries; some including, some excluding "political" strikes; and taking different approaches to lay-offs of workers in associated industries to that experiencing the strike'[8]. Bearing this in mind, however, comparisons have been made. One study for the period 1963-69 'suggested that Britain came sixth or seventh of fifteen industrial nations, with Ireland, Italy, Canada, United States and Australia repeatedly appearing in a worse light, while West Germany, Japan and others had notably better records'[9].

The summer of 1996 illustrated that strike action is still regarded by many workers as a viable form of political protest. In August, Seumas Milne pointed out that 'the proportion of unions taking industrial action has doubled over the past six months compared with the same period last year, and unions report sharp increases in yes votes in strike ballots, up to 63 per cent from 51 per cent last winter'[10]. The most common reason for strike action was pay but 'the proportion over redundancies has nearly doubled to one in five, with changes to working practices and hours accounting for 29 per cent'[11]. Notably, there were strikes by postal workers, rail workers and by those employed on the London Underground. The mood was summed up by John Monks, the T.U.C. General Secretary, 'People are fed up with being taken for granted, fed up with feeling insecure and fed up with those at the top reaping rich rewards which aren't shared by the workforce'[12]. In the light of this industrial action, the Labour Party was keen to continue to distance itself from the unions. Some commentators felt that the aim was to 'make Labour more like the American Democrats to whom the unions give money but with whom they have only limited institutional influence'[13]. *The Times* asserted that 'Public sympathy with strikes has diminished hugely in the past decade or so, particularly if they inconvenience consumers. And strikers rarely gain from their actions, particularly in the long term'[14]. Likewise, the *New Statesman* stated, 'the public will move against them if they cause sustained inconvenience in pursuit of grievances that are incomprehensible to the customer and the taxpayer'[15]. The wave of strikes in 1996 illustrates that the strike remains an important political tool but the criticism that this industrial action provoked demonstrates that New Labour was correct to weaken its ties with the unions in order to attain electoral success.

The Labour Party has, traditionally, had close links with the trade unions. Indeed, any assessment of Labour Party history focuses heavily upon its ties with the trade unions[16]. These bonds have come under increasing scrutiny throughout the late 1980s and the 1990s. New Labour, in particular, has sought to distance itself from being too closely associated with them. It has been noted that 'Labour's internal polling continues to show that the unions are a deep negative in the minds of a large portion of the electorate'[17]. Tony Blair and others have shown themselves to be eager to present a firm stance against the trade unions. Blair has 'insisted he would stand firm against the unions, warning them: "I'll simply say 'No'"[18]. Likewise, David Blunkett, prior to becoming Education Secretary, asserted that 'There was not a democracy in the world that barred all strikes. But there is no place whatever for strike action in terms of government policy on admissions or inspection or the rigours of testing ... I don't think that withdrawing your labour and leaving children without a teacher assists in raising standards or raising the esteem of the teaching profession'[19].

The wave of strikes and related forms of industrial action that took place during the summer of 1996 prompted calls for a reappraisal of the relationship between the Labour Party and the trade unions. Blair's attitude towards trade unions, described as 'lukewarm'[20], is a crucial aspect of New Labour's general approach. There has been intense speculation as to how Labour will deal with the trade unions now that they are in office. The *New Statesman* asserted that 'The signs are unambiguous: it will give no favours; pull no punches; raise no wages in deference to sentiment, tradition or sympathy. A minimum wage - important to moderate the worst employment practices - will be implemented and unions will have the right to representation in workplaces where the majority wish it. Beyond that, business as usual'[21]. Blair, in particular, talks of 'fairness, not favours'[22] with respect to Labour's attitude towards the trade unions. Clearly, the Labour leadership deems it necessary to demonstrate a firm stance towards the trade unions. The perception remains that the Labour Party had to appear in control *vis-a-vis* the unions otherwise it would have lost its lead in the opinion polls and, more importantly, its potential for electoral success.

New Labour has been accompanied by New Unionism. The unions have adapted in the light of the Thatcherite legislation and, some may claim, changing public perceptions with relation to the role of trade unions. As Leadbeater states, 'If trade union leaders are to be believed, a renaissance of unionism is just over the horizon, as they deploy newly crafted corporate strategies, backed by modern marketing techniques, to launch a recruitment drive that will play to a widespread sense of work-place insecurity bred by downsizing, delayering and restructuring'[23]. John Monks, the T.U.C. General Secretary, has suggested that new unionism means that we are likely to see a sharp rise in union membership. He claims that there are '5 million "union wannabes"'[24] that the T.U.C. could tap into. These potential union members are 'more likely to be women working in small firms in the private sector'[25].

New unionism is evident at the higher echelons too. According to Hugill, 'Central to new unionism is "partnership". The new breed of trade union leader is as likely to talk of "stakeholding" as "solidarity" and old notions of class struggle have been dispatched to the dustbin'[26]. Clearly, unions have modernised and, as we approach the new millenium, they offer a wide range of facilities; recently '36 new schemes have been introduced, including discount mortgages, accountancy schemes, stress counselling and 24-hour legal help-lines. Many unions provide private health cover and cheap credit-card deals'[27]. As is implicit in the title, New Unionism appears to represent a marked departure from old-style trade unionism, 'The "brothers" of old were not only male, they were predominantly white. The dockers, famously militant in the 1950s and 1960s, actually stopped London docks for a day in support of Enoch Powell's call for repatriation of "coloured" immigrants. The new unionism is targeting ethnic minorities and is actively involved in numerous anti-racist campaigns'[28]. This is not to say that new unionism has attained all of its goals. Increasing their membership amongst younger employees is certainly a target. It is worth noting that, 'the average trade union member is 46, while the average British worker is 31' and that 'young people are more likely to work as casuals or on short-term contracts. Many face long periods of unemployment. If any group of workers needs representation it is this one'[29]. Perhaps this is what is meant by the 'McDonaldisation' of employment practices?

The importance of the strike weapon should not be overlooked. As Lenin stated, 'action by the masses, a big strike, for instance, is more important than parliamentary activity at *all* times'[30]. Hain, in his text *Political Strikes*, highlights the fact that there have always been those 'who have seen strikes as vehicles for political transformation'. He goes on to cite a trade union militant who sees the advantage of a strike as being that it 'increases the enmity between labourers and capitalists, and compels workmen to reflect and investigate the causes of their sufferings ... The fruit of such reflections would be a violent hostility against the capitalist class'[31]. This may constitute an exaggerated account of the impact of strike activity upon the participants but the research undertaken for this book reveals that we should not underestimate the impact of strikes upon the participants.

There are other opportunities available for individuals to voice their opinions other than by taking part in strike activity. As one commentator puts it, 'Everyone's doing it. There's a new spirit of protest in Britain, as well as round the world. Where in the 1980s a self-serving "Not In My Backyard" (NIMBY) attitude prevailed, increasing numbers are now questioning the whole process by which decisions are being made ... Roads, quarries, open cast coal mining, traffic congestion, water companies, incinerators, airports, shops, ports, banks, waste - you name it - are being opposed by groups of increasingly organised people'[32]. The extent of the involvement in such groups is worthy of emphasis as, 'according to MORI, one in 10 people is a member of an environmental organisation, compared to one in 25 who belongs to a political party'[33]. It appears though that there is a discrepancy of opinion as to the extent of political protest and participation that is currently taking place. Another observer cites Scargill's supporters and poll tax protesters as manifestations of protest in the eighties but believes that 'these belligerent attitudes have, by now, all but disappeared to be replaced by cynicism or affectless disgruntlement. The idea of spending Saturday protesting no longer seems attractive, and few people, young or old, are prepared to do it anymore. Instead they watch football, parent, or push the trolley around the supermarket - and they seem not much to mind, or even notice, the absence of a coherent and absorbing public culture.' The critique continues in the same vein, 'British protest has reduced itself to the scale of the local and intimate. And it is coloured green. The heroes of our time - personified by Swampy - get down in front of road-diggers on the A30 by-pass or are run down by the Brightlingsea trucks carrying calves to the slaughter. They are admired by young people because they display no interest in general ideas about society and little concern with abstractions'[34]. By way of an aside, it is perhaps worth pointing out that Swampy, aka Daniel Hooper, has become something of a sex symbol! His idealism has been described as 'the quality which makes him irresistible'. For women, he irepresents a departure from 'lads and narcissists - Chris Evans and Peter Andre - and reminded them that caring isn't uncool or effete'[35].

This book examines the links between strikes and politicisation, it constitutes **a critical analysis of the aftermath of the 1984/5 Miners' Strike.** It also involves the detailed examination of one particular community starting more than four years after the 1984/5 Miners' Strike.

A plethora of books, journals and other literature has been written about the Miners' Strike, much of which is analysed throughout the course of this book but, it is held that the concept of the politicisation of communities and the significant after-effects of the strike have not been given enough detailed investigation and have not been the subject of a great deal of debate. Since the end of the Strike, interest has to a certain extent 'tailed-off', although the 1992/3 coal dispute did place it back in the political spotlight. This research sheds more light on politicisation and any lasting impact of the Strike. The information accrued as a result of this research, using both the primary *and* secondary sources, is important because of what it reveals both about the question/concept of politicisation and also about the impact of the Miners' Strike on one specific mining community.

It is felt that the chosen topic is important because the state of the coalfields has been a crucial issue in British politics since the 1970s. Its importance was indicated when Cecil Parkinson, Secretary of State for Energy 1987-1989, unveiled the Government's plans to privatise British Coal; a privatisation which is described in Jonathan Winterton's article (*The Times Higher Education Supplement* 11.1.91) as '*Cecil Parkinson's promise of the "ultimate privatisation"*'. Parkinson notes in his book, 'Right at the Centre', that he made this claim at the 1988 Conservative Party Conference; 'Coal will be privatized. By the next parliament, we shall be ready for this, the ultimate privatization'[36]. He goes on to say, 'What was ultimate about the proposed privatization of coal was that it would mark the end of the political power of the National Union of Mineworkers and would make the coal industry what it should always have been, another important industry, no more and no less important than many others'[37]. It is worthy of emphasis, however, that although the book is important because the question of coal is important, the wider question of politicisation constitutes the crux of the debate and, therefore, the primary reason why the work is of interest to political scientists and academics in the field of Politics/Industrial Relations.

This book seeks to examine whether Hemsworth can be regarded as a microcosm of the coal community as a whole. Are the lessons to be learnt from this study of Hemsworth applicable to other communities? Other industries, perhaps? Given that Hemsworth is (was?) a typical example of a mining community, it is a valid and representative example to use. This will be illustrated in subsequent chapters.

This research topic, strikes and politicisation, can be seen as original for a number of reasons; firstly, many political observers, at least up until the October 1992 pit closure announcements, regarded the coalfields as 'old hat', almost a 'fait accompli' - they neglected the current developments, for example, privatisation, flexible working hours, etc.; secondly, the author has actually lived in the area which was subject to investigation. She is/was part of that community, not an (possibly patronising) outsider. It is worth stating, however, that care needs to be taken with this point as the author may not originally be a geographical outsider but the very nature of conducting the research and investigations means that she *is* to some extent an outsider; thirdly, the fact that the researcher is female might lend itself to a slightly different political perspective. This raises the question as to whether the sex of the interviewer will elicit a different response from the interviewees; perhaps it might also contribute to the development of a feminist research methodology? Obviously, male researchers may be feminist in their outlook and so care needs to be taken in terms of avoiding over-emphasising this point.

Politicisation

An examination of the notion of politicisation is obviously of central importance to this investigation. What exactly is meant by the term politicisation? Say, for example, that a member of this community attends a few more political meetings, or even that they begin to attend meetings, does this necessarily mean that they are politicised and, notably, politicised as a direct result of the Strike? To infer this linkage would appear to be a premature conclusion. It *may* be the case that political awareness has been heightened due to the Miners' Strike but the political scientist requires firm evidence in order to attempt to prove this and must be clear whether changes are due to the Strike or to some other variable. Chapter Two and subsequent chapters that reveal what the interviewees had to say attempt to shed light on this debate.

The task here is two-fold; firstly, an attempt must be made to define politicisation and secondly, it is necessary to be able to pin-point specific examples when that politicisation can be said to have manifested itself. It follows too, that a distinction must be made between politicisation which occurred during the Miners' Strike and politicisation/political awareness which existed prior to the Strike. It might be interesting and informative to interview a political activist but how useful is this exercise if it emerges that their political interest came about, for example, after having watched televised news reports of the Saltley depot incident of February 1972, or, less directly applicable perhaps, the Falklands conflict of 1982? Obviously, as is emphasised in Chapter Two, we can not have a re-run of the 1980s *without* the Miners' Strike to discover whether levels of politicisation would have remained the same. Unlike the physical sciences, the social sciences have difficulty in isolating observable and measurable criteria in a controlled environment. This aside, however, the evidence of the in-depth interviews reveals that a significant number of the inhabitants of Hemsworth do believe that their level of politicisation has increased. We can not simply discount both their statements and more tangible evidence such as increased levels of electoral turnout in mining constituencies after the 1984/5 Strike.

This question of politicisation is, then, more complicated than at first appears. There may be a school of thought that equates politicisation with class consciousness/class awareness but it may be fair to say, that politicisation is more than a sense of belonging to and recognising the existence of social class. For the purposes of this work, a tripartite definition of politicisation is employed which embodies the following elements; political participation, political awareness and behavioural changes. Full details and further discussion of each of these components is given in

Chapter Two. It could be said that politicisation includes a genuine interest in and/or significant degree of involvement in politics on both a macro and micro scale. That is to say on both a national and a local level, which may, for example, include personal politics (gender). Political involvement on both a national and international level is also examined. The tripartite definition of politicisation, highlighted in Chapter Two, is utilised because it is quantifiable. It is factually ascertainable. A relatively narrow definition of politicisation is necessary in order to establish a focus for the thesis and to provide a yardstick with which to determine any changes.

It is necessary to examine what the interviewees *say* has happened to them since the Strike in terms of any psychological changes and differences in terms of beliefs and attitudes. It is also important to examine factually ascertainable aspects such as increased participation in various political organisations - attendance at party/political meetings, membership of various political organisations - and behavioural changes on a personal level, such as, any alterations or modifications regarding the sexual division of labour.

As stated above, class consciousness (Chapter 8 in Penny Green's book[38] is useful here) does enter into the politicisation equation. Perhaps it could be shown that a significant proportion of the local community became aware of their own social class during the Miners' Strike in a way which hitherto had eluded them. So, was the Strike a politicising event to the extent that citizens became aware of their own positions within society and where they fit into the scheme of things? Did the Strike reinforce a 'them and us' mentality? Although, for reasons given in Chapter Two, class consciousness is not chosen as a component in *this* definition of politicisation it is, nevertheless, worthy of note. These are just some of the questions tackled in this book.

Politicisation and Hemsworth

Accepting the preliminary definition of the concept of politicisation above, an attempt can be made to assess the extent to which politicisation has occurred in Hemsworth both during and after, but definitely as a direct consequence of, the 1984/5 Miners' Strike. Many of the interviewees did profess to having experienced a great surge of political interest during the Strike. They were galvanised by their own individual experiences, by the revelations of friends and acquaintances and by the view(s) expressed via the mass media (whether or not it correlated to their own perceptions of a particular event) into taking more of an interest into what was going on around them, into having a more questioning (cynical perhaps) approach towards the events unfolding in their own backyards (literally, in one case!). Politics, for them, had become more than just a distant activity taking place in the environs of Westminster and in the television studios. For many, their only previous political experience had been the marking of a cross on a ballot paper, now they were on picket lines, running 'soup' kitchens and even, for a handful, evading the taunts of pickets as they attempted a premature return to work. Many would agree with the sentiments of Betty from Woolley, 'I've had three months up to now on the picket lines and my political education is being acquired at a gallop'[39].

A variety of commentators discussed the existence of politicisation during the 1984/5 Miners' Strike[40] but an examination of the extent to which it occurred, specifically in Hemsworth, and also its lasting impact and manifestations, is the object of this book.

Methodology

Before moving on to the main body of the book, it is worthwhile looking in greater depth at the methodology employed in order to obtain the empirical data. The methodology utilised in this study is highlighted in this first Chapter because it is pertinent to give a little detail regarding the relevance and significance of the manner in which the investigation was conducted. It is necessary to explain why this approach was taken and also what are the positive and negative aspects of the methods employed.

It was felt appropriate to use qualitative methodology as only this particular approach would reveal a detailed and full understanding of the effects of the 1984/5 Miners' Strike. Quantitative research, such as a questionnaire, could have been employed but, whilst this would have revealed raw statistical data, it would not have provided the depth and insight which the method utilised did. Having said this, an EXIT poll was carried out on the day of the Hemsworth by-election (7th November 1991). The EXIT poll involved questioning voters regarding their views on the Labour Party's choice of candidate to fight the by-election. This survey is examined in detail in Chapter Six but, suffice to say at this particular juncture, the EXIT poll provides a useful addition to the qualitative methodology employed as the main way of gathering data for this research. The EXIT poll furnishes some useful results and illustrates that the researcher, whilst preferring the qualitative stance, does not have an aversion to other methodological approaches.

As stated, sixty in-depth interviews were carried out reflecting a cross-section of the population of Hemsworth. This was a deliberate ploy in order to ensure that, as far as possible, the whole community would be represented by this research. (*A brief outline of the interviewees is given in Table 1.0.*)

TABLE 1.0:

No.	Date	Gender	Biographical Data
1	8.11.89	F	Elderly woman. Widow of a miner. Contributed to Strike effort by baking scones for soup kitchen. Sons also miners.
2	29.11.89	M	Miner, employment relocated to Selby coalfield.
3	29.11.89	F	Miner's wife. Clerical worker.
4	17.11.90	M	Political activist. Instrumental in setting up a branch of the Green Party. House-husband.
5	27.1.90	M	Former Member of Parliament.
6	18.2.90	M	Former councillor. Local doctor.
7	7.3.90	M	Councillor.
8	8.3.90	F	Miner's wife. Shopworker.
9	8.3.90	M	Former miner.
10	8.3.90	M	Former miner. Now insurance collector.
11	28.3.90	F	Active in Support Group.
12	28.3.90	F	Active in Support Group.
13	2.5.90	F	Active in Support Group.
14	9.5.90	M	Former councillor. Active in Support Group.
15	16.5.90	F	Active in Support Group.
16	17.7.90	M	Londoner, married woman from Hemsworth.

17	17.7.90	F	Active in Support Group. Met husband in London whilst collecting for miners.
18	17.7.90	M	Hemsworth resident. No personal connection with mining industry. Single. Musician.
19	17.7.90	F	Hemsworth resident. No personal connection with mining industry. Shop-keeper.
20	26.7.90	M	Former miner. Now school caretaker and also a school governor.
21	12.9.90	F	Active in Support Group. Divorcee. Works part-time.
22	19.9.90	F	Active in Support Group. Works part-time.
23	19.9.90	F	Active in Support Group. Works part-time.
24	17.10.90	F	Active in Support Group.
25	15.11.90	M	Miner.
26	15.11.90	F	Miner's wife. Works full-time.
27	21.11.90	F	Active in Support Group. Works part-time.
28	21.11.90	M	Miner.
29	28.2.91	M	Teacher.
30	28.2.91	M	Teacher.
31	28.2.91	F	Teacher.
32	28.2.91	F	Teacher.
33	28.2.91	F	Teacher.
34	22.10.91	M	Miner.
35	22.10.91	F	Miner's wife. Works full-time.
36	31.10.91	M	Former miner. Currently self-employed.
37	5.11.91	M	Student.
38	5.11.91	M	Student.
39	24.1.92	M	Hemsworth resident. No personal connection with mining industry. Joiner.
40	5.2.92	M	Former miner. Currently self-employed.

41	28.7.92	F	Miner's wife. Works full-time.
42	28.7.92	M	Miner.
43	28.7.92	M	Retired miner.
44	28.7.92	F	Retired miner's wife.
45	11.11.92	F	Full-time clerical worker.
46	18.11.92	M	Retired miner.
47	26.11.93	M	Member of Parliament.
48	3.12.93	M	O.A.P. Ex-paratrooper.
49	4.12.93	F	O.A.P. Used to do a variety of part-time jobs.
50	4.12.93	M	Unemployed former mineworker.
51	4.12.93	M	Unemployed former mineworker.
52	4.12.93	M	Unemployed former mineworker.
53	4.12.93	M	Unemployed former mineworker.
54	4.12.93	M	Unemployed former mineworker.
55	4.12.93	M	Unemployed former mineworker.
56	18.1.94	M	Miner. Union official.
57	19.1.94	M	Journalist.
58	26.1.94	M	Union official.
59	22.2.94	M	Clergyman.
60	22.8.94	M	Hemsworth resident. No personal connection with mining industry. Employed in a bakery.

The interviewees were originally selected from responses to an article in the local newspaper, the *Hemsworth and South Elmsall Express*. This then snowballed as interviewees were able to recommend colleagues and friends who might prove beneficial to the research and who would willingly agree to an interview. In addition, a number of interviewees were specifically targeted because of their occupation (such as a number of local teachers) or because of their involvement in local politics either on a casual or full-time basis. One of the pitfalls encountered by researchers undertaking a study such as this one is the problem of the self-selecting sample, this is where the 'type' of people who come forward to be interviewed in response to such tactics as the aforementioned letter in the local press tend to be very similar. This is to say that the people who respond to letters requesting interviews, on the whole, tend to be the more out-going, perhaps more articulate and opinionated members of society, therefore, their representativeness is open to question. This problem of the self-selecting sample was partly rectified by targeting potential interviewees. This means, basically, that people representing all sectors of the community were deliberately approached in an attempt to ensure that the interviewees would constitute a definite cross-section of the population.

As stated, an attempt was made to ensure that the interviewees represented a cross-section of the community. This was achieved by drawing up a check-list of the groups within the community which it is felt ought to be included in such a detailed ethnographical study. The inclusion of the following sectors of the community was deemed necessary; miners, both striking and non-striking, miners' wives, local politicians - providing representation at both national and local levels, business people, teachers, trade unionists, clergy, police, a doctor and a section who could be classified as having no familial connections with the mining industry but who, nevertheless, inhabit the community of Hemsworth. These sectors were then deliberately targeted and, as far as was possible, interviewed over the course of the four year research period.

With respect to non-striking miners, whilst a determined effort was made to interview them, this was not forthcoming. They were very difficult to identify with any degree of certainty; many of them are clearly reluctant to be identified, also there were relatively few of them who returned to work during the Strike and many of them have subsequently left the Hemsworth area. This meant that the search proved to be a fruitless task. One notable success was in terms of interviewing a woman who married a miner who returned to work before the end of the Strike. This is what she had to say on the matter; 'I met him [her husband] in the twelve months after the Strike. He went back to work. Nobody knows that. I've never told my mother but yes he went back to work towards the end of the Strike. He went back to work because he was going to kill himself. He couldn't stand it any longer. He'd no money, his father and mother had no money. His father was on strike and he was on strike. He went back to work after Christmas because he said it was the worst Christmas of his life'. When asked whether her husband suffered any intimidation, the interviewee stated, 'Yes, he did. Greatly. In fact, when I met him we went to Castleford for a drink and we were sat in this pub and this bloke came up to him and said "Scab, scab, scab" and I was looking round and thinking "Who's this?" And he [her husband] never said anything to me and I think he was totally embarrassed. We just left our drinks and walked out of the pub. I thought at first the man might have been talking to me, (I've been out with hunt saboteurs, you know). We went on to the next pub and he never said anything to me, he was really quiet. And we went back to his mum and dad's and he told me and I said "So what? The Strike's over. I'm not bothered". He said "Oh, I was really frightened about telling you". I said, "I'm not bothered. It's over and done with, the Strike. It's in the past"'. It is interesting that this interviewee reacted in this way because she claimed that during the Strike she was very much in favour of strike action. In response to a question about being able to see both sides when she was so strongly in support of the Strike herself, she stated, 'Yes, I could see both sides when I spoke to him. I can understand *why* he went back to work. He couldn't stand the pressure at all, not having any money and nothing to do'. When asked whether her husband had any regrets about going back to work, she said, 'No. He says he wished that he'd gone back earlier'. A point to note, however, was that this interviewee had still, more than seven years after the end of the Strike, not told her mother that her husband returned to work before the end of the Strike. The interviewee said, 'No. I don't know why I've never told her but, I mean, it's personal, private. We don't have many secrets in our family but I've never told my mother because I don't know how she'd react'.

The methodology employed in order to gather the information required was 'in-depth interviews'. Sixty interviews were conducted over a four-year period. The interviewees constitute a cross-section of people, 37 men and 23 women, from the small mining town of Hemsworth. These people include a former and the then current M.P. (Alec Woodall and Derek Enright, respectively), a local councillor, a doctor, teachers, clergy, the police, miners' wives and also, of course, miners, as it transpired, exclusively strikers although with differing levels of activism. An attempt was made to interview the former M.P., George Buckley, but, unfortunately, this did not materialise as he died in 1991 and had previously been too busy to be interviewed as '...on Mondays to Fridays I am in London on my Parliamentary duties to the House of Commons and on Saturdays and Sundays I have commitments in the constituency'[41].

Initially, the intention was to distribute detailed questionnaires to a wide cross-section of the people of Hemsworth, say 5,000 inhabitants, in order to analyse the extent of political literacy and level of political socialisation. It was decided that this tactic would raise a number of problems, such as the validity of the questions and the reliability of the responses received. In addition, the in-depth interviews stand on their own and do not need to be supplemented by a potentially dubious questionnaire. For reasons summarised below, qualitative methodology was deemed to be the most appropriate strategy for addressing the topic of this book and does not automatically require buttressing with quantitative research. The local newspaper, the *Hemsworth and South Elmsall Express*, was approached in order to request that people come forward. The Central Library in Doncaster was visited in order to unearth and examine data from the 84/85 Strike. An attempt was made to locate articles from 84/85 and to examine the accuracy of any predictions. The Job Centre and the D.S.S. in Hemsworth were visited in order to obtain statistics relating to re-deployment.

With respect to the in-depth interviews, each interview lasted, on average, forty five minutes and was based around a questionnaire (a copy of which is included in the appendices). Interviews usually took place in the interviewee's own home unless it was more appropriate and accessible to see them at their place of work. For example, the teachers were interviewed during school hours at their relevant educational establishment. All the interviews were tape-recorded onto a dictation machine and then transcribed at a later stage. Additional questions were included in the interviews, as current events have necessitated, (during the course of the collation of the primary investigative material), for example, the allegations relating to the National Union of Mineworkers' finances as revealed in the *Daily Mirror* and on the *Cook Report*[42] in March 1990, as well as the 1991 Hemsworth by-election and the row over candidate selection.

In addition to the inclusion of extra questions, the actual conduct of the interviews themselves was adapted and changed during the information-gathering period. Most notably the duration of the interviews was trimmed from the mammoth three and a half hours of the initial interview to the more sensible and manageable half an hour to an hour length of subsequent interviews. This is indicative both of the developing confidence of the interviewer and of a growing realisation that quantity does not necessarily equate with quality! The skills of the competent interviewer were, hopefully, learnt and expanded upon during the course of the interviews being conducted.

The Questionnaire

It is worthwhile discussing the questionnaire at this particular point as this gives an insight into why particular questions were included and it is relevant at this stage given that it is appropriate to discuss the methodological approach taken. The questionnaire (Appendix Three) begins with what are termed 'personal' questions. This is to enable a biography of the interviewees to be built up and to ensure that a cross-section of the community is encountered. The intention was to locate people from all sectors of the community and not just those who were directly involved in the Strike. The next two questions ask 'How clearly do you remember the Miners' Strike?' and 'Do you think the experience changed you in anyway?'. Whilst these are obviously important questions, they are, nevertheless, introduced at an early stage to get the interviewee 'talking', to enable them to relax and gain confidence both in themselves and in the interviewer. At this stage it is imperative that they feel able to trust the interviewer.

The questions were, for greater ease and to facilitate a smooth progression of the interview, grouped together into a number of sections. The headings were as follows; politics, community, the police, during the Strike, looking back, the government. Obviously, because the interviews are conducted over a period of time - approximately four years - further questions become appropriate with the passage of time. For example, as stated earlier, further questions regarding the allegations of financial irregularities against Arthur Scargill, the leader of the National Union of Mineworkers and questions concerning the 1991 Hemsworth by-election were necessary. It might also have been worthwhile to ask for their views on certain political issues such as privatisation, the sale of council houses, unemployment, inflation, patriotism. It was for this reason that Greenberg's book 'Workplace Democracy. The Political Effects of Participation'[43], was examined in order to gain more of an insight into politics in a way which is perhaps more measurable. A further question to add could have been whether the Strike had an impact on gender relationships i.e. did it 'enter the house'? Judy Wajcman's book 'Women in Control'[44], about a group of women who set up and ran an all-female co-operative in the early 1970s, was helpful here. It may be that the answers to these questions would have emerged without any prompting but, obviously, by including them in the questionnaire from the outset it avoided any omissions. Consequently, questions relating to the above issues (allegations of financial irregularities against the leader of the National Union of Mineworkers, about the 1991 Hemsworth by-election and concerning the issue of gender relationships) were added. It was decided, however, that questions relating to specific issues such as privatisation and unemployment, interesting though they may be, would not add significantly to the overall thesis.

When it was felt necessary, questions were included which targeted specific individuals. The person who set up a branch of the Green Party in Hemsworth, for example, was asked a series of questions related to the connection between Hemsworth and environmental politics. Likewise, when a number of teachers were interviewed the questions were specifically geared towards the link between the Strike and the educational establishment.

With regards to the actual wording of the questions care was taken to ensure that the language used was accessible to the interviewees. It goes without saying that jargon and using polysyllabic words simply for the sake of it has to be avoided if an honest and thorough response is to be elicited. Leading questions need to be avoided too. The question regarding the Government's privatisation plans, for instance, prompted a positive response from virtually all those interviewed and for that reason it is felt that it was not as probing and as discriminating as perhaps it could have been.

The politics section of the questionnaire followed the questions about mining in general as it was thought appropriate to get the interviewees on familiar ground and begin with what they expected to be discussing. It was anticipated that it would be unwise to use unlocated questions about politics, that these might turn people off and make them suspicious of the motives of the interviewer. It is important to get people talking, to establish trust, it makes them feel easy - *before* the more 'abstract' issues get discussed. This whole question of trust-building is obviously an important one - the question of whether or not to tape the interviews was closely allied to this.

Retrospective Evidence

An added problem which this research had to surmount was the issue of retrospective evidence; that is to say, events which occurred more than a decade ago are referred to and interviewees are asked to delve into the annals of time and rely upon, often, incomplete memories and this obviously entails the researcher questioning the reliability of the information and evidence unearthed. It is difficult, sometimes, to recall one's movements, feelings and aspirations of, say, a month ago and yet here interviewees are asked to remember just that from almost ten years previously. It would detract too greatly from this research, however, if retrospective evidence was to be regarded as an insurmountable problem. The events relating to and emanating from the Miners' Strike of 1984/5 are of such significance that it is hardly surprising that, for many of those, both directly and indirectly, involved, they have remained in focus in their mind's eye with a sharpness and clarity which is remarkable given the time which has elapsed. Indeed, it could also be argued that the delay between the end of the Strike and when the research was carried out does have positive elements. This is to say that a more coherent and reflective stance might be taken by some of the interviewees with the benefit of hindsight. The cliched standpoint has it that time is 'a great healer' and this may, to a certain extent, contain a grain of truth in that those involved in the events of 1984/5 may, on reflection, have mellowed with time or may have modified many of the ideas and opinions which they originally held. This was one of the ideas behind embarking upon the research in the first instance. Had the research been undertaken immediately after the Strike had ended then feelings would have obviously still been running high and this may have led to a distortion of the results. The use of retrospective evidence, therefore, can have both positive and negative aspects. One problem with this research is the fact that these events occurred a relatively long time ago. We are dealing with an event, monumental and influential as it was, but which, nevertheless, occurred more than ten years ago now. Any researcher dealing with historical events has to face the problem of retrospective evidence. How reliable is the evidence if much of it is based upon the human memory with all that its fallibility entails?

This problem of retrospective evidence can be partly solved by reference to any evidence which may exist regarding the views and actions of the people of Hemsworth during the Strike - newspaper articles (all the copies of the local newspapers from during the Strike were examined), television programmes, videos, pamphlets, personal letters, letters to the newspapers, etc. One resident of Hemsworth kept a particularly detailed diary and this was of great help in enabling a detailed picture of the Strike and of Hemsworth to be built up. (For example, (9th February 1985) 'The Strike is still with us causing a lot of worry and unhappiness. The girls and men at the Alpha still cook the dinner and this week there is the promise of a food voucher which will help the families along...'. (17th May 1985) 'So much was lost in the 12 months' Strike. Even now after working three months there are people who don't know which way to turn. Everything is just so expensive'.) There is such a wealth of detailed information in this diary that it would benefit from publication as a separate entity. It is fair to say that, although the Strike did take place ten years ago, there is enough surviving primary investigative material to ensure that it is not merely confined to the annals of history and that the spirit can be resurrected by use of the range of aforementioned sources.

Analysis of Data

In terms of the analysis of the interview data, the transcribed responses were examined with a view to ascertaining whether the interviewees could, in fact, be said to have become politicised. The tripartite definition of politicisation, referred to earlier in this Chapter and examined in detail in Chapter Two, was used as the yardstick to determine the extent to which politicisation had occurred. Additionally, an assessment was made as to whether this politicisation, if it had taken place, was as a direct result of the 1984/5 Miners' Strike. A detailed scrutiny of the transcripts took place in an attempt to assess the extent to which the interviewees claimed to have been politicised. This assessment involved focusing upon specific responses, such as those grouped around the role of the police or those which referred to the women of mining communities. In addition to recording specific and detailed comments made by the interviewees, a relatively simplistic attempt was made (given that the focus is on qualitative methodology) to produce statistical data from the comments put forward by the interviewees. The results obtained from this exercise are included in the relevant chapters. The analysis of the data unearthed a number of very interesting and thought-provoking results. These are highlighted throughout the course of this study but, suffice to say, in particular, the impact upon the women and the roles played by both the police and the media throughout the 1984/5 dispute led to some very interesting findings regarding the nature of the politicisation process.

The research process in general

An assessment of the research process in general concludes that there are obviously both advantages and disadvantages involved in focusing upon the use of qualitative methodology. These benefits and pitfalls have already been highlighted but it is worthwhile making a brief summary of the main points to note. Qualitative research, research which is not based upon precise measurement and quantitative claims, has many strong and influential arguments in its favour. Qualitative research has the potential to produce data which is rich and unique. It is capable of bringing people's experiences to the fore, making visible that which may have been neglected or simply overlooked. It enables us to attempt to understand the meaning of certain experiences, an understanding which may be missed by the use of other methodological approaches. Reducing data to raw statistics may lead to the eternal problem illuminated by the old adage 'Lies, damned lies and statistics'. Statistical data has the potential to be interpreted in a myriad of different ways. This is one problem which the qualitative approach may be able to overcome. It gives a fuller picture than does a simple reliance upon raw statistics.

On the other hand, qualitative methodology does not offer a universal panacea. It suffers from a number of shortfalls. Firstly, it lacks precision and it is often difficult to make comparisons on the basis of qualitative data. It is, by its very nature, not easily quantifiable. It, by necessity, tends to be based upon small-scale research and this, inevitably, leads to a questioning as to its wider applicability. Can universal or simply more general conclusions be drawn on the basis of qualitative methodology? In addition, qualitative methodology may require significant amounts of time in order to decode it. This inevitably leads to it being criticised as time-consuming and expensive and to it having a tendency to rely on a relatively small sample size. Can generalisations be made from such small numbers?

In terms of assessing the overall research process, it is necessary to refer again to the problem of retrospective evidence and also to the issue of the self-selecting sample. Both these factors have been discussed at length throughout the course of this first chapter but, again, any assessment of the whole research process cannot choose to ignore these thorny problems. They have to be taken into account as issues which need addressing even if the only option is to do little more than simply flag them up as a potential weakness. Attempts can be made to circumnavigate both of these obstacles but the success of these measures is a matter of contentious debate.

Thus, an attempt has been made to assess the research process. There are both positive and negative aspects associated with the methodology employed throughout the course of this book but, on the whole, the positive factors prevail and hence provide the reasoning and justification for the approach taken.

The central thesis

To reiterate then, the basic contention embodied in this thesis is the notion that the 1984/5 Miners' Strike was a great politicising event. The work claims that the Strike made a significant number of people more interested and more active in politics. As clarified in Chapter Two, politics is interpreted in both a narrow and a wider sense. The thesis employs a case study approach. This is in order to ascertain what lessons can be learnt via a detailed examination of one particular mining community. The use of qualitative methodology is felt to be the most appropriate way of shedding light upon the actual contention that the Strike was a great politicising event.

Structure of the book

The community examined here is Hemsworth, in West Yorkshire; the book attempts to ascertain whether the people of Hemsworth were 'politicised' as a direct result of the Miners' Strike. A number of factors are central to this work. After giving a detailed descriptive and historical account of the community of Hemsworth, it is necessary to concentrate upon; firstly, the mining industry in general; secondly, the mining industry and Hemsworth; thirdly, the Miners' Strike in general terms; fourthly, the Miners' Strike and Hemsworth; fifthly, the concept of politicisation; sixthly, the politicisation of Hemsworth; and finally to marry the two major themes, - were the people of Hemsworth politicised and, if so, were they politicised as a direct result of the Miners' Strike or as a result of other factors? It is necessary to establish whether there is a causal relationship between the Miners' Strike and politicisation. The book examines the community of Hemsworth, including details of its historical background, socio-economic structure, numbers employed in the mining industry and a brief resume of the Strike and Hemsworth. The following Chapters will then examine: the question of politicisation; secondly, the background to the Strike and a profile of Hemsworth; the role of the police and the women, respectively; the politics of Hemsworth; and finally, the concluding chapter will draw all strands of argument together and summarise the evidence to see whether the Miners' Strike was a great 'politicising' event.

It is also necessary, in examining the basic theme of this research (politicisation), to get at the *processes* of change - how and why did any changes occur? With this in mind, it would be useful to look at evidence regarding specific events and issues, such as; the ballot debate, the Nottinghamshire Miners, the police behaviour, Orgreave, the media, etc.

Thus the scene is set with respect to this book and the approach taken. The relevance of the work as an important area for investigation, the nature of the subject matter and the basic 'theme' of the work are outlined. The methodological approach taken is explained and justified. It is necessary at this stage to move on to an examination of the basic theory behind this research which obviously entails an examination of what exactly is meant by the concept of politicisation. This is dealt with in Chapter Two.

Notes

---

[1] Quote from a striking miner. Interviewee number 17.

[2] Quote from a striking miner. Interviewee number 10.

[3] Quote from a picket. Interviewee number 4.

[4] Quote from an activist who became involved with the miners in their dispute. Interviewee number 17.

[5] Woman relative of striking miners. Interviewee number 22.

[6] Charlesworth, A. *et al.* (1996) *An Atlas of Industrial Protest in Britain: 1750-1990*, (Basingstoke: Macmillan), p. 51.

[7] Ibid., p. 123.

[8] Ibid., p. 179.

[9] Ibid.

[10] Milne, S. 'Rise in Strikes Forecast', *The Guardian*, 30th August 1996.

[11] Ibid.

[12] Ibid.

[13] 'Love of Labour Lost', editorial *The Times*, 12th September 1996.

[14] Ibid.

[15] *New Statesman*, 'Labour's one-trick pony', editorial, 13th September 1996, p. 5.

[16] See, for example, Pelling, H. (1965) *Origins of the Labour Party*, second edition, (Oxford: Oxford University Press).

[17] *New Statesman*, 'It's time we all grew up', editorial, 6th September 1996, p. 5.

[18] Carvel, J. 'Labour warns off teachers', *The Guardian*, 1st April 1997.

[19] Ibid. David Blunkett in a speech to a press conference at the National Union of Teachers' Conference in Harrogate, March 1997.

[20] Hugill, B. 'Brothers in law strike back', *Observer*, 4th August 1996.

[21] *New Statesman*, 'Mr Blair and the unions', editorial, 26th July 1996, p. 5.

[22] Lloyd, J. 'With one bound ...', *New Statesman*, 9th August 1996, p. 14.

[23] Leadbeater, C. 'The hole in the heart of Britain's economy', *New Statesman*, 1997 Trade Union Guide, p. 3.

[24] Halsall, M. 'Monks aims at 5m "union wannabes"', *The Guardian*, 10th September 1996, p. 8.

[25] Ibid.

[26] Hugill, B. *Op. Cit.*

[27] Ibid.

[28] Ibid.

[29] Gallagher, J. 'Workers United? Not us', *New Statesman*, 30th August 1996, p. 30.

[30] Lenin, V. I. (1969) *Party Work in the Masses*, (Moscow: Progress Publishers), p. 99.

[31] Hain, P. (1986) *Political Strikes*, (Harmondsworth: Penguin), p. 16.

[32] Vidal, J. 'DIY Democracy', in 'One Thousand Days', supplement in *The Guardian*, 5th April 1997, p. 13.

[33] Wheale, S. 'Action, Lights', in 'One Thousand Days', supplement in *The Guardian*, 5th April 1997, p. 14.

[34] Fraser, N. 'Manon, the force', in 'The Week' section, *The Guardian*, 5th April 1997, p. 1.

[35] Raven, C. 'New lads out, new man Swampy in', *The Guardian*, G2, 22nd April 1997, p. 5.

[36] Parkinson, C. (1992) *Right at the Centre*, (London: Weidenfeld), p. 208.

[37] Ibid., p. 208.

[38] Green, P. (1990) *The Enemy Without. 'Policing and Class Consciousness in the miners' strike'*, (Milton Keynes: Open University Press).

[39] North Yorkshire Women Against Pit Closures, (1985) *Strike 84-85*, (Leeds: North Yorkshire Women Against Pit Closures), p. 56.

[40] See, for example, Goodman, G. (1985) *The Miners' Strike*, (London: Pluto).

[41] Letter from G.J. Buckley, M.P., dated 8th March 1990.

[42] The *Cook Report* was shown on I.T.V. on Monday 5th March 1990.

[43] Greenberg, E.S. (1986) *Workplace Democracy. The Political Effects of Participation*, (New York: Cornell University Press).

[44] Wajcman, J. (1983) *Women in Control*, (Milton Keynes: Oxford University Press).

2   Miners and Politics

Having set the parameters for this book in Chapter One and before outlining the mining community in question, it is now necessary at this particular juncture to focus upon the ideas/concepts that lie at the centre of the debate. Although the emphasis of this work is centred around a detailed examination of one particular mining community, the key concern is the extent to which politicisation occurred within the people of that community. The notion of politicisation and whether the 1984/5 Miners' Strike was a great politicising event is, therefore, the central concern of this study.

What is politics?

Before focusing explicitly upon the concept of politicisation, it is necessary to take a step backwards and begin by briefly outlining what is meant by politics. It is fair to say that there exists both a narrow and a broad definition of politics [see Adrian Leftwich's 'What is Politics?' for a detailed summary[1]]. The narrow definition of politics refers to activity with respect to the state, to 'Politics and institutions', as Schwarzmantel states, 'politics deals with relations of power and that it is fundamentally concerned with one central political institution, the state'[2]. The second definition refers to politics and conflict and this relates more to political awareness as it is a much broader definition. Under this second definition, wherever you have a dispute or conflict then politics comes into play, over the allocation of scarce resources, over whether, for example, more money should be spent upon defence or upon welfare. There may also be moral and religious disagreements, for example, over the issue of abortion. Disagreements may take place between groups in society, such as social class, race and gender divisions. Politics, therefore, involves disagreements and reconciliation of disagreements. The conflict which takes place may be about goals or it may concern methods of achieving those goals.

Under this second, much wider, definition, politics can be seen as encompassing all human activity. As Crick and Crick state, 'The activity of politics arises from the basic human problem of diversity'[3]. Madgwick highlights the 'necessity of political activity: we simply cannot manage without it. Politics is about society's conflicts and disagreements, and it is hardly imaginable that these should not exist'[4]. Using this broader definition, the personal becomes political. This includes, therefore, sexual politics, for example, the sexual division of labour. Millett, in her text, 'Sexual Politics', illuminates this much broader definition when she speaks of politics as being about power relationships, sexual 'power relationships'[5].

Millett sheds further light upon this debate when she asks the question, 'Can the relationship between the sexes be viewed in a political light at all?'[6]. She continues, 'The answer depends on how one defines politics'[7]. She 'does not define the political as that relatively narrow and exclusive world of meetings, chairmen and parties. The term "politics" shall refer to power-structured relationships, arrangements whereby one group of persons is controlled by another'[8]. Obviously, Millett feels that it is pertinent to focus upon the broad definition of politics. Likewise, Siltanen and Stanworth argue that 'the private woman-public man conception misleads as to the relationship of the political to both private and public, and that it fosters misunderstanding of the character and genesis of the political potential of both women and men'[9]. They continue, 'The private world - the world of personal relations and marriage, of friendships and family, of domestic routine and child-care - is, as feminists have persuasively demonstrated time and again, political as well as personal'[10].

Another political scientist who has emphasised this broader definition of politics is Schwarzmantel. He states that, 'Politics exists in any context where there is a structure of power and struggle for power in an attempt to gain or maintain leadership positions. In this sense one can speak about the politics of trade unions or about "university politics". One can discuss "sexual politics", meaning the domination of men over women or the attempt to alter this relation. At the present time there is much controversy about race politics with reference to the power, or lack of it, of people of different colour or race in various countries'[11]. This goes far beyond his earlier account of politics relating to 'state' activity.

The narrow definition of politics could be referred to as Party Politics or politics with a capital 'P', whereas the broader definition expands 'politics' to include activities on a number of different levels. Sexual politics and worker/employer relations, as illustrated, can be included within this definition. It is evident that many more people are likely to be seen as having been politicised as a result of the 1984/5 Miners' Strike if the broader category is used than if the focus is purely upon those who entered the party political arena. In addition, it can be argued that the first definition excludes significant sectors of the population, for example, as this research seeks to show, women. It is worth stating that the gender dimension became very important to this research, the extent to which it did so being one of the unanticipated outcomes of this work. That is to say, at the outset it was appreciated that gender was likely to be an important factor but exactly *how* important was a surprising revelation.

Politicisation

Having outlined various approaches to the question of what is politics, this begs the next question, therefore, of what exactly is meant by politicisation? There are obviously a myriad of ways in which this concept can be interpreted. Five basic components can be identified: political participation, political awareness, behavioural changes, political knowledge and class consciousness. However, in order to be precise and focused and to produce an empirically measurable definition, for the purposes of *this* book a tripartite notion was adopted which embodies political participation, political awareness and behavioural changes. This was utilised because these aspects are manageable, measurable and, to a certain extent, they subsume the others. Before examining each criterion in turn it is necessary to state that, as far as this text is concerned, all three elements are necessary in order to be able to state categorically that politicisation has occurred but, nevertheless, there are varying degrees of politicisation and it may be the case that only one, or perhaps two, of the criteria have been realised. It is possible to have one element without the others (although they are more likely to occur in concert) but this is an issue to which we will return at a later stage. As Gavin Williams states, 'Nobody is totally politicised and nobody is totally apoliticised'[12] and obviously, therefore, there are inherent difficulties in trying to come up with a measure of politicisation. Perhaps the best that can be hoped for is to be able to produce a continuum of politicisation?

A fuller discussion of the *process* of politicisation is given later on in this Chapter but prior to this discussion, it is necessary to expand upon the various components which, it may be said, constitute politicisation.

Political participation

One of the major aspects of politicisation is, of course, political participation. It is worthwhile clarifying at this particular stage that participation is not solely concerned with participation in *party* politics. It is broader than that; it is not simply concerned with formal aspects of politics such as, voting, campaigning at election time or joining a political party. It includes, therefore, activities such as, involvement in pressure groups, going on protest marches and demonstrations or joining suppport networks and informal groups like those set up during the Miners' Strike.

Numerous political scientists and political sociologists in particular have examined the intriguing question of why some people participate in politics whereas others do not. Rush[13] has identified a number of pertinent issues which are crucial to this debate. He highlights the fact that there are problems involved in trying to define political activity and also that there are problems in trying to explain *why* individuals get involved in politics. He emphasises that there are a number of factors which influence whether or not individuals get involved in politics. These include knowledge, values, attitudes, experience and personality.

Political participation is linked to the notion of democracy. The extent to which citizens participate in the political process is the major indicator of the extent to which democracy prevails. The two 'types' of democracy are direct and indirect (or representative democracy). Direct democracy flourished mainly in ancient Greece, though even in Athens women and slaves could not vote! With respect to direct democracy, however, Parry *et al.* believe that new technology has the potential to allow 'a 'voting machine' to be installed in every home', a futuristic occurrence they term 'this brave new democratic world'[14]. This aside, the usual form of participation constitutes indirect democracy given that, for the mass of the populace, involvement often terminates after they have cast their vote in periodic elections (if indeed they choose to do this)[15]. Low levels of participation were highlighted by Almond and Verba[16], who discovered that 81 per cent of Britons were not even passive members of a political group (apart from a political party) and although they published in 1963, many of their findings appear to be still applicable today.

Other pertinent issues surrounding political participation include discussion of what purpose participation is meant to serve. Why should anyone want to participate? One theory states that people participate in order to protect their own interests, be that property or other resources. This is borne out by the increase (if instances cited in the media are indicative) in the numbers of the so-called NIMBY's, the 'Not In My Backyard' brigade, who campaign and participate only when it is an issue which directly concerns them.

Examination of the population as a whole reveals that even though levels of participation are low, recent decades have witnessed some degree of increase. Another potential explanation of increased levels of participation is the growth of youth culture[17]. The emergence and expanding numbers of teenagers, fuelled in the 1960s by the 'coming of age' of the baby-boomers led to substantial numbers of young people who, motivated by a social and political conscience, protested and participated in political activity against or in support of a wide range of issues. These included campaigns against the Vietnam War, protests over nuclear armament and marches to draw attention to the issue of sexual equality. An era when there was a feeling in the air that ordinary citizens could change the status quo and tackle the establishment. Increasing numbers of students entering higher education also played a part in this phenomenon. It is necessary to consider whether a youth culture is, as the name implies, a transient stage to be attributed to the folly of youth perhaps, something which you 'grow out of' or whether it lasts into middle and later life. What has happened to the sixties radicals? Are young people today just as willing to participate and get involved in political activity? Certainly, the youth culture thesis has much to offer and appears, in part at least, to explain increasing levels of participation.

It has been argued that a great deal of participatory activity tends to be reactive in that pressure groups, for example, are often formed to oppose some aspect of government activity (such as opposition to the siting of the then proposed third London airport) rather than striving to obtain something which they do not already possess. Parry *et al.* believe that under indirect or representative democracy, the citizens are '"controllers" rather than "participants"'[18]. Although perhaps even this is debatable given the extensive room for manoeuvre that many political actors have once in office and the difficulties, some would say impossibility, involved in attempting to remove an incumbent politician from elected office. Is it the case that participants always get what they want and that any decisions taken are 'better' decisions? It might seem reasonable to claim that the more people that are consulted before a particular decision is taken by those in positions of power, the greater the likelihood that the course of action chosen will be a true reflection of the 'wishes of the people'. A further issue revolves around whether or not participants are simply articulate minorities and, therefore, unrepresentative of the population at large? Surely, too, one cannot be sure that the 'most worthy' causes will have the most articulate advocates.

It is worthwhile contemplating whether there are more intrinsic values attached to participation. What about self-fulfilment or some kind of internal satisfaction? Again, Parry *et al.* have alluded to this aspect. They highlight the 'self-development or political education'[19] which may derive from participation. This is where participation is regarded as more than simply a means to an end (with the end being 'better' decisions emerging). It is regarded as an end in itself. Using this interpretation it does not matter so much if you do not achieve your goals as, merely by having participated, an individual will benefit. Higgins and Richardson cite John Stuart Mill's 'preference for being a human being dissatisfied rather than a pig satisfied'[20]. Surely, however, this point about the self-fulfilling, life enhancing nature of participation depends upon how society regards participation as a *value*? It is necessary for participation *per se* to be held in high esteem.

Pateman's work on the politicising role of participative democracy is worthy of mention at this particular juncture[21]. Pateman's study constitutes a critique of revisionism. She believes that the revisionists have turned democratic theory on its head and that the revisionists' view of democracy is really elite rule. Pateman puts forward a convincing case for the retention of a participatory theory of democracy and tries to bring together two themes; these themes are a sense of personal efficacy which draws upon the work of Rousseau, John Stuart Mill and G.D.H. Cole and also an emphasis upon workplace democracy. Together these constitute her theory of participatory democracy. It is worthwhile having a look at Pateman's work in a little depth in order to shed further light upon the process of politicisation.

Pateman is critical of contemporary theory. As she states; 'in the contemporary theory of democracy it is the participation of the minority elite that is crucial and the non-participation of the apathetic, ordinary man lacking in the feeling of political efficacy, that is regarded as the main bulwark against instability'[22]. Pateman believes that this is a misconception and that real benefits are to be gained through having a fully participatory society. She is of the opinion that 'the evidence supports the arguments of Rousseau, Mill and Cole that we do learn to participate by participating and that feelings of political efficacy are more likely to be developed in a participatory environment'[23]. She is keen to emphasise the links between democratic participation and individual characteristics, 'the experience of participation itself will develop and foster the "democratic" personality, i.e. qualities needed for the successful operation of the democratic system'[24]. She believes that there are psychological traits which can be cultivated through having a participatory society. She explains that 'socialisation, or "social training", for democracy must take place in other spheres in order that the necessary individual attitudes and psychological qualities can be developed. This development takes place through the process of participation itself. The major function of participation in the theory of participatory democracy is therefore an educative one, educative in the very widest sense, including both the psychological aspect and the gaining of practice in democratic skills and procedures'[25]. Pateman dismisses the notion that a participatory society would lead to a loss of political stability, 'there is no special problem about the stability of a participatory system; it is self-sustaining through the educative impact of the participatory process. Participation develops and fosters the very qualities necessary for it; the more individuals participate the better able they become to do so. Subsidiary hypotheses about participation are that it has an integrative effect and that it aids the acceptance of collective decisions'[26].

Pateman employs a wide definition of the term 'political' and thus does not confine her theory to the national or local government spheres. She regards industry as a most important area in which participation should be increased and where benefits will accrue. She believes that greater participation in industry is crucial. Building upon Cole's work regarding self-government in the workshop and his emphasis upon Guild Socialism, Pateman's belief is that 'individuals and their institutions cannot be considered in isolation from one another'[27]. Participation in areas such as industry, higher education and local government would, according to Pateman, 'enable the individual better to appreciate the connection between the public and private spheres'[28]. She thus puts forward a powerful critique of the revisionists' arguments and offers her thesis relating to the participatory theory of democracy and the benefits to be gained through a participatory society. The main justification for her theory 'rests primarily on the human results that accrue from the participatory process'[29]. As she says, 'One might characterise the participatory model as one where maximum input (participation) is required and where output includes not just policies (decisions) but also the development of the social and political capacities of each individual, so that there is "feedback" from output to input'[30].

Having presented Pateman's case and highlighted the positive aspects of participation, it is worthwhile considering the arguments against greater political participation. It is beneficial to look at why it might not be regarded as a good idea. One argument could be that democracy can, to a certain extent, be a painful process. That is to say that, the more that the 'people' are consulted, the longer it takes. Also greater consultation is likely to mean increased costs. In addition, it might be argued that a relatively acquiescent population leads to greater political stability. Surely, too, it is necessary to distinguish between participation and influence? What is the point of participation if nothing is achieved? In terms of the policy making process, perhaps it is also important *when* participation takes place. That is to say it might be easier to effect change at certain stages in the procedure rather than at others, for example, at policy germination stage rather than at policy implementation stage[31]. Another, possibly negative, aspect is the difference of opinion of those in positions of power compared with the population at large. An oft cited example concerns capital punishment, where opinion polls have consistently indicated that public opinion favours its reintroduction whereas Members of Parliament continue to vote against it. Does it matter that elite opinion appears to be 'out of sync' with the views of those they are elected to serve? One possible scenario is that greater political participation will lead to the articulation of extremist views.

If initial difficulties regarding the concept of politicisation are placed to one side for the moment, it seems reasonable to claim that the five basic components (political participation, political awareness, behavioural changes, political knowledge and class consciousness) may be used to constitute politicisation. Political participation is reasonably easy to define, that is to say an increase in terms of joining a political party or attending political meetings for example. Political awareness simply means becoming more conscious of what is happening around us in terms of political life. The third aspect, behavioural changes, not surprisingly, could be interpreted in terms of a change in behaviour, that is to say that an individual has been so affected by political 'happenings', that this may have resulted in them changing their lifestyle because of what they have witnessed or participated in. So, behavioural changes may involve change in lifestyle but it *is* worth emphasising that some behavioural changes do not concern formal politics. Many of the changes which are identified throughout the course of this book, such as, movement towards shared domestic responsibilities, do not concern the formal political arena but, nevertheless, they are still classified as behavioural changes. Re-emphasis upon the notion that the 'personal is political' adds to and clarifies the debate at this particular stage.

Obviously, it has already been stated that the first criterion involves increased activity so how is this to be distinguished from the third element? The main point to note here is that the third aspect involves a *qualitatively* different form of behaviour. Political knowledge means becoming more factually aware. A distinction must be made between the second and the fourth dimensions. As stated, political knowledge refers to the acquisition of facts and it is likely to occur as a side-effect of political awareness. Political awareness and political knowledge are most likely to be found together. Politicisation could also be interpreted as a dawning awareness of class consciousness. The following section examines these five components separately and explains why, as stated above, this research concentrates on three of these elements.

What is politicisation? Towards a working definition

Firstly, **political participation**. This is perhaps one of the most straightforward of the five factors to test because it is more factually ascertainable. Political participation and political knowledge are both factually ascertainable but is difficult to say which criterion is the easier to quantify. Voting, standing for office, trade union activity, membership of a political party, attendance at party meetings, school governorships and activism in general. These are all, as Parry, Moyser and Day clearly show, more or less, relatively easy to measure. Apart from more overtly ascertainable aspects like, for example, voting in a general election, Parry et al believe that what they term the 'less episodic forms of participation'[32], such as complaining to the council, can also be assesssed. This research examines the extent to which participation levels in a number of areas increased or decreased after the 1984/5 Miners' Strike and whether any change can be attributed to the Strike or if other factors provide the root cause. Change should not automatically be attributed to the Strike itself. For example, a branch of the Green Party was set up in Hemsworth. On analysis it appears, however, that this was basically a continuation of a national trend in the growth of the Green Party and not something specific to the community of Hemsworth. The local branch of the Green Party was set up in August 1989 after the Party had achieved 15% of the national vote in the June 1989 Elections to the European Parliament. Was Hemsworth just riding along on the crest of the electoral wave? [It is interesting to note that the Green Party did not provide a candidate in the 1991 Hemsworth by-election. Was this a result of financial expediency or does it indicate something more significant?]

The second aspect is **political awareness**. This involves an understanding of what is happening in the world around us in terms of politics (at both a national and local level). Thackrah prefers to call this concept political perception. As he says, 'First, there is the **perception** of what is done to us by government and external forces, that is force, authority and order. Second, there are the perceptions of our human identity, i.e. what we think we are, what is done to us and what should not be done to us. These concern rights, individuality, freedom and welfare. Last there are perceptions of different kinds of relationships, between "them" and "us" or between "order" and "individuality" or government and the governed, i.e. concern with justice, representation and influence'[33]. In one sense, political awareness involves change at a deeper level than that of acquiring knowledge of political facts. It embodies a different outlook or approach to 'life' in general, for example, an understanding that politics pervades our everyday existence, a recognition that politics is omnipresent. Political awareness involves a dawning realisation that events and experiences *are* political. The implication is that this is a perception which you may not have had before. Thackrah's definition, whilst shedding some light upon political awareness, is not entirely appropriate because it does place slightly too much emphasis upon the formal political arena and activity. For the purposes of this research, political awareness involves a sort of gut reaction and appreciation of political 'life'. It may also involve a perception of what we as individuals can do - be that through formal political activity or through such action as strikes. Political awareness means understanding that issues are 'political' even though you may not necessarily be more politically knowledgeable. It can also be argued that there is a direct causal link between behavioural changes and political awareness, that is to say that political awareness may lead to behavioural changes. This investigation seeks to discover the level of political awareness which exists in the community of Hemsworth in the post-Strike scenario. Have the inhabitants of Hemsworth become more politically aware as a result of the Strike?

The third factor involved in this assessment of politicisation is **behavioural changes**. This implies that those involved in the Miners' Strike may have undergone an experience which led to their behaviour being, either permanently or temporarily, altered[34]. These changes relate to actions both inside and outside of the domestic environment. Many people may be politicised not in terms of formal political participation but in terms of changing their lives in other ways - for example, a number of miners' wives, as is highlighted in Chapter Six, did decide to go to university as a result of their experiences during the Miners' Strike.

Looking at behavioural changes will, therefore, enable an assessment to be made of the extent to which change took place regarding the sexual division of labour. As with some of the other dimensions of politicisation there may be a degree of overlap. For example, behavioural change may coincide with an increase in political participation. Thus, behavioural change requires a change in attitudes but it must also be accompanied by positive action (no matter how small that action might be). This is what distinguishes behavioural changes from the second dimension of politicisation, political awareness. By way of example, if a miner switched from reading the *Sun* to reading the *Guardian*, as a result of the Strike, that is regarded as behavioural change. Likewise, if a miner began to participate more in household chores and shared in tasks previously performed solely by their wife/partner then that too is deemed to be behavioural change. In terms of behavioural change then, it might not involve formal political activity but it does involve changes that are caused by a growing political awareness.

Political knowledge is the fourth aspect. One way of testing it would be to commission a sort of general knowledge test on quite a wide scale. This constitutes a fairly ambitious task but it would not be impossible to administer. The difficulty is in knowing, firstly, which questions are appropriate and why and, secondly, how to assess the levels of political knowledge prior to the Strike. Once again, the problems of retrospective evidence surface. This concept needs to be distinguished clearly from political awareness - because, as the name, political knowledge, implies, it is centred around the acquisition of political facts. In fact, it might have perhaps been better to discuss political knowledge first as this is, in one sense, the 'lowest' level of politicisation. An individual may become more knowledgeable about political facts and issues but it does not necessarily follow that they will become more politically aware. Certainly, on a national scale, political literacy, or rather the lack of it, is an issue which deserves to be addressed (one only has to examine the Hansard Society's investigation into the political awareness of school-leavers[35], which was published in 1977 and where, for example, 44 per cent of those questioned thought that the I.R.A. was a Protestant organisation, to appreciate that this important topic cannot and should not be ignored). For the purposes of this research, political knowledge is not really excluded from the definition of politicisation offered here, but it is not really part of the operationalisation of the concept and also it is, to a certain extent, subsumed by the concept of political awareness.

To reiterate, the reasoning behind the exclusion of political knowledge from the definition of politicisation is that, on a basic level, the depth of political knowledge may be factually ascertainable but what does this prove? (Although, even here, there may be problems relating to how does one actually conduct a feasible survey of political knowledge, can it be measured?) Placing these practical limitations aside, the attainment of a relatively high score in terms of political knowledge does not necessarily mean that you are politically aware. An individual may have a good memory and be able to recite 'political' facts verbatim but it is no indicator as to their level of political awareness and understanding. Political knowledge is not 'strong enough' as a concept to merit inclusion in the overall definition of politicisation. It can be seen, therefore, that the inclusion of political knowledge is unnecessary and does not add to the overall concept which this book aims to analyse, namely politicisation.

In some respects, possibly the most contentious area is **class consciousness**. This is a very difficult element to examine[36] and, therefore, whilst noting its role as a component of this debate and illustrating an awareness of its existence, it is largely ignored as far as this book is concerned as much of the discussion around class consciousness *per se* falls outwith the remit of this study. This work necessarily focuses upon a relatively narrow definition of politicisation that is manageable, measurable and which, to a certain extent, subsumes the other concepts. To do otherwise would be to dilute the significance of this book and open up a whole 'can of worms' which would constitute an unnecessary distraction from the crux of the debate. Class consciousness involves controversial theoretical issues as to how we define class. In addition, there are also empirical problems involved in the class consciousness debate. How, for example, could one assess levels of class consciousness pre-Strike? The definition of politicisation employed here is, therefore, whilst not simple, much more straightforward than one involving class consciousness. Having said this, the two concepts, politicisation and class consciousness, are not mutually exclusive and, therefore, a great deal of the literature on working class consciousness is relevant to this debate. It is worth noting that there is overlap between political awareness and class consciousness in that, at a very basic level, class consciousness requires a perception of belonging to a particular group or social class and, clearly, this links in with political awareness.

Emphasising and studying the community in terms of three facets of politicisation does not mean that the study has less theoretical value and intellectual weight than if all five components are used, merely that it enables many of the pitfalls and problematic conceptual obstacles inherent in any detailed discussion of class consciousness and political knowledge to be successfully negotiated or at least by-passed. The definition of politicisation used here is more straightforward and less complicated ensuring that the focus is placed upon the community as a whole and not just upon the miners themselves. There is obviously a relationship and a shared extension between politicisation and class consciousness, factors which may reveal class consciousness are also indices of politicisation so the links are definitely there. The fact remains, however, that politicisation, in view of the fact that the parameters of the debate and the terms of reference have been set throughout this book, begs fewer questions.

Class consciousness enters the debate later on in this chapter when reference is made to those who have written on the thorny topic of social class but, suffice to say at this point, that class consciousness can, justifiably, be excluded because this book constitutes, in part, a community study and is not just an investigation into the mining industry. It does not seek to prove that everyone in Hemsworth constitutes part of the working class. Hemsworth was primarily a mining community but, nevertheless, it does contain people from all walks of life. Its inhabitants represent a variety of social strata and are employed in a myriad of different occupations.

Additional factors

There are a whole host of debates concerning the concept of politicisation. Part of the debate surrounding politicisation entails contemplating what makes people interested in politics and, consequently, why are some people more interested in politics than others. Coxall and Robins highlight the fact that there are a number of factors which predispose some people to be more interested in politics than others. As they state, 'The most influential agencies are the family, education, peer groups, the mass media and important political events or experiences': They go on to say that 'every individual stands in the middle of a network of social influences'[37]. Obviously, as Coxall and Robins suggest, there are a whole host of influences which affect people's political views and their political behaviour but this book expounds the view that certain 'political events and experiences' can have an important influence upon the politicisation process. There are a number of examples of 'events' which may have had a positive or negative influence upon political opinions and behaviour; such as World War Two, the 1978/9 'Winter of Discontent', the 'Falklands Factor', the rise and fall of the Social Democratic Party[38], the poll tax. Likewise, the 1984/5 Miners' Strike can be seen to have had a significant effect upon the attitudes and behaviour of the inhabitants of mining communities.

Having defined the various components of politicisation, it is essential, at this stage, to give a fuller discussion of the *process* of politicisation. It is vital that an attempt is made to establish what links, if any, exist between the three dimensions of politicisation. It is necessary to assess their relative importance. Can they, for example, be ranked? In addition, an examination needs to be made as to whether there is some continuum between them.

The focus is upon the three dimensions, political participation, political awareness and behavioural changes, as already set out in this Chapter. Having given a detailed definition of each of these components, it is fair to say that an attempt can be made to place them in some kind of rank order. As far as this book is concerned, behavioural changes constitute the most important aspect of the equation. In terms of rank order, behavioural changes would head the list, closely followed by political awareness and then political participation. The reasoning behind this assertion is that behavioural changes encompass a change in behaviour or lifestyle which, as stated earlier, is 'qualitatively different' from one's previous existence. Its very definition implies that a change has taken place. Attendance at party political meetings is factually ascertainable but it does not tell you anything about the state of mind of that particular activist. It does not tell you, for example, the reasoning behind their attendance. They may have ulterior motives for attending political meetings. By way of example, it is often said that many members of the Conservative Party join the organisation in order to enhance their social life as opposed to being deeply commited to the goals and aspirations of the Party. The coffee mornings and jumble sales may provide the so-called 'blue-rinse brigade' with more of an incentive for activism than any expose of the basic tenets of conservatism could ever hope to achieve. A cynic might argue that behavioural changes could, likewise, be instigated by ulterior motives. It could be the case that a miner begins to take on more of the household chores because he regards it as a way of keeping in favour with his spouse and not necessarily due to a belief in the basic equality of the sexes. But in this case behavioural change as defined here has not occurred because the miner helping in the home is not accompanied by that, all important, change in attitude. It is fair to say that this example might, on the surface, seem like behavioural change because positive action has occurred but it is imperative that attitudinal change is also present. In a sense, it is all about combining a change in activity with 'thinking differently'.

With political awareness, an appreciation of political life in general and a realisation that events *are* political does not necessarily mean that an individual is then galvanised into doing anything about that political awareness. Political awareness, if the task of attempting to rank the three components is continued, should be placed above political participation in the hierarchy because it does, at least, require an individual to be more conscious of what is happening around them in political terms. The process of reasoning is, at least, beginning to take place in this dimension. It is, however, ranked lower than behavioural changes because it does not necessarily mean than any action is taken as a result of a growing awareness nor does it necessarily imply a change in attitude. An individual may, for example, be made aware of the existence of racism but it does not necessarily transpire that they are then moved to drop their own bigoted beliefs.

So, in terms of this rank order, behavioural changes is placed at the top. Political awareness is ranked second and political participation follows in third place. What if one of these components exists without the other two?

Can politicisation be deemed to have occurred? It could be argued that it depends on the combination and that behavioural change (which implies awareness) is, to some extent, enough. For the purposes of this book, however, the tripartite definition is employed precisely because it permits a greater degree of accuracy regarding our assessment of whether or not politicisation has taken place. It is more detailed and, hence, as stated, more accurate. Having said this, it is fair to claim that there are degrees of politicisation and one possibility is to produce a continuum of politicisation. If political participation is the only component which has occurred that is, nevertheless, a change. It perhaps means that an individual has, metaphorically speaking, boarded the bus towards politicisation even if they have not necessarily arrived at the final destination.

Politicisation and the Miners' Strike

This book seeks to establish that there is a direct causal relationship between the 1984/5 Miners' Strike and the extent to which politicisation occurred in mining communities (using the case study of Hemsworth by way of example). Basically, the hypothesis is that politicisation was at one level before the Strike and that it reached another, much higher, level after the Strike. At issue is also the strength of any change which has occurred. The hypothesis goes on to claim that the increase in politicisation levels can be directly attributed to the events which took place during the 1984/5 Strike itself, i.e. *that the Strike was a great politicising event.* Bearing in mind that it is impossible to eliminate all the alternative arguments, both theoretical and practical/empirical, it is necessary that they are at least highlighted as alternative explanations and theories. We may wish to look at why alternative explanations of politicisation do not apply in this instance. As stated earlier, this obviously involves an examination of why people are interested in politics but it also necessitates discounting theories which claim that other factors supersede the 'Miners' Strike' argument. What other factors could be put forward as politicising events or issues? It could be the case, for example, that a political scientist might claim that factors such as age, levels of education, incidence of divorce, exposure to political information via the media, etc. are important politicising factors and that it was one or a combination of these criteria which produced the increased levels of politicisation after the 1984/5 Miners' Strike and that the Strike itself had no part to play in the procedure, that is to say, that it was merely coincidental that the post-Strike scenario witnessed increased politicisation. Obviously, as stated, it is impossible to eliminate all the alternative arguments on theoretical grounds, the main requirement is to ensure that they are at least 'flagged up', recognised and taken into account.

Apathy

A further debate concerns whether or not apathy is, in fact, a political act. The distinction between positive and negative abstention is clearly important here. If the focus is purely upon voting behaviour then positive abstention is, for example, where all the alternatives are examined and the voter does not like what is on offer so they make a conscious decision not to bother to vote. Negative abstention includes the voter simply not being bothered to vote or being deterred by the fact that it rains on polling day. Michael Rush has examined this notion of lack of political involvement. He states that 'Non-involvement in politics has been variously ascribed to apathy, cynicism, alienation and anomie'. He proceeds to further distinguish between these categories, 'apathy is a lack of interest, cynicism is an attitude of distaste and disenchantment, while alienation and anomie both involve a feeling of estrangement or divorce from society, but where alienation is characterised by hostility, anomie is characterised by bewilderment'[39]. It could be suggested that a certain degree of apathy is an essential ingredient of any realistic theory of democracy. Sir Ian Gilmour is quoted as saying that 'Political apathy is to some extent rather a good sign. It means that people aren't all that worried; they are reasonably contented'[40]. With respect to the 1984/5 Miners' Strike, an attempt can be made to ascertain whether the inhabitants of mining communities became disillusioned and whether this manifested itself in higher levels of non-participation. This issue will be tackled in greater depth when an analysis is made of the findings of this study. It could be the case, for example, that the Strike was a demotivating and de-politicising force and that it actually led to some of the inhabitants of the community under investigation turning away from formal political activity and behaviour, i.e. perhaps they became disillusioned.

Voting Behaviour

It is pertinent to examine different types of political participation. Psephological inquiry is relevant at this point. Voting could be described as the minimum form of political participation but, for most people, it is also the maximum. Figures relating to electoral turnout provide interesting, possibly dismal, reading. In addition, questions such as why does the working class tend to vote Labour and what accounts for working class Conservatism are also relevant to the debate surrounding the concept of politicisation.

The study of voting behaviour constitutes a very interesting area of political science. Political scientists differ, however, in terms of their explanations as to why people vote the way that they do. There are many different theories and models about voting behaviour. Some studies concentrate upon the social backgrounds of individual electors, others concentrate upon party identification (attachment to a specific political party) and the third most often cited model stems from rational choice theory[41]. These models and their intrinsic components change over time, for example, religion is less important nowadays as a determinant than it perhaps was at one stage. Psephology can never be an exact science, especially considering the secret ballot but, nevertheless, we can make a number of assumptions regarding the factors which influence the way that people vote. Despite class dealignment[42], social class is held by many political scientists to be a major, if not the major, factor which influences the way that people vote. The impact of class may have declined since Peter Pulzer's now infamous claim that 'Class is the basis of British party politics: all else is embellishment and detail'[43] but the importance of social class as a determining factor should not be ignored[44].

It is generally held that there are both objective and subjective factors which can be utilised in order to pigeon-hole electors into specific social classes. Objective factors include the socio-economic characteristics such as occupation, wealth, etc. and the subjective aspect is the way that the voter regards him/herself. There may be contradictions here too, for example, objectively, a voter might be termed working class but, subjectively, they may think that they are middle class and vote accordingly. This is used, in part, to explain working class Conservatism - although deference is also proposed as a theory to explain why a certain proportion of the working class votes Conservative, i.e. they regard the Conservatives as the 'natural party of government', the born leaders. It is worth noting that there is only a contradiction if you expect people who are 'objectively' working class to behave politically in a certain way, i.e. to vote Labour.

There is evidence that deference is declining in importance[45] and that 'secular' or pragmatic explanations have become more important.

A third explanation, therefore, proposes that members of the working class vote Conservative for secular reasons, i.e. on the basis of specific policies, they are attracted to the Conservative Party. The sale of council houses, which the Conservatives first offered to the electorate in 1979 and which was enacted under the 1980 Housing Act, is claimed to be a case in point. It is worth emphasising that without substantial working class support the Conservatives would never have won any election this century[46]. Middle class Labourism is partly explained by reference to working class origins, sticking to their 'roots', and by the fact that these deviants tend to work in what are deemed to be caring professions, such as health workers or teachers[47].

Apart from social class, other factors have been postulated in an attempt to explain voting behaviour. These factors include, for example, age, gender, ethnicity, region, trade union membership, family[48]. These cleavages are said to have an effect upon the way that people vote. It is unnecessary to go into a great deal of detail regarding the various aspects but it is worthwhile noting that psephologists differ as to how much weight they attach to these criteria.

The 1980s and 1990s have witnessed a great deal of partisan dealignment. That is to say, there has been a weakening of voters' loyalty to specific parties and a subsequent increase in electoral volatility. Voters are more willing to change the way that they vote rather than to provide consistent support for a political party irrespective of the particular policies which that party embodies. There is also evidence that secular voting is on the increase. Voters are voting for parties which they feel will best serve their interests. It is generally held that electors 'shop around' more. There is also the view that sectoral cleavages are more important than class alignment - the public/private sector cleavage being the main one. The theory behind this notion of consumption cleavages is that the voter's choice is influenced by their pattern of consumption. The idea being that those who use private health care are more likely to vote Conservative and those who, for example, use state schools are more likely to vote Labour. Dunleavy and Husbands emphasised sectoral cleavages as an influence upon voting behaviour. They noted that the postwar period has witnessed 'the increasing importance of sectoral cleavages'[49] and that this has had a marked effect upon voting behaviour.

The analysis of voting behaviour may, superficially, appear to be an easy task. One can point to the existence of quantifiable data, statistics, etc. As evidenced above, however, psephological inquiry constitutes a very contentious area of investigation and political scientists differ as to the importance they attach to the various explanations. Indeed, the truth may be akin to the insight offered by Sanders that 'Many activists, on both sides of the party political divide have long been convinced of what they regard as a simple truth of electoral politics: that the incumbent government stands an extremely good chance of getting re-elected if enough people believe that "I'm alright, Jack"'[50].

Other forms of political participation include pressure group activity and a wide variety of campaigns which involve collective action. The extent of involvement varies, as Dowse and Hughes state, 'people participate in politics in many different ways, with different degrees of emotional involvement and at different levels of the system'[51]. Nevertheless, involvement in pressure groups is, relatively speaking, a major way in which people participate in politics. Trade union activity, as examples of protective pressure groups, provide opportunities for involvement but, setting aside sporadic strike action, levels of participation, on a day to day basis, are usually low.

Much of the discussion has, so far, concentrated upon political participation. This is, to a certain extent, dictated by the available literature but also because it is slightly easier to measure than the two other elements, namely political awareness and behavioural change. These two components were broached earlier but it is necessary to examine them in greater depth.

Political awareness or political perception, as Thackrah notes, refers to a kind of political awakening or dawning consciousness. This obviously applies to both sexes but there is a growing body of literature which specifically relates this to changes which have occurred in women. Tolleson Rhinehart, in her text on 'Gender Consciousness and Politics', recalls that she has 'spoken not merely of political participation but of political *engagement* to indicate the spectrum of politicization, from internal feelings of confidence and interest, the connection to the political system and the commitment to acquire political information, to the performance of actual participatory acts'[52]. This continuum is relevant to the discussion and clearly highlights that political awareness should not be ignored.

As far as behavioural changes are concerned, again much of the previous literature regarding political participation is pertinent. In addition, a major change concerns focusing on the political aspects of the private domain, the home and familial life for example, as well as the public domain, in order to ascertain whether behaviour has altered. This is particularly important for our purposes in the light of the post-Strike scenario. Sociological studies, such as those which attempt to define and analyse the concept of the 'New Man'[53], are appropriate here.

Related works

As stated earlier, although not concentrating upon class consciousness some of the literature relating to class imagery is, nevertheless, relevant to this debate because it involves studies of working class communities. Lockwood's work[54] is particularly relevant because of his characterisation of the traditional proletarian with miners. Miners are regarded as the ultimate example in terms of knowing where their industrial and political interests lie. Lockwood distinguishes between various working class images of society. He believes that the working class possess a variety of different perceptions of society. The three models which he identifies are; firstly, a power or dichotomous model of society; secondly, a status or hierarchical model; and thirdly, a 'pecuniary' model. The power model is where there is a perception of there being two classes in a relationship of opposition. The status model involves a belief that society is composed of different strata or levels and, in its simplest format, there are higher, lower and equal strata. The pecuniary model focuses primarily upon the cash nexus. Class divisions are mainly perceived in terms of income difference and difference in terms of material possessions. In this vein, work is regarded merely as a means to an end.

Lockwood believes that traditional proletarians exist in industries 'which tend to concentrate workers together in solidary communities and to isolate them from the influences of the wider society'. They experience a 'high degree of job involvement and strong attachments to primary work groups that possess a considerable autonomy from technical and supervisory constraints'[55]. It can clearly be seen from Lockwood's description of the traditional proletarian how miners fit into this model; 'The isolated and endogamous nature of the community, its predominantly one-class population, and low rates of geographical and social mobility all tend to make it an inward-looking society and to accentuate the sense of cohesion that springs from shared work experiences'. He goes on to highlight the 'awareness of "us" in contradistinction to "them"'[56]. Again, the evidence unearthed during the course of the research for this book indicates that this notion of a 'them' and 'us' mentality definitely exists in mining communities and was a point which was made on numerous occasions during the course of the interviewing process.

In his study, Lockwood proceeds to highlight the way in which work contacts carry over into leisure-time pursuits. Again, this is an important aspect of mining communities. Work colleagues also tend to be drinking partners and leisure-time companions. Rees, too, has alluded to this aspect of mining communities; 'miners are conceptualised as an essentially homogeneous social grouping, whose characteristic experience of dangerous and unpleasant work underground is reinforced by communal forms of social activity in geographically isolated "mining communities"'. He continues 'These shared conditions of production and social reproduction, in turn, combine to provide the structural basis for highly solidary forms of social relations, which are expressed in the peculiarly "macho" and intense forms of industrial and political militancy which are characteristic of the coalfields and in which the miners' union plays a central role'[57].

Lockwood identifies at least three different types of worker. It is evident that the miner fits into the '"proletarian" variety whose image of society will take the form of a power model'[58]. Their view of society is most probably 'a dichotomous or two-valued power model' whereby there are 'two classes standing in a relationship of opposition'. Lockwood maintains that 'the social divisions of the workplace, the feeling of being subject to a distant and incomprehensible authority, and the inconsiderable chances of escaping from manual wage-earning employment' all contribute to the fact that miners hold this belief. This belief is said to be strongest amongst those who have an 'awareness of forming a quite separate community'. It is also strongest amongst those who 'have a high degree of job involvement and strong ties with their fellow workers'[59]. So, these are all factors which contribute to the belief in a dichotomous class ideology, a belief held by many of those who live and work in mining communities.

Lockwood believes that the traditional proletarians, such as miners, have 'horizons of expectations' which 'do not extend much beyond the boundaries of the communities in which they live'. He sees this as being mainly due to their 'social isolation and social stability'. As Lockwood states; 'Workers in such environments are as unlikely to change their patterns of consumption as they are their political loyalties, because in both cases they are encapsulated in social systems which provide them with few alternative conceptions of what is possible, desirable and legitimate'[60]. The evidence unearthed by this research certainly accords with Lockwood's description of the traditional proletarian community.

Lockwood believes that because of the traditional proletarian's 'membership of the work gang and his participation in the system of communal sociability' this leads to their 'conception of a "class-divided" society'. They see "strata" or "classes" as active social formations and not merely as amorphous aggregates of individuals' and they have a strong sense of 'group affiliation'[61]. The evidence unearthed during the course of the research for this book certainly supports the view that miners and many of those who live in mining communities do have a notion of a 'class-divided' society. The class consciousness of the traditional proletarian is, as Lockwood states, acquired via 'his involvement in solidary work groups and communal sociability'[62].

Class is a concept which has been examined in detail by a number of political scientists and sociologists. Bulmer, Parkin, Mann, Gallie and Scase[63], amongst others, have all added to the debate about class imagery. Bulmer emphasises the 'complexity of the inter-relationships between objective class situation and perceptions of that situation'[64]. Bulmer makes a distinction between 'the study of images of society and of stratification, and the study of political and industrial class consciousness'[65]. They are related but they are not the same. Bulmer's work has implications for this book as he focuses upon class imagery as opposed to class consciousness because 'class consciousness ... presupposes its articulation in a coherent ideological form'. Whereas class imagery 'may be fragmentary, ambiguous or uncertain'. He goes on to say that 'How far they cohere to form unitary images is open to question'. In order to study class consciousness, it is necessary to examine 'The collective political and industrial organisation and articulation of class sentiment'. Class imagery, on the other hand, 'focuses upon the unorganised and often diffuse representations of social structure held by members of particular occupational groups'[66]. Using this explanation, and bearing in mind Bulmer's added belief that 'the relationship between social imagery and class consciousness is problematic'[67], this lends weight to the decision to abandon class consciousness as a criterion in the definition of politicisation. Bulmer clearly illustrates how analysing class imagery is a more straightforward task as opposed to attempting to tackle the notion of class consciousness.

Scase has also put forward an analysis of social class and, like many before him, concedes that class, as a concept, is 'probably the most ambiguous, confusing and ill-defined'[68]. He believes, however, that 'It is only by reference to class, as determined by the social relations of economic and social organizations, that it is possible to understand the changing composition of occupational order and, related to these, patterns of privilege and disadvantage'[69]. Scase, like Mann, highlights the way that workers accept the status quo; 'As long as employees perceive that they receive "fair rewards" for "fair effort", that wage differentials are reasonably legitimate, and that they are able to earn enough money to meet their personal needs, they are unlikely to become engaged in collective action directed towards the destruction of capitalism'[70]. Scase does not, therefore, foresee the overthrow of capitalism as 'The overwhelming majority of people in capitalist society accept the personal costs of class exploitation because it offers them compensatory benefits'[71]. The image of social class relationships presented by Scase, therefore, is one of relative stability.

A further addition to the debate about class imagery is provided by Gallie. He, in particular, has examined the impact of technological change upon social class. He has compared workers at oil refineries in both France and in Britain and he is of the opinion that 'theories that automation *necessarily* leads to a high degree of social integration, and theories that it *necessarily* leads to new forms of class conflict are both mistaken'[72]. He believes that factors other than the impact of the technology have more of an effect upon the nature of class relations. 'The crucial variables ... are factors like the managerial ideology, the typical structure of power in social institutions, and the ideology and mode of action of the trade union movement characteristic of the specific society'[73]. Another point made by Gallie is that technological change has involved a degree of enskilling but that men have benefited more. Continuing this brief snap-shot of class imagery, Parkin has highlighted the increasing professionalisation of work and the emphasis which tends to be placed upon qualifications. His analysis of social class relationships highlights the role played by professionals. Parkin is a neo-Weberian[74] who, as might be expected, highlights the limitations of Marxism. He believes that a rethinking of class analysis is due 'now that racial, ethnic, and religious conflicts have moved towards the centre of the political stage in many industrial societies' and that 'any general model of class or stratification that does not fully incorporate this fact must forfeit all credibility'[75]. He maintains that the high levels of working class allegiance to social democracy 'suggests that the alternatives on offer are felt to have even fewer attractions, the revolutionary Marxist alternatives included'[76]. An interesting aspect of Parkin's work is the way he distinguishes three 'major meaning-systems'. These are the 'dominant value system', the 'subordinate value system' and the 'radical value system'[77]. These describe different responses to the nature of class relationships and are expressed in varying degrees by the working class. They involve either adopting the views and ideology of the dominant class, accommodating their viewpoint or opposing it. Different conclusions may be reached regarding the justice or injustice or the inevitability of one's lot in society or as to the possibility of any alternative to it.

With respect to this notion of related works, two further examples are Goldthorpe and Lockwood's classic 'Affluent Worker' Studies[78] and Devine's reappraisal of the earlier work, entitled 'Affluent Workers Revisited'[79]. They are relevant to the extent that they constitute detailed examinations of one particular community, namely Luton. Using qualitative research methodology, they look at the political dimensions of the interaction between work and home life. It is not necessary to over-emphasise their applicability to this book but, nevertheless, they are worthy of a brief mention as being of interest to those studying working class communities and to those interested in class imagery.

As stated, Mann has also produced work which examines class imagery. He offers a comparison of working class consciousness in a number of western European nations, notably, Britain, the U.S.A., France and Italy, in an attempt to examine whether the working class is a revolutionary force. Mann believes that the worker has a 'pragmatic acceptance'[80] of the status quo rather than having shared values with those who occupy the positions of power. He states that the worker, 'Normally confronted by an employer who will budge on economic but not on control issues, ... takes what he can easily get and attempts to reduce the salience of what is denied him'[81]. This means that 'Forced to alienate his own productive powers in return for economic rewards, the worker develops a *dualistic* consciousness, in which control and money, work and non-work, become separated'[82]. Perhaps this is the only way in which the worker is able to survive his/her oppression by denying or failing to recognise its full significance?

Mann identifies four elements of class consciousness[83]. These are **identity**, believing yourself to be working class; secondly, the notion of being in **opposition** to another class (to the middle class and to capitalism); thirdly, class **totality**, the belief that this sense of identity and notion of opposition define one's total situation; fourthly, a belief in an **alternative** type of society. He believes, however, that the fourth element which he highlights, namely that of a vision of an alternative society, is rarely found. He argues that 'a realistic appraisal of alternative structures is lacking even among the most class-conscious workers in the most explosive situations'[84]. Mann believes that 'If the working class and its organisations accept as the framework for part of their activities an economism that does not challenge the structure of capitalism, then their collectivism does not escalate into an aggressive societal force but turns in upon itself'[85]. This leads Mann to the conclusion that 'It seems rather unlikely that the proletariat carries *in itself* the power to be a class *for itself*'[86]. For him, the notable factor is the way in which the workers appear to acquiesce in their own oppression and, as stated, do not possess a realistic vision of an alternative society.

Mann highlights the limits to the extent of working class consciousness. He has identified the four elements of class consciousness (identity, opposition, totality and alternative vision) but he does believe that it is very difficult to progress from one to four. Mann highlights the essentially conservative nature of British workers and believes that it is highly unlikely that an explosion of consciousness will occur. It appears to be the case that it is very difficult to get workers to progress from identifying themselves with a particular social class and from having an awareness of a 'them' and 'us' type of society to an appreciation that this pervades their whole lives and all aspects of their existence. If they do not possess this notion of totality then it hardly seems likely that they will then proceed to think in terms of an alternative vision of society.

This book may, in some small way, be able to add to the debate about the limits of working class consciousness due to the fact that it focuses upon one particular community. Given that Hemsworth was a mining community with a high percentage of the population either employed by the coal industry or heavily connected to the mining industry, it is reasonable to expect that class consciousness would take place. Certainly, the interviews conducted for this book reveal that the inhabitants of Hemsworth do have a strong sense of working class identity and most of them have then proceeded to acknowledge the existence of a class in opposition to them. In many respects, however, the notion of totality was lacking and only a relative few of the inhabitants had gone as far as recognising the way in which social class impinges upon their whole existence. Likewise, this vision of an alternative society appears to have escaped most of the interviewees. Most seem to have accepted their 'lot' in society and to have acquiesced in the scheme of things. There was no real evidence that any of the interviewees wanted to see the overthrow of the state and the replacement of capitalism and capitalist structures by alternative forms of government and politics. It is fair comment, however, that even though this overthrow, by violent or any other means, does not appear to have been a serious consideration for most of the interviewees, the Miners' Strike does appear to have led the inhabitants to question their own place within the class structure and to consider the implications for them of a society based upon the premise of two main classes acting in opposition to each other. They became more aware of class divisions due to Miners' Strike but, in accordance with Mann's observations about class consciousness, they did not then proceed to think in terms of an alternative society.

What, if anything, would have made the interviewees move forward towards thinking about an alternative society and alternative structures? This is a very difficult question to answer and, to a certain extent, is outwith the scope of this book. It leads to a questioning as to whether an explosion of class consciousness could ever really take place in contemporary society if a community as homogeneous and as solidary as a mining community, fighting not just for pecuniary measures, but for the very survival of jobs and communities, is unable or unwilling to move towards the imposition of an alternative society which is not based upon the capitalist mode of production and the exploitation of their labour power. Is it the case then that British workers, even traditional proletarians like miners, are essentially conservative by nature and in the late twentieth century are more concerned about percuniary measures as opposed to overthrow of the state and its related structures?

It is necessary, at this particular juncture, to discuss the relevance of this literature to the degree and quality of change needed for politicisation levels to increase. The texts examined above all shed some light upon the issue of social class and help in terms of thinking about how the working class perceives society. Whilst they are not directly concerned with the notion of politicisation, especially the tripartite definition employed by this research, they are helpful in terms of the light which they shed upon class imagery. The literature illustrates, however, that it is very difficult for the requisite change to occur. If we accept, as Mann does, that the working class is essentially conservative in nature and that the potential for an explosion of class consciousness often gives way to economism and an emphasis upon mere financial rewards, then the literature illuminates the difficulty involved in achieving the levels of change required for politicisation.

On a positive note, the literature, focusing as it does upon class imagery and studies of working class communities, aids our understanding of politicisation partly because it illuminates that for any politicisation to have taken place at all during the 1984/5 Miners' Strike is a commendable factor. This is especially true if the essentially conservative nature of the working class, the high levels of working class allegiance to social democracy and the propensity of the working class to conform and to accept the status quo is considered. Surely, in this context any politicisation whatsoever is a noteworthy feature. This leads to the observation that the high levels of politicisation and the degree and quality of change which occurred during the Miners' Strike and which is evidenced through this book, may be even more remarkable than was initially perceived.

Thus it can be seen that there are a whole host of texts which shed some light upon the thorny and contested concept of social class and class imagery. In agreement with Edgell, however, this is 'not to suggest that class is the only factor that structures economic and political life, but it is arguably the most fundamental'[87]. Obviously, class does occupy an important position within this investigation of one particular mining community and its importance as a factor in the equation should not be underestimated.

Conclusion

To sum up this chapter, five elements of politicisation were identified. These are; political participation, political awareness, behavioural changes, political knowledge and class consciousness. Each factor was examined, but for the purposes of this book, a tripartite definition was adopted to determine whether or not politicisation had occurred. If political participation begins or increases, if political awareness is initiated or increases and if behavioural changes occur then politicisation is deemed to have taken place. A three-way definition was chosen because it is felt that this offers the most comprehensive framework for the analysis. It has already been noted that politicisation is a difficult concept to identify, if it was less so then perhaps it would be less interesting to the political observer. Three 'measurable' factors offer a more watertight definition of politicisation but, as stated, this book does acknowledge that there are degrees of politicisation, that one person may have become 'highly' politicised by the Strike and another person less so but nevertheless politicisation might still have taken place (for example, investigations, namely the in-depth interviews conducted for this book, reveal that those striking miners who went on to the picket lines became more politicised than striking miners who did not operate as pickets). This issue is examined in greater depth in Chapter Four which examines the role of the police. So, the tripartite definition is used but it is necessary to reiterate the fact that there are degrees of and different dimensions of politicisation.

Once the criteria for politicisation were decided upon, it was necessary to ascertain how politicised the community was *before* the Strike. The problem of retrospective evidence resurfaced here. Memories fade or become distorted so it was necessary to unearth as much documented material as possible. Due to retrospective evidence, this was obviously a difficult concept to test.

An examination of what happened during the Strike is necessary. This book needs to look at the ways in which the community did become politicised. The next stage is to analyse the extent to which the community is still politicised, if at all. This will be difficult to assess. What criteria will be used? Finally, an attempt will be made to see if there are any predictions for the future in terms of decreasing or increasing politicisation. In all of the above categories, this book will investigate whether one section of society (for example, women or men, young or old, mineworkers/non-mineworkers) became more politicised than the rest. This is to say, were there *different* degrees of politicisation *among different groups*?

Having set out the parameters within which this book operates, it is necessary to examine the Miners' Strike and Hemsworth in order to ascertain the degree to which politicisation occurred and the extent to which lessons can be learnt from the Miners' Strike in terms of politicisation. Given that the Strike lasted virtually twelve months and that approximately 30 per cent of the male population was, at one time, employed in the mining industry, one can reasonably deduce that firstly, most, if not all, of the local population would be aware of the Strike and secondly, for many people the Strike would represent a significant learning experience which would have a profound and lasting impact. Mere deduction is, however, not enough. It is necessary to buttress this supposition with hard evidence.

Evidence, gleaned mainly from sixty in-depth interviews with people from Hemsworth, supports this argument in that most of the interviewees *do* claim that the Strike changed them in many ways. The problem of the self-selecting sample needs emphasis here, i.e. the ones who have been interviewed are the ones who are most likely to come forward and who are already very political. Correspondingly, those who are not very political are unlikely to answer newspaper advertisements or to express a willingness to be interviewed. The interviewer's skills, both investigative and interpersonal, are put to the test here as attempts are made to overcome the self-selecting sample phenomenon. Most of the interviewees claim that post-Strike they came to have a totally different outlook upon life (again see Stead's *Never the Same Again*[88] for details of the changed experiences [post-strike] of women in general), that the Strike had such a profound impact upon their lives and even if it did not induce any change in behaviour (such as joining a political party or a pressure group) it at least meant that they would never think in the same way again. For the majority of those interviewed it meant a much more critical approach towards the police in particular but also towards the media. Many came to distrust all sources of information, they became much more cynical and disbelieving. Having said this, although people did become distrustful of certain media, they nevertheless attempted to keep abreast of the images and (as they saw it) propaganda that television and radio in particular conveyed.

There have been debates in the press[89] regarding lack of political activism in general and perhaps lessons can be learnt from recent debates, i.e. have those in mining communities become less active as a result of the 1984/5 Miners' Strike? It remains the case, however, that we need to be wary of the interpretations which are imposed upon phenomena such as supposed increased apathy. Can increasing politicisation encourage citizens not to give, not to buckle under the weight of political despair but to give them hope and confidence in their ability to change things - be it their own domestic arrangements or the existing social order? A decline in political activity may actually signify *increased* rather than decreased politicisation. It may, in actual fact, mean that people have become much *more* demanding of the Labour Party, for example, and hyper-critical of existing parties in general. So we do need to be wary about jumping to the wrong conclusions!

To conclude, this Chapter has attempted to define politicisation using three specific criteria - namely political participation, political awareness and behavioural changes - other elements, political knowledge and class consciousness, were explored but, for reasons already stated, they were not used in the main framework for analysis. From the evidence unearthed via the literature explored and the in-depth interviews conducted with the people of Hemsworth it seems that the Miners' Strike was directly responsible for the significant degree of politicisation which took place within that community either during or post-Strike.

Now that the parameters of politicisation have been defined and illustrated, the next step awaits. Namely, to examine, in subsequent chapters, the Strike and Hemsworth, the roles which the police, the mass media and the women played during the Miners' Strike and to see the impact, if any, of the increasing politicisation, which this research has identified, upon those roles. Finally, the political scenario in Hemsworth is examined in Chapter Seven before the overall conclusions are reached in Chapter Eight.

Notes:

[1] Leftwich, A. (Ed.) (1984) *What is Politics?*, (Oxford: Blackwell).

[2] Schwarzmantel, J. (1987) *Structures of Power*, (London: Wheatsheaf), p. 2.

[3] Crick, B. and Crick, T. (1987) *What is Politics?*, (London: Edward Arnold), p. 6.

[4] Madgwick, P.J. (1984) *Introduction to Politics*, (London: Hutchinson, third edition), p. 15.

[5] Millett, K. (1977) *Sexual Politics*, (London: Virago), p. 24.

[6] Ibid., p. 23.

[7] Ibid., p. 23.

[8] Ibid., p. 23.

[9] Siltanen, J. and Stanworth, M. (1984) *Women and the Public Sphere*, (London: Hutchinson), p. 195.

[10] Ibid., p. 196.

[11] Schwarzmantel, J., *Op. Cit.*, p. 2.

[12] Interview conducted with Gavin Williams, Oxford University, March 1992.

[13] Rush, M. (1992) *Politics and Society*, (London: Prentice Hall).

[14] Parry, G., Moyser, G. and Day, N., *Op. Cit.*, p. 4.

[15] See Rose, R. (1989) *Politics in England*, 5th Edition (London: Macmillan), esp. chapter 6, for further detail regarding low levels of political participation. Also Moodie, G.C. (1971) *The Government of Great Britain*, third edition (London: Methuen).

[16] Almond, G. and Verba, S. (1963) *The Civic Culture*, (Princeton, N.J.: Princeton University Press), Chapter 14.

[17] Beer, S. (1982) *Britain Against Itself*, (London: Faber).

[18] Parry, G. *et al.*, *Op. Cit.*, p. 5.

[19] Ibid., p. 432.

[20] Higgins, G.M. and Richardson, J.J. (1976) *Political Participation*, (London: Politics Association), p. 9.

[21] Pateman, C. (1970) *Participation and Democratic Theory*, (Cambridge: Cambridge University Press).

[22] Ibid., p. 104.

[23] Ibid., p. 105.

[24] Ibid., p. 64.

[25] Ibid., p. 42.

[26] Ibid., pp. 42-3.

[27] Ibid., p. 42.

[28] Ibid., p. 110.

[29] Ibid., p. 43.

[30] Ibid., p. 43.

[31] See Forman, F.N. (1985) *Mastering British Politics,* (London: Macmillan), Chapter 13, for further details on the policy making process.

[32] Parry, G., Moyser, G. and Day, N. (1992) *Political Participation and Democracy in Britain*, (Cambridge: Cambridge University Press), p. 3.

[33] Thackrah, J.R. (1987) *Politics*, (London: Heinemann), p. 4.

[34] See, for example, Stead, J. (1987) *Never the Same Again*, (London: The Women's Press).

[35] Stradling, R. (1977) *The Political Awareness of the School Leaver*, (London: Hansard Society).

[36] See, for example, Mann, M. (1973) *Consciousness and Action Among the Western Working Class,* (London: Macmillan). Marx, K. (1968) *Selected Works of Karl Marx and Frederick Engels*, (London: Lawrence and Wishart). Weber, M. (1948) *Essays in Sociology*, (London: Routledge and Kegan Paul). Parkin, F. (1972) *Class Inequality and Political Order*, (St. Albans: Paladin).

[37] Coxall, B. and Robins, L. (1989) *Contemporary British Politics*, (London: Macmillan), p. 31.

[38] See Denver, D. and Bochel, H. (1994) 'Merger or Bust: Whatever Happened to Members of the S.D.P.?', *British Journal of Political Science*, (Cambridge: Cambridge University Press, Vol. 24, pp. 403-417).

[39] Rush, M. (1992) *Politics and Society*, (London: Prentice Hall), pp. 126-7.

[40] Browne, S. (Ed.) (1986) *Is Democracy Working?*, (Newcastle, Tyne Tees Television), p. 4.

[41] See Sanders, D. 'Voting Behaviour in Britain', *Contemporary Record*, (February 1991, pp. 2-6) for a more detailed analysis of the main theories of voting behaviour.

[42] See Butler, D. and Stokes, J. (1974) *Political Change in Britain*, (London: Macmillan, second edition) for further details.

[43] Pulzer, P. (1967) *Political Representation and Elections in Britain*, second edition 1975 (London: Allen and Unwin).

[44] Heath, A., Jowell, R., and Curtice, J. (1985) *How Britain Votes*, (Oxford: Pergamon).

[45] See Butler, D. and Stokes, J. (1974) *Political Change in Britain*, second edition (London: Macmillan) for further details. Denver, D. and Hands, G. (1992) *Issues and Controversies in British Electoral Behaviour*, (Hemel Hempstead: Harvester Wheatsheaf), pp. 64-5 gives a more recent analysis.

[46] Cocker, P.G. (1986) *Government and Politics*, (London: Edward Arnold), p. 65.

[47] Coxall, B. and Robins, L. (1989) *Contemporary British Politics*, (London: Macmillan), p. 269.

[48] Ibid., Chapter 12, pp. 264-282.

[49] Dunleavy, P. and Husbands, C.T. (1985) *British Democracy at the Crossroads*, (London: Allen and Unwin), p. 24.

[50] Sanders, D., 'Voting Behaviour in Britain', Contemporary Record, (February 1991, pp. 2-6), p. 6.

[51] Dowse, R.E., and Hughes, J.A. (1972) *Political Sociology*, (London: John Wiley), p. 289.

[52] Tolleson Rhinehart, S. (1992) *Gender Consciousness and Politics*, (London: Routledge), p. 128.

[53] See, for example, Segal, L. (1990) *Slow Motion: Changing Masculinities, Changing Men*, (London: Virago).

[54] Lockwood, D. (1975) 'Sources of Variation in Working Class Images of Society', in Bulmer, M., (Ed.), *Working-Class Images of Society*, (London: Routledge and Kegan Paul).

[55] Ibid., p. 17.

[56] Ibid., p. 18.

[57] Rees, G. (1993) 'Class, Community and the Miners: The 1984-85 Miners' Strike and Its Aftermath', *Sociology*, (Vol. 27, part 2, pp. 307-12), pp. 307/8.

[58] Lockwood, D., *Op. Cit.*, p. 17.

[59] Ibid., p. 18.

[60] Ibid., p. 21.

[61] Ibid., p. 21.

[62] Ibid., p. 23.

[63] See bibliography for further details relating to each of these authors.

[64] Bulmer, M. (Ed.) (1975) *Working-Class Images of Society*, (London: Routledge and Kegan Paul), p. 4.

[65] Ibid., p. 5.

[66] Ibid., p. 5.

[67] Ibid., p. 6.

[68] Scase, R. (1992) *Class*, (Buckingham: Open University Press), p. 1.

[69] Ibid., p. 26.

[70] Ibid., p. 81.

[71] Ibid., p. 89.

[72] Gallie, D. (1978) *In Search of the New Working Class*, (Cambridge: Cambridge University Press), p. 300.

[73] Ibid., p. 318.

[74] See Giddens, A. (1973) *The Class Structure of the Advanced Societies*, (London: Hutchinson) for an overview of Weber's ideas.

[75] Parkin, F. (1979) *Marxism and Class Theory: A Bourgeois Critique*, (London: Tavistock), p. 9.

[76] Ibid., p. 202.

[77] Parkin, F. (1972) *Class Inequality and Political Order*, (St. Albans: Paladin), p. 81.

[78] Goldthorpe, J.H. and Lockwood, D. (1968) *Affluent Worker: Political Attitudes and Behaviour*, (Cambridge: Cambridge University Press). Goldthorpe, J.H. *et al.* (1969) *The Affluent Worker in the Class Structure*, (Cambridge: Cambridge University Press).

[79] Devine, F. (1992) *Affluent Workers Revisited*, (Edinburgh: Edinburgh University Press).

[80] Mann, M. (1973) *Consciousness and Action Among the Western Working Class,* (London: Macmillan), p. 30.

[81] Ibid., p. 32.

[82] Ibid., p. 33.

[83] Ibid., p. 13. Gallie also provides a concise outline of the elements of class consciousness. [See Gallie, D. (1983) *Social Inequality and Class Radicalism in France and Britain*, (Cambridge: Cambridge University Press), p. 27.]

[84] Mann, M., *Op. Cit.*, p. 69.

[85] Ibid., pp. 71/2.

[86] Ibid., p. 73.

[87] Edgell, S. (1993) *Class*, (London: Routledge), pp. 114/5.

[88] Stead, J., *Op. Cit.*

[89] See article in *The Guardian*, 25th September 1993, (p. 10), by Seyd, P. and Whiteley, P.

3   A Study of the 1984/5 Miners' Strike and its effects upon Politicisation

Hemsworth; a brief profile

The community upon which this research is based, Hemsworth, is a small market town located between Pontefract and Barnsley, at a point where the A628 bisects the B6421. The town itself is a definite geographic entity as it is (relatively speaking) isolated from neighbouring towns and villages. Hemsworth is also the name of the local Parliamentary constituency although here the area extends to cover nearby Kinsley, Fitzwilliam, South Kirkby, South Elmsall, Upton and Ackworth.

Hemsworth is a peculiar kind of industrial community in that its history remained mainly agricultural right up until the sinking of the local mines towards the end of the last century. Apart from the mining industry, the area has never possessed any other heavy industries - a factor in itself of no small significance given the recent decline in the coal mining industry.

According to Bulley, the author of 'Hemsworth in History', 'The casual visitor to Hemsworth, and no doubt many of its residents, too, may question whether it is a place worthy of historical research'[1]. On the face of it, it might seem that Hemsworth has little to offer in terms of its scope for investigation but, given its rich history and firm links with the mining industry, it would be unwise to dismiss Hemsworth too readily. The evidence and insight revealed via the in-depth interviews lends weight to the argument that Hemsworth *is* a place worthy of research. Subsequent chapters which highlight what the interviewees had to say reiterate this point. This book seeks to examine how Hemsworth has changed, changes both on a communal and on an individual basis which occurred due to the Miners' Strike.

It is perhaps worth giving a few historical details about Hemsworth. The first settlers in the Hemsworth area arrived during Saxon times. As already stated, the community remained mainly agricultural right up to the second half of the nineteenth century; the Industrial Revolution does not appear to have had much impact on Hemsworth. However, rapid change was brought about by the coal-mining industry. Two pits were sunk in the Hemsworth area in the final quarter of the last century. This brought with it an increase in population and the Hemsworth of the 1880s emerged: a community dominated by the coal industry. Hemsworth Colliery opened in 1882 and was closed in 1968; after merging with South Kirkby Colliery in July 1967. South Kirkby Colliery was opened in 1885 and closed in 1988. Ferrymoor Riddings (formerly Brierley Colliery) opened in 1978 and closed in 1988. Kinsley Drift was what is known as a 'short-life' pit, it opened in 1979 and closed in 1986.

In terms of man-power at these collieries, it is worth examining the statistics immediately prior to and just after the 1984/5 Miners' Strike. These clearly illustrate a decline in the numbers employed after the Strike;

Manpower Figures	1981	1982	1983	1985
Ferrymoor Riddings	555	568	532	405
South Kirkby	1,495	1,552	1,436	1,147
Kinsley Drift	450	469	432	300

(Source: N.U.M.: Yorkshire Area Headquarters, Barnsley)

For a thorough historical account of the growth of Hemsworth, it is useful to examine 'Hemsworth in History'[2]. There are other references to Hemsworth in such publications as, the Parish Registers (in the Yorkshire Parish Registers Society Series) but nothing else constitutes an extensive chronological account.

In terms of population growth, the census figures from 1801 for the parish of Hemsworth are thus;

1801 - 803	**1871** - 993	**1951** - 13,750
1811 - 811	**1881** - 1,665	**1961** - 14,413
1821 - 963	**1891** - 2,887	**1971** - 14,851
1831 - 937	**1901** - 6,283	**1981** - 14,529
1841 - 1,005	**1911** - 10,173	**1991** - 14,063
1851 - 997	**1921** - 11,235	
1861 - 975	**1931** - 13,001	
(Source: Census Returns)		

It is not until after 1871 that the population increased significantly. The population grew notably in the last quarter of the nineteenth century and up to the First World War. As the statistics clearly illustrate, during a period of approximately thirty years Hemsworth's population increased six-fold. It is necessary to examine why.

In the nineteenth century, the birth-rate was higher than the death-rate in the Parish of Hemsworth yet the population did not increase significantly until the end of that century. It appears that people were moving from Hemsworth to work in the more industrialised parts of West Yorkshire. When the pits were sunk in the vicinity this stopped the population drain and resulted in a fairly dramatic local population increase. According to Baylies, in Hemsworth 'new migrants made up 20 per cent of the 1901 population'[3].

With the creation of the mines at Hemsworth and South Kirkby, there 'was now an opportunity for the young man of Hemsworth to find a livelihood in his own parish, not only in mining, but also in building and in the provision of essential services for the growing community'[4]. It is also interesting to note that in 1891 in Hemsworth there were '206 unmarried males to each 100 unmarried females aged 25-35'[5]. There were more males due to immigration and also many females went to work in domestic service.

Bulmer refers to the migration which took place in mining communities and emphasises that it is not a purely British phenomenon; 'Mining development, moreover, like the beginnings of industrialisation in general, has been marked by the migration of labour, predominantly from rural areas to towns or industrial villages. This is so whether the labour is brought by a recruiting agency from an African village to the Rand or Copper belt, from a Russian mir to the Don mines, or from Ireland to Lancashire'[6].

In addition to the population increase attributed to the sinking of the mines, there was also a great deal of immigration into the Hemsworth area which appears to have been facilitated by the Railway Age. In the 1870s a colliery was created in Fitzwilliam and two new housing estates were set up at Fitzwilliam and Kinsley. In the mid-1860s the Wakefield to Doncaster Railway line was installed and in the 1880s the Barnsley to Hull railway line was laid. In Hemsworth itself, the rows of terrace houses were built at the areas known as Common and West Ends.

The Act of 1894 set up the parish council and rural district council system. Hemsworth Parish Council was first elected in December 1894. It had eleven members and the chairman was Mr. F. Buckle. It was not until 1921 that the Hemsworth Urban District Council was created, at this time the population was in excess of 11,000 and the rateable value was £42,239.

According to 'Population Bulletin No 6', published by Wakefield Metropolitan District Council (Planning Department) in July 1988, the South East District Plan Area, which covers Ackworth, Hemsworth and Elmsall, has the highest birth-rate of the three areas which compose the Wakefield Metropolitan District. This increase is offset by population migration, estimated at 0.5 per cent of the total population of the area between 1983 and 1987. This overall decline in population is blamed, in part, on the large number of miners who transferred to the Selby Coalfield.

Information gleaned from the 1981 Census reveals that the constituency of Hemsworth was at that time composed of; 35 per cent owner occupiers, 45 per cent local authority tenants. 0.5 per cent Black/Asian citizens, 30 per cent fitted into the Registrar-Generals C1 category and 8 per cent into the Professional/Managerial classification. The 1991 Area Profile[7] reveals that the ethnic minority population of Hemsworth remains at 0.5 per cent, well below the national average figure of 5.5 per cent ethnic minority population.

The 1981 figure of 35 per cent owner occupiers increased to 52.7 per cent in 1991; again this compares with the national figure of 66.7 per cent so Hemsworth is still below average in terms of owner occupation. The percentage of local authority tenants has declined in 1991 from the previous figure of 45 per cent to 36.9 per cent. This is a significant drop but perhaps not as large as one might have expected given the Government's 1980 Housing Act which introduced the Right to Buy policy, the effect of which ought to have been felt by 1991.

In terms of the Registrar-General's classifications; the previous 8 per cent in the Professional/Managerial category increased to 9.7 per cent in 1991. This compares with a national figure of 23.0 per cent. It can be clearly seen that Hemsworth is a predominantly working class area. The figure of 8.7 per cent of those employed in Energy, which includes coal mining, clearly indicates the extent to which Hemsworth has suffered due to the decline of the coal mining industry[8].

One notable feature to emerge from the Census data is the changed nature of the occupational structure of Hemsworth. A number of changes have taken place in this area but, especially marked, is the growth in the employment of women. As the 1991 Area Profile reveals, many more women are now going out to work. A significant number of these women have taken up employment in low-level service sector work. For example, as care assistants in residential homes for the elderly, dinner ladies, school cleaners, working in light industry at a nearby Japanese electronics factory. Not all but a great deal of this work is part-time and low paid; lacking in job security and promotion prospects, it is usually routine and unskilled work.

This changed occupational structure has implications for this study because it may alter the gender relationships and roles within the household unit. No longer is it the case that the majority of women remain as housewives. As stated, many of them have taken up paid work outside of the home. This may, in turn, have led to changes relating to the sexual division of labour within the domestic environment. In addition, it may be the case that because of their wider horizons these women have become more receptive to the politicisation process. The workplace may lead to an interest and involvement in trade union politics. These are obviously aspects which this investigation needs to bear in mind.

Communities like Hemsworth have thus not been immune from change. It is pertinent to discuss both continuity and change with reference to Dennis, Henriques and Slaughter's study of Featherstone in the 1950s. Their study, aptly entitled *Coal is Our Life*, provides useful comparative data. They put forward a detailed and accurate portrayal of a community which is very much as Hemsworth was prior to the demise of the coal mining industry. The overriding importance of the colliery and the coal industry in general, coupled with the close-knit nature of the local community is realistically reflected in the Dennis text. Parallels can clearly be drawn between this study of Hemsworth and their sociological inquiry into Featherstone (or Ashton as they call it). Dennis *et al.* build up a holistic picture of the community by examining the role of the miner at work, by looking at the influence of the National Union of Mineworkers, exploring leisure activities and seeking to establish the nature of familial and gender relationships within this community.

The similarities between 'Ashton' and Hemsworth are marked. A number of changes, however, have taken place in Hemsworth in the post-1984/5 Strike scenario. These are mentioned in detail throughout the course of this investigation but, suffice to highlight at this particular juncture, some of the key elements. These include; the increase in female participation in the workforce, increasing numbers reliant upon income support and various other benefits, closure of a number of small businesses, a degree of migration out of the area (in the immediate post-Strike period a number went to the Selby coalfields), some interviewees spoke of the seemingly higher incidence of vandalism, drug, alcohol and solvent abuse, whilst others painted the picture of what they termed a virtual 'Ghost Town'. Perhaps the strongest point to be made in terms of continuity is the existence of a community spirit which many of the interviewees maintained had not been crushed or extinguished by the demise of the coal mining industry. It was felt that, although demoralised, the people were still basically the same.

Returning briefly to the Census data, the population figure for Hemsworth from the 1991 Census does show a slight decline but, according to the Planning Department at Wakefield Metropolitan District Council, this is a relatively small decline and is partly explained by people moving out of the area due mainly to the decline of the mining industry and partly by minor boundary changes.

'Change without sacrifice is a rare feature in history'[9]. This is the opening sentence of Bulley's concluding paragraph in his text on the history of Hemsworth. It is a statement which is directly applicable to the situation after the 1984/5 Miners' Strike. Such sacrifices as there were during the Strike, what has been the impact of those events upon the community of Hemsworth?

Thus section one has set the scene regarding the constituency of Hemsworth. A brief profile in terms of its history, population and socio-economic make-up is given. It is appropriate now to examine the political scenario in Hemsworth.

Introduction to the Politics of Hemsworth

Chapter Seven is devoted exclusively to Hemsworth and its politics but it is necessary to at least introduce the topic at this stage in the book in order to be able to shed light upon the chapters which examine the roles fulfilled by the police and the women.

Hemsworth, it appears, is a famous name electorally. Waller, in his 'Almanac of British Politics', states that 'This is the seat which has produced the largest Labour majority in so many General Elections, remaining over 30,000 from 1950 to 1974. This is where it is said that the Labour votes are weighed and not counted'[10].

Waller continues that the constituency boundaries were redrawn in the light of Local Government Reorganisation in 1974. This was because constituencies could not cross county boundaries. It resulted in the loss of certain areas such as Cudworth, Goldthorpe, Thurnscoe and Bolton on Dearne (these were lost to Barnsley East) and the notable addition of Featherstone, 'Featherstone is a large mining village of 10,000 souls, with a famed community spirit - its rugby league team has frequently reached the Cup Final at Wembley'[11].

One pertinent factor which Waller refers to, in his *Almanac of British Politics,* is the fact that 'Together with Bolsover in Derbyshire, a higher proportion of its population is employed in the coal industry than any other constituency in the U.K. - in 1981 over 30%'[12]. In 'The British General Election of 1970'[13], Hemsworth is cited as having 40.7 per cent of its population employed in the mining industry, which puts it at the top of a league table of the '50 Most Mining Seats'. Bolsover comes second with 40.3 per cent. By October 1974 those figures had fallen to 32.9 per cent for Bolsover and 32.4 per cent for Hemsworth. Obviously, these figures have declined even further in the aftermath of the Miners' Strike.

Alec Woodall was the Member of Parliament for Hemsworth between February 1974 and 1987. He was replaced by George Buckley in 1987. Buckley was elected with 67 per cent of the total vote and a majority of 20,700 (49.8 per cent). As with most mining constituencies, both Woodall and Buckley have strong links with the N.U.M.

The replacement of Alec Woodall by George Buckley is an issue which will be returned to at a later stage (in Chapter Seven) as the precise nature and details of this changeover are still the subject of a degree of controversy. Alec Woodall was a 'victim' of mandatory re-selection between the 1983 and 1987 general elections. The exact circumstances of this event were affected, to a considerable extent, by the Miners' Strike itself. Alec Woodall was one of only a handful of Labour M.P.s who were deselected prior to the 1987 General Election - a factor in itself of no small significance, that is to say that the small number of those who were actually de-selected illustrates the strength of feeling against Woodall.

Byron Criddle writes in 'The British General Election of 1987'; 'For only the second time since its introduction in 1980, Labour's mandatory reselection process was applied to all 177 Labour M.P.s seeking to retain their seats'[14]. He continues 'by 1986 [reselection] had claimed the scalps of six M.P.s, four from the right of the party and two from the left. Two of the six were ostensibly casualties of the 1984-5 miners' strike. Michael McGuire, the 59-year old N.U.M.-sponsored M.P. for Makerfield, ... Alec Woodall, another little-heard and little-known N.U.M.-sponsored member, who had represented Hemsworth since 1974, was ousted for similar reasons. He too paid for his non-Scargillite views; he had praised the local police in clashes with striking miners in July 1984. He also had his age (67) against him, though he was at pains to point out that "in all its long history, the Yorkshire N.U.M. has allowed its M.P.s to die in office, or retire with honour: I am the first to be sacked for no reason". His replacement, after a 60-28 vote defeat, was another local miner, 50-year-old George Buckley'[15].

George Buckley's untimely death in 1991 prompted the Hemsworth by-election in November of that year. Derek Enright won the by-election for the Labour Party and remained its Member of Parliament until his death in 1995 but, as will be discussed in Chapter Six, this 1991 by-election was not quite so straightforward as might have been assumed.

After noting the impact which the arrival of the coal industry had upon the growth of the community of Hemsworth, witnessing the high numbers employed in the industry by the time of the latter half of the Twentieth Century, and emphasising the influence which the N.U.M. has had upon Hemsworth via its sponsorship of Members of Parliament, it is no surprise, therefore, that the 1984/5 Miners' Strike would have a deep and lasting effect upon this particular community. The extent of that effect is the subject of this book.

The 1984/5 Miners' Strike

It is pertinent at this stage to give a brief outline of the 1984/5 Miners' Strike. Perhaps it is relevant also to emphasise, as Winterton does, the fact that 'The greatest problem which anyone researching the strike must acknowledge is that there is no single "correct version" of such a complex phenomenon'[16]. This is definitely a factor to be taken into consideration when analysing the events of 1984/5.

Given that the Strike is discussed and analysed in a number of key texts (see, for example, Adeney and Lloyd's *Loss Without Limit*, Beynon's *Digging Deeper*, Callinicos and Simon's *The Great Strike*, Coulter *et al*'s *State of Siege* amongst others) it is not necessary to duplicate their work here, merely to highlight the aspects of the 1984/5 Miners' Strike. Aspects, many of which, are now already deeply embedded in the national consciousness.

The Miners' Strike began on the 12th March 1984 in response to the Government's announcement, on the 1st March 1984, that it was going to close Cortonwood Colliery. The N.U.M. believed that Cortonwood was going to be closed for political rather than for economic reasons. The ensuing national strike which lasted for virtually twelve months was regarded by miners and their families as a struggle to protect their jobs and their communities: Many of them felt that their very existence was under direct attack. As Rees says 'the **object** of the strike itself was new; for the first time in the mining industry, it was the preservation of jobs and communities, rather than wages or working conditions, which was sought - a development which struck at the heart of the organisation of a nationalised industry and raised the issue of "management's right to manage"'[17]. The twelve months following the Government's decision to close Cortonwood Colliery in March 1984 brought considerable change to the British mining industry and to the trade union movement as a whole. After all, the miners have traditionally been regarded as the vanguard of the trade union movement.

Proponents of the Strike, such as Arthur Scargill and Mick McGahey, argued that Cortonwood represented the beginning of a mass closure programme which threatened the lives of pits and communities throughout the country. The Government's case was that closures were based on the economics of mining, they wanted to close what they deemed to be uneconomic pits but, as Glyn[18] points out, the definition of uneconomic is not so clear cut as the Government made it appear. It could be argued that the Conservatives, because of their intention to pursue a monetarist economic policy, needed to defeat the miners in order to keep a tight rein upon public expenditure. In addition, there is also the widely held view that the Thatcher Government wanted to exact revenge for previous humiliation suffered at the hands of the mineworkers, namely Saltley in 1972 (see Chapter Four) and the loss of the February 1974 General Election. The 1978 Ridley Report also indicated the Government's intentions with respect to the mining industry. The appointment of Ian MacGregor as Chair of the National Coal Board, given his legacy at British Steel, also revealed the determination on the part of the Government. Strike leaders, therefore, saw the closure of Cortonwood as provocative and the closures themselves as political dogma and a naked attempt to emasculate the N.U.M. and the trade union movement at large.

The Government's preparations and determination to win are also illustrated by Hain and McCrindle, 'There are all the hallmarks of a carefully-planned strategy ... Anti-union laws; restrictions on picketing; the extension and centralisation of police powers; new social security regulations to ensure that families of people on strike cannot survive on state benefits; the use of U.S.-style management tactics, first at B.L., then at British Steel, followed by the deliberately provocative appointment of MacGregor; the creation by government policy of regional unemployment; the deliberate shift in energy policy towards nuclear power; the curbing of local authorities' ability to protect their communities from the worst effects of redundancy and the collapse of heavy industry; the use of the media to discredit and abuse the leadership of any union likely to mount serious resistance'[19]. Obviously, Hain and McCrindle are writing from a definite political position but they do, nevertheless, highlight many of the measures which the Government took, even if in a less than impartial manner.

The Strike was significant in several ways. Perhaps the overriding image which remains in the minds of many people are the violent scenes (notably from the coking plant at Orgreave) which were broadcast from the picket lines. As Waddington *et al.* illuminate 'The dominant media representation of the violence was one of the police reacting defensively in the face of extreme provocation by the pickets ... This causality is strongly disputed (Waddington *et al.*, 1989) but helped to legitimize police aggression and turned public opinion against the miners (ibid.)'[20]. This raises questions regarding coverage of the Strike by the various media and its impact on the support by the public of the miners' case.

Police tactics during the Strike were controversial for a number of reasons. They are examined in detail in Chapter Four but it is relevant at this stage to highlight their significance. Unlike the 1974 Strike, the police seemed determined to gain the upper hand. Innovations such as setting up the National Reporting Centre were regarded by some critics as moving towards the establishment of a 'national' police force instead of county based forces. Although, to be fair, as Waddington *et al.* reveal, 'Throughout the strike senior members of the Association of Chief Police Officers (A.C.P.O.) insisted that the N.R.C. was merely a convenient device for ensuring the efficiency of "mutual aid" between forces'[21]. It is necessary to reiterate, however, that the curtailment of freedom of movement - the stopping and turning back of vehicles carrying miners, various incidents of alleged police brutality and random arrests when pickets were subsequently released without charge, illustrate the lengths to which the Government, via the police, was prepared to go in order to settle the Strike on their terms.

If police methods were regarded as controversial then many miners, trade unionists and politicians of the 'Left' considered the leadership of the N.U.M. to be equally suspect. It was this lack of a consensus between the 'Scargillites' and those who would have preferred a ballot that ultimately led to the defeat of the N.U.M.

It was the Nottinghamshire area where the demands for a ballot were strongest and it was here that the N.U.M. split and the Union of Democratic Mineworkers was formed, with Roy Lynk at its head. The U.D.M. was not formed until the end of the Strike ['19 October 1985 "Nottinghamshire Area miners vote by a majority of 72 per cent to form a new union, the Union of Democratic Mineworkers"'[22]] but it was definitely a product of the events which took place during the 1984/5 coal dispute. The incumbent General Secretary of the Trades Union Congress, Norman Willis, was heckled and 'threatened' with a noose when he spoke against picket line violence at a South Wales rally. It was not until almost the end of the Strike (January 1985) that Neil Kinnock, the Labour Leader, publicly declared his support by joining a Welsh picket line. All of these incidents serve to demonstrate how deeply divided the Labour movement had become over the Strike.

One positive factor to have emerged during the Strike, however, was the growth of the Womens' Support Groups. Originally set up to provide miners with meals, they soon developed in to a network of fund- and political consciousness-raising bodies. A testimony to their commitment is the fact that many of these groups have survived the end of the Strike. It is interesting to note that the recent coal dispute, sparked off by the Government's announcement of pit closures in October 1992, also led to the setting up of many support groups and a significant number of women engaged in protests and demonstrations against the Government's intended actions. During Easter 1993, for example, four women, Elaine Evans, Dot Kelly, Lesley Lomas and Anne Scargill took part in a sit-in for four days down Parkside colliery at Newton-le-Willows in order to raise public awareness regarding the miners' plight. They later went on to campaign to help miners in Cuba.

In purely numerical terms it appears that the Government's 'attack' was real enough. In 1979-80 there were 233,163 miners in the U.K.; by 1988-89 this figure was reduced to 81,739[23]. By September 1994, there were only 8,000 miners in 16 collieries left in the British coal industry, 14,000 employees if all the white collar and ancilliary workers are included[24].

Although the Strike can only be regarded as a defeat for the N.U.M., Arthur Scargill's argument about pit closures and job losses has largely been vindicated. Allied to this, there has been, arguably, a discernible and lasting increase in the political awareness of mining communities. Many people living in the mining communities and representing all parts of the political spectrum, were galvanised into political activity. Their political participation was either instigated or increased. People, who previously had never professed an interest in politics, appear, preliminary inquiries reveal, to have been motivated by the Strike into taking positive action. It is this increased political activity and political awareness in Hemsworth which this research seeks to address.

On this question of political awareness, it is interesting to cite a passage from 'The British General Election of 1987' by David Butler, 'Increased political awareness also produced higher turnout. The clearest example is mining constituencies which used, in the 1950s, to have the highest turnout in the country but where, from 1966 onwards, turnout has been declining at an above-average rate. In 1987 the passions felt on both sides of the dispute amongst the miners over the 1984-5 strike were evident. In the 18 constituencies with over 15% employment in mining, turnout rose 4.4% on average and in the nine with over 20% employment it jumped 5.2%. As a result, turnout in mining seats is now once again higher than the national average, even though most are safe seats; turnout in 1987 averaged 76.5% in the 33 constituencies with most mining. It is noteworthy that this rise in voting occurred in both Arthur Scargill's Yorkshire bastion and in the Nottinghamshire stronghold of opposition to his leadership of the strike. Mansfield, the headquarters of the Notts miners, had the third biggest rise in turnout in Britain, whilst Hemsworth and Barnsley East, the two most solidly mining Yorkshire constituencies, lay seventh and fifteenth in that league table'[25]. It is interesting to note that the national turnout was 74.5 per cent in 1987, having risen from the 1983 figure of 72.7 per cent. Turnout at the 1992 General Election was 77.8 per cent but, according to Professor David Butler, there was no significant increase in turnout in mining constituencies as there was in 1987. 'Turnout in mining seats used to be among the highest in the country. But that's no longer the case'[26]. So, in terms of turnout, mining constituencies did witness a post-Strike increase in 1987: the extent to which this rise in turnout illustrates a heightened politicisation as a result of the Miners' Strike is worthy of detailed examination at a later stage.

Apart from examining the turnout figures, it is interesting to scrutinise the electoral swing in mining constituencies in 1987 and 1992 and to compare these with the national average. On a national basis, in 1987 there was a 2.8 per cent swing from Conservative to Labour and in 1992 there was a 3.0 per cent swing from Conservative to Labour[27]. In Hemsworth, no swing was registered in 1987 but, in 1992, there was a 1.2 per cent swing to Labour. By way of further example, in Bolsover, Derbyshire, there was a 0.8 per cent swing to the Conservatives in 1987 and a 5.7 per cent swing to Labour in 1992. In Barnsley East in 1987 there was no recorded swing but in 1992 there was a 1.3 per cent swing to Labour. These figures illustrate that mining constituencies tended, on the whole, to mirror the national picture. It is difficult to draw any firm conclusions, however, as these statistics may simply be a reflection of the national trend. It would be hard to substantiate any claim that these swings to Labour in mining constituencies were due to factors exclusively associated with the mining industry and its 'problems'. Nevertheless, these fluctuations in voting patterns are still worthy of note.

The Strike lasted for virtually twelve months. A number of important issues were raised as a result of this Strike, including; the question of strikes and ballots, the role of the police, the role of the media, the support given by the women of the miners' support groups, the question of economic/uneconomic pits and the very existence of the communities themselves.

The 1984/5 Miners' Strike and Hemsworth

This section constitutes a brief analysis of the Miners' Strike and its impact upon Hemsworth. Support for the strike was more or less solid in Hemsworth throughout the whole twelve month duration, with only a handful of miners returning to work prior to the ending of the Strike. Numbers did begin to creep up gradually around Christmas 1984 but, nevertheless, in comparison with other mining areas, support remained relatively solid right up until the end of the Strike. The local newspaper, the *Hemsworth and South Elmsall Express*, reported in its review of the year that it was on November the 12th 1984 that 'The first group of miners crossed picket lines at local pits to return to work'[28]. This event resulted in mounted police being called in the next day to 'patrol picket lines in South Kirkby and South Elmsall as 600 pickets gathered outside Frickley colliery and violence erupted throughout the area'[29]. In early January it was reported that more than 93 per cent of Yorkshire's 55,000 miners were still on Strike[30].

On January 24th 1985 the *Express* stated that 'Locally there has been a steady rise in the number of men crossing picket lines since the pre-Christmas levelling off. The [coal] board said 53 miners returned to work in the "Express" area at the start of the week. Most of them were turning in at Nostell Colliery, where 19 miners were working, and South Kirkby Colliery where 14 men returned. South Kirkby Colliery's N.U.M. president, Mr Frank Clarke, said he was proud of the way local miners had stayed solidly behind the Strike and that only 53 out of an approximate 5,000 local pit men had crossed picket lines. He said: "I'm pleased to see we are sticking together. We came out on strike together and we will go back together. The 'Express' area pits have been one of the strongest and most solid areas in the country"'[31].

Numbers crossing picket lines increased slowly until the seven local collieries covered by the *Hemsworth and South Elmsall Express* newspaper; Nostell, South Kirkby, South Kirkby East Side Coal Preparation Plant, Ferrymoor-Riddings, Grimethorpe and Kinsley, had a combined figure of 100 men returning to work in late February 1985[32]. Just before the end of the Strike, it was reported that at South Kirkby Colliery 36 men had returned to work[33]. Therefore, according to the figures, the Strike remained solid in the Hemsworth vicinity. This was reiterated once the return to work had started, 'The vast majority of miners at the collieries in the "Express" area have remained solid and up to last week, less than 100 had crossed picket lines and returned to work'[34].

One of the noteworthy aspects of the Strike, although this was obviously not an activity confined to Hemsworth, was the setting up of the local Miners' Wives Support Group. This is examined in detail in Chapter Five but suffice to say that this Group was formed when the Strike was in its infancy and continued to function even after the Strike had ended. The main remit of this group was to provide at least one good meal a day to the striking miners of the immediate vicinity but it also proved to be a haven for many of the women. Here they could leave the relative isolation of their domestic situation and share experiences and mutual support. For some of the women, it also provided an introduction to and an interest in politics. One woman claimed that, after having voted for Mrs Thatcher in 1979, her experiences in the Support Group enhanced her subsequent realisation that all women in politics were not the same.

An article, headed 'Providing 100 Meals', referring to the Support Group appeared in the *South Elmsall and Hemsworth Express* on the 31st May 1984. It states 'An action group is now providing more than 100 meals every weekday for striking miners. Formed with the intention of offering "practical help", the group consists of miners' wives and those sympathetic to their cause. Financial help was given by Hemsworth Town Council and the group is now using facilities at the Alpha Working Mens' Club. A spokeswoman said they were now in the process of writing letters to businessmen stressing that their motives were "non-political" and asking for donations'[35]. So, like many other groups up and down the country the Support Group was intended primarily to provide practical help but in certain cases it appears to have gone further than this; it encouraged a much wider interest in politics amongst the women. This became apparent during interviews with various members of the Support Group and, as stated, it is examined in depth in Chapter Five.

Apart from the setting up and running of the support group, the other noteworthy event which happened in Hemsworth was the so-called 'riot'. This took place on the 13th July 1984 and many interviewees alluded to it during the course of this research.

The riot is mentioned in Brown's article entitled 'Hemsworth's pigs' (*Spectator* 21 July 1984). He believes that Hemsworth 'is an excellent place in which to study the attitudes of the hard-core striking miners'[36]. He goes on to say 'Last week £100,000 worth of damage was done to the pit above ground during a small riot in which the Hemsworth police station was besieged; and further trouble followed at the weekend'[37]. The riot appears to have been instigated when a group of policemen marched into the Blue Bell public house on Cross Hills in the centre of Hemsworth. Many of those involved, questioned by Brown, believe that these policemen came from Huddersfield. The significance of this being that animosity towards the police could be directed towards police from outside the immediate vicinity. Surprisingly, perhaps, they do not appear to feel any animosity towards the local constable believing that he was overruled by his superiors.

According to the *Hemsworth and South Elmsall Express*, 19 July 1984, 'Police in riot gear were involved in a pitched battle with local men as violence erupted in Hemsworth town centre on Friday night'[38]. It goes on to say that eyewitnesses severely criticised the role of the police and estimates of the numbers involved are put at 120-150 police and 40-50 local men.

Following this incident a special press conference was held at Hemsworth police station. Alec Woodall met the the West Yorkshire Chief Constable, Colin Sampson. The latter met Hemsworth residents on the Saturday evening and Sunday afternoon following the 'riot'. A special police inquiry was held culminating in a Report to the Police Authority on the 25 July (see Appendix Four).

It is obvious that this event in Hemsworth was particularly significant due to the level of interest which it aroused. It represented an escalation in the scale of the violence from the picket lines and into the mining communities themselves. '*Scenes reminiscent of Belfast*' is an oft quoted phrase. In retrospect, the fears were not fully justified for this was a somewhat isolated incident. Nevertheless, the events in July served to underline the extreme feelings which were aroused on either side.

By the time that Brown returns to Hemsworth in February 1985, there has been a definite mood change. Now it seems that 'an honourable settlement'[39] will suffice in place of victory. Brown argues that the 'mistakes the miners made were all the fault of other people. The timing of the strike had been wrong - but then it was provoked by the Coal Board; the violence on television had been counter-productive - but then it was provoked by the police'[40]. There appears to be more than a hint of sarcasm in Brown's tone here.

Continuing this examination of Hemsworth and the Miners' Strike (both during and after); one post-strike event has been the setting up of a local branch of the Green Party in Hemsworth. This is examined in Chapter Six but it is worthwhile highlighting it at this stage. The local Greens were launched in August 1989, branch chairman Steve Ely stated, 'We believe that our input into local politics will begin to change the face of our area ... Who knows, at the next General Election, the electors of Hemsworth may choose a Green Party candidate to represent them in the House of Commons'[41].

It remains to be seen, as we approach the new millennium, whether the Greens will actually change the face of Hemsworth's politics and whether or not any direct link can be traced to the politicising impetus which may or may not have been provided by the Miners' Strike of 1984/5. The Greens are obviously a new political phenomenon in the Hemsworth area and the reasons for their emergence are worthy of investigation. It may be that Hemsworth's Greens are more a product of the national tide of events and a result of the surge of support clearly illustrated by the June 1989 European Electoral successes. The Green Party gained 15 per cent of the total vote but no seats in the European Parliament due to the First Past the Post electoral system used by the United Kingdom.

The local Greens did not put forward a candidate at either the November 1991 Hemsworth by-election or the 1992 General Election, presumably the cost involved was the major obstacle for the Party. They did, however, field a candidate at the 1996 by-election (Peggy Alexander obtained 157 votes). With further respect to the electoral fortunes of the Green Party at national level, Ghazi notes, in the *Observer*, that 'In the 1992 general election, the party's vote slumped to 1.3 per cent; in the recent [1994] local elections, it averaged 5 per cent. Membership has slumped from 18,500 in 1989 to less than 6,000'[42]. Weale, in the *Guardian*, also highlights the way in which the electoral fortunes of the Green Party have changed. In the 1994 European elections the Green vote plummeted 'from its high of 15 per cent five years ago to just over 3 per cent ... After the heady days of the 1989 European elections when the Greens emerged triumphant as Britain's fourth party, this time only three candidates out of 84 managed to poll the 5 per cent of the vote required to save their £1,000 deposits'[43].

It could, arguably, be the case that the Green's former success was part of the national phenomenon but the extent of any heightened political awareness stimulated by the Miners' Strike is, nevertheless, worthy of investigation to either prove or disprove this theory.

Conclusion

The debate surrounding the politicising impact of the Miners' Strike makes Hemsworth an interesting constituency to study; primarily because of the remarkably high numbers employed in the mining industry and also by virtue of the fact that for many years it was the highest Labour majority in the country. Allied to this there is the almost rock-solid support for the Miners' Strike, with only a very small handful of mineworkers returning before the end of the dispute[44]. Also, as Harrison stated, as far back as 1978, in 'The Independent Collier', 'we need more historical, micro-comparative studies of coal mining communities'[45]. Add to this the question of politicisation and interest is sure to be aroused in the lessons to be learnt from this one particular community and the impact of the 1984/5 Miners' Strike.

Notes

[1] Bulley, J. (1957) *Hemsworth in History*, p. 5.
[2] Ibid.
[3] Baylies, C. (1993) *The History of the Yorkshire Miners*, Volume 2, 1881-1918, (London: Routledge), p. 17.
[4] Bulley, J., *Op. Cit.*, p. 70.
[5] Baylies, C., *Op. Cit.*, p. 22.
[6] Bulmer, M.I.A. (1975) 'Sociological Models of the Mining Community', *Sociological Review*, (Volume 23, pp. 61-92), p. 62.
[7] See Appendix One for further details.
[8] See Appendix One for further details.
[9] Bulley, J., *Op. Cit.*, p. 74.
[10] Waller, R.J. (1991) *Almanac of British Politics*, (London: Routledge), p. 229.
[11] Ibid., p. 230.
[12] Ibid., p. 229.
[13] Butler, D. and Pinto-Duschinsky, M. (1971) *The British General Election of 1970*, (London: Macmillan).
[14] Butler, D. and Kavanagh, D. (1988) *The British General Election of 1987*, (London: Macmillan), p. 191.
[15] Ibid., p. 192.

[16] Winterton, J. (1987) 'The Miners' Strike: Lessons From the Literature', *Industrial Tutor*, (Volume 4, part 4/5, pp. 92-106), p. 92.

[17] Rees, G. (1985) 'Regional restructuring, class change and political action: preliminary comments on the 1984-1985 miners' strike in South Wales', *Society and Space*, (Volume 3, pp. 389-406), p. 399.

[18] See Glyn, A. (1985) The Economic Case Against Pit Closures, (Sheffield: National Union of Mineworkers) for further discussion of this matter.

[19] Hain, P. and McCrindle, J., 'One and All: Labour's Response to the Miners', *New Socialist*, (October 1984, Number 20, pp. 44-46), p. 44.

[20] Waddington, D., Wykes, M. and Critcher, C. (1991) *Split at the Seams? - community, continuity and change after the 1984-5 coal dispute*, (Milton Keynes: Oxford University Press), p. 8.

[21] Ibid., p. 8.

[22] Ibid., p. 205.

[23] Answer given by the Energy Minister, Mr. Michael Spicer, to a parliamentary question. Reported in the *Guardian*, 11th April 1989.

[24] British Coal London Headquarters, 8th September 1994.

[25] Butler, D. and Kavanagh, D., *Op. Cit.*, p. 345.

[26] Professor David Butler, Nuffield College, Oxford University. Letter received July 1994.

[27] Butler, D. and Kavanagh, D. (1992) *The British General Election of 1992*, (London: Macmillan), p. 322.

[28] The *Hemsworth and South Elmsall Express*, 3rd January 1985.

[29] Ibid.

[30] The *Hemsworth and South Elmsall Express*, 10th January 1985.

[31] The *Hemsworth and South Elmsall Express*, 24th January 1985.

[32] The *Hemsworth and South Elmsall Express*, 21st February 1985.

[33] The *Hemsworth and South Elmsall Express*, 28th February 1985.

[34] The *Hemsworth and South Elmsall Express*, 7th March 1985.

[35] See the *Hemsworth and South Elmsall Express*, 31st May 1984.

[36] Brown, A. 'Hemsworth's Pigs', The Spectator, 21st July 1984, p. 15.

[37] Ibid.

[38] See the *Hemsworth and South Elmsall Express*, 19th July 1984.

[39] Brown, A. 'Return to Hemsworth', *The Spectator*, 9th February 1985, p. 15.

[40] Ibid.

[41] See the *Hemsworth and South Elmsall Express*, 16th August 1989.

[42] Ghazi, P., article in *The Observer*, 12th June 1994.

[43] Weale, S., article in *The Guardian*, 14th June 1994.

[44] See the *Hemsworth and South Elmsall Express*, January-March 1985.

[45] Harrison, R. (1978) *The Independent Collier*, (Hassocks: Harvester Press), p. 14.

4 The Role of the Police

Introduction

As one of the key 'participants' in the dispute, the police cannot be ignored as a possible agency of politicisation. If the Miners' Strike did constitute a great politicising event then was the role of the police the pivotal or an important factor? The policing of the 1984/5 Miners' Strike, alongside the role of the women and the role of the media, remains, for many observers, the over-riding memory which they have of the events of 1984/5. The way that the police were used by the Thatcher Government in order to control the dispute, to discourage mass picketing and to patrol the mining communities raised questions in many quarters about the existence of a real-life '1984' police state.

In this chapter, therefore, attention turns to the role of the police during the Miners' Strike. The policing of the Strike will be examined at both national and local level. In addition, was there anything specific about the way that the police operated in Hemsworth? This Chapter examines public perceptions of the police force, the extent to which those attitudes have changed since the Strike? How the people themselves think that they have changed and what the police did which brought about those changes?

So, the bulk of this chapter is not so much about the police but what people *think* about the police. The main part of the chapter concentrates upon reporting and analysing what the interviewees have said. The focus is on people's political attitudes; on what the interviewees said about the policing of the strike and about policing in general. An examination is also made of how attitudes have evolved since 1984/5. It is necessary to examine whether police tactics during the Strike constituted something new or whether they were just part of a wider phenomenon? An attempt will be made to analyse just how pervasive the role of the police was during the

1984/5 Miners' Strike. In addition, no analysis of the role of the police would be complete without the inclusion of the police's perspective. It was for this reason that the view of a senior police officer was sought. An interview with the Chief Constable of West Yorkshire Police, Keith Hellawell, is included within this Chapter.

This Chapter also seeks to highlight whether the interviewees think that the policing of the Strike was very different from that which had gone before - in terms of previous industrial disputes, previous miners' strikes and policing of the community at large. Due to the fact that the *extent* of the policing was perceived to be so *different*, this helps our understanding of precisely why it had such an impact upon people's political opinions. Also, it was not just the extent of the policing but the fact that many 'new' tactics were used. These were approaches which had not previously been employed in an industrial dispute in Britain. These methods, which will be examined in detail at a later stage, include the use of the National Reporting Centre, the use of the Police Support Units and the process of binding over' and the various bail-terms.

Forms of policing

As stated, the policing of the Strike took many forms. Key features were the National Reporting Centre, the Police Support Units, the targeting of pickets travelling to Nottinghamshire, the bail conditions which often imposed a curfew on striking miners (meaning that they were more likely to be gaoled if they re-offended), the deployment of huge numbers of police at Orgreave, South Yorkshire, in order to combat mass pickets, the heavy police presence in many mining communities and the use of police convoys to accompany the relatively small numbers of miners who began to go back to work towards the latter end of the Strike.

It is worthwhile at this point saying a little about the situation at Orgreave. As stated in Chapter Three, Orgreave witnessed some of the bloodiest scenes of the entire twelve month dispute. Mass pickets were organised at Orgreave, South Yorkshire in May/June 1984 in an (unsuccessful) attempt to stop fuel supplies from Orgreave coke works reaching Scunthorpe steelworks[1]. As Callinicos and Simons state 'The result was the greatest violence seen in a British industrial dispute since before the First World War'[2]. Whether the blame for the violence is attributed to the police or to the miners, the events at Orgreave cannot be ignored and are relevant both in terms of the policing of the Strike and also in terms of the media portrayal.

Policing progressed from simple control of pickets at the various coal mines to stopping people on their way to picket, to the use of 'out of area' police, etc. It quickly became (apparently) a measure of the Government's resolve to contain the Strike and to break the determination of the miners. It could be argued that the purpose of the policing was to ensure that striking miners were not allowed to intimidate miners who wanted to work. On the other hand, the police are regarded by certain political commentators as having become a political tool used by the Conservative Government in order to oppress, what had previously been regarded as, the backbone of the trade union movement.

John McIlroy provides an example of the latter view. He argues that the Thatcher Government was influenced by the '72 and '74 strikes and by the 1978/9 Winter of Discontent in terms of realising the potential power which the labour movement had at its disposal. According to John McIlroy, who writes in Hugh Beynon's *Digging Deeper* (Chapter 5 'Police and Pickets'), the mass pickets emerged during the first few weeks of the Strike and the debate over whether to use the full force of the legal armoury open to the Government ensued. He cites an article from the *Times* which described 'an atmosphere of mounting confrontation reminiscent of the 1972 and 1974 disputes'[3]. The fact that the miners contributed, in no small part, to the downfall of the Heath Government in February 1974 must have weighed heavily on the Thatcher Government's strategy with regards to the policing of the strike. To quote McIlroy, 'The scar the events of the early 1970s left on Tory perceptions of law and order and the proper regulation of trade unions - Saltley Gates mingling with the demise of Heath in 1974 - was a permanent one'[4]. Likewise, the effect of the 1978/9 'Winter of Discontent' should not be underestimated on Tory consciousness.

The Ridley Report (a secret report drawn up by Nicholas Ridley, the radical right-winger, for Mrs Thatcher), as early as 1978[5], highlighted the fact that the Conservatives saw the major industrial threat as coming from the miners and that preparations would be made in order to minimise that threat. It listed measures which a future Conservative Government could take to deal with a threat from the trade unions, mainly the miners[6]. The sheer scale of the policing of the strike illustrates the extent to which the Conservative Leadership took heed of the Ridley Report.

A variety of measures came in to being, however, much earlier than the late 1970s. As McIlroy states, 'Police support units which could intervene in industrial disputes had been developed since 1970'[7]. These Police Support Units are described by Jonathan and Ruth Winterton as constituting 'Twenty men, two sergeants and one inspector, trained in riot-control techniques and equipped with riot shields, helmets and flame-proof boiler suits) from as many as fourteen different forces, under the direction of a "ground commander"'[8].

Another innovation was the National Recording Centre. This was to co-ordinate the 43 police forces, (given that Britain is supposed to have a police force which is based on a local level). It was 'used during the inner-city riots of 1981, the prison officers' dispute of 1980-1, and the Pope's visit in 1982'[9]. It emerged as a result of the 1972 Miners' Strike and, although it was activated during the 1974 Strike, it was not used to the same extent as it was during the 1984/5 Miners' Strike. The National Recording Centre, based in Room 309 at Scotland Yard, was used extensively during the Strike to co-ordinate the movements of both police and pickets. This is a very important aspect of the policing of the strike because, effectively, a national police force was in operation as illustrated by the fact that police were moved at relatively short-notice to potential 'trouble-spots' around the country.

Apart from the use made of the National Recording Centre, the tactics employed by the police also caused concern. Their use of roadblocks, of riot control tactics, of police support units (or P.S.U.s), their deployment of dogs and of mounted police raised a great deal of opposition. There had been nothing like it before, as Geoffrey Goodman states in *The Miners' Strike*, 'The practical use of riot-squad police in other industrial disputes, such as Grunwick and the Eddie Shah confrontation with the National Graphical Association at Warrington, offered no real parallel'[10]. During the first week of the Strike, the National Recording Centre sent 8,000 men to areas where trouble was expected. The main resistance by miners to the Strike came from Nottinghamshire so roadblocks were set up around that area and cars suspected of carrying pickets were turned back. This tactic obviously raised questions regarding civil liberties - a question which many magistrates, at a later stage, did not choose to answer. A question, too, which the media failed to adequately address.

Goodman highlights the fact that 'a virtual military command system'[11] was in operation. He continues 'Thousands of police, specially trained to contain civil disorder, were already being housed in army barracks near to the Yorks, Notts and Derbyshire coalfields'[12].

One important point about the policing of the Strike was the apparent initial reluctance on the part of the Government to use their employment legislation which had been passed in the early 1980s. The 1980 Employment Act (The Prior Act) and the 1982 Employment Act (The Tebbit Act) were not used. Goodman postulates two reasons as to why this should be the case; firstly, a political backlash may have been anticipated by the Government in that other unions would possibly have come out in support of the miners had the legislation been invoked; secondly, perhaps more importantly, there was no real need to utilise the new Statutes when existing tactics were achieving success. It is, however, worth pointing out that this apparent reluctance on the part of the Government only extended to the earlier part of the Strike. The Employment Laws were used to great effect against the National Union of Mineworkers from the middle of 1984. For example, the South Wales Area N.U.M. was fined £50,000 for contempt of court and they had their assets seized on the 30th July 1984.

The views of Margaret Thatcher, especially with regards to the policing of the Strike, are recounted in her memoirs, *The Downing Street Years*. She states that 'The militants knew that if it had not been for the courage and competence of the police the result would have been very different ... their [the militants] mouthpieces in the Labour Party began a campaign of vilification against them'. She continues in the same vein, 'Mob violence can only be defeated if the police have the complete moral and practical support of government. We made it clear that the politicians would not let them down'. Quoting herself on a Panorama programme Mrs Thatcher states, 'The police are upholding the law. They are not upholding the Government. This is not a dispute between miners and government. This is a dispute between miners and miners ... it is the police who are in charge of upholding the law ... [they] have been wonderful'. With specific reference to Orgreave, she asserts, 'The police were pelted with all kinds of missiles, including bricks and darts, and sixty-nine people were injured. Thank goodness they at least had proper protective riot gear'. Still on Orgreave, Thatcher continues, 'The sheer viciousness of what was done provides a useful antidote to some of the more romantic talk about the spirit of the mining communities'[13]. Later in her memoirs, she defends her usage of the phrase 'the enemy within' and claims that her meaning was distorted. 'Back in July [1984] I had addressed an eve of recess meeting of the '22

Committee on the subject of the "enemy within". The speech had attracted a good deal of hostile comment: critics had tried to distort my meaning by suggesting that the phrase was a reference to the miners at large rather than the minority of Marxist militants, as I had intended'[14]. Mrs Thatcher is in no doubt that the strike was unnecessary, 'The N.U.M.'s position throughout the strike - that uneconomic pits could not be closed - was totally unreasonable ... Yet the coal strike was always about far more than uneconomic pits. It was a political strike'[15].

The scale and extent of the violence on the picket lines remain as vivid memories of the 1984/5 dispute. It is worth pointing out, however, as Hain states, 'The violence in 1984-5 pales into insignificance compared with widespread violence during previous miners' strikes. During the 1867 coal dispute in South Lancashire there was large-scale violence against "blackleg" labour imported by the pit owners to break the strike, and in one incident in Wigan 5,000 miners marched to every pit still at work, smashing property and driving out imported blacklegs. In 1893, soldiers fired on an unarmed crowd of striking miners at Featherstone in Yorkshire; two were killed and thirteen injured ... Violence is a normal part of the history of strikes in Britain'[16]. This may be so but McIlroy believes that 'the scenes of picket line confrontation, crystallised in Tory minds around the death on the night of 15 March of David Jones, a Yorkshire miner, focused Mrs Thatcher on the law and order issue'[17]. The death of David Jones was, especially for the Yorkshire miners, one of the over-riding events of the Strike but in terms of the Government, the media and the public it was the events at Orgreave that were to remain as the more important issue. Mrs Thatcher was able to use the images of picket line violence to her advantage but the images of the events at Orgreave remain for many participants and observers, even today, a key politicising event - as the qualitative data will reveal at a later stage.

Policing the communities

The way that the policing of the Strike spilled over into the mining communities cannot be ignored. 'One important contributory factor, to the far-reaching nature and massive impact of the policing on the striking communities, was the penetration into the villages themselves. Police activity was focused as much on the villages as it was at the pithead gates and therefore brought all members of the community within its experience'[18]. This was indeed a very important aspect of the policing and one which, this research attempts to prove, fundamentally affected the politicisation of the people in the community of Hemsworth.

Adeney and Lloyd lend support to this viewpoint, 'The concentration of action in the last months of the strike in and around the pickets' home pits brought police into prolonged daily contact not just with pickets, but with the communities from which they came. It was this interaction which brought about some of the bitterest and most emotional reactions of the strike, and perhaps some of the longest-lived. It is the behaviour of the police in the villages, not so much in the heat of the picket line confrontation, that many miners are most bitter about. Those who are critical blame the out-of-town police, often the London Metropolitan, for their behaviour'[19].

There were a number of specific clashes between the police and mining communities. To quote Jonathan and Ruth Winterton 'On the evening of 9 July after the incidents at Rossington described in Chapter three [*Coal, Crisis and Conflict*], the police retaliated with a series of attacks and arrests in the villages of Hemsworth and Fitzwilliam'[20]. Incidents like these signified a marked departure from the style of policing which took place during the miners' strikes of the early 70s. Policing of an industrial dispute, which had at one time been confined to the picket lines, moved into the areas where the miners lived and not just those where they worked. So, besides focusing upon other workplaces (such as Orgreave) and on motorways, the police also operated, to a significant degree, in the communities themselves.

The style of policing must have contributed to the anger felt by many in the mining communities. 'At the end of the strike the anti-police bitterness in many mining communities was without parallel - far worse than in the 1926 general strike. Miners and their families had become convinced that the police, and the courts, were being used in a calculated manner as an instrument of oppression against the union'[21].

A number of texts exist which examine the Miners' Strike in general terms but there is a dearth of books specifically on the role of the police. Three notable exceptions are *Policing the Miners' Strike* by Fine and Millar, *State of Siege* by Coulter, Miller and Walker and Spencer's *Police Authorities During the Miners' Strike*. A more recent exception is *The Enemy Without* by Green. Winterton endorses the Fine and Millar text by describing it as, 'The most comprehensive analysis of policing in the miners' Strike'[22].

Adeney and Lloyd highlight the extent to which the miners and the police came into conflict. 'The police were deployed in larger numbers than had ever before been seen, deployed with growing efficiency by the National Reporting Centre in London, camped for weeks on end in Nottinghamshire, Derbyshire and Yorkshire. The riot control techniques which had been in ever more frequent use during riots in inner cities, football grounds and in such industrial conflicts as the 1980 steel strike were employed with skill against pickets who were, though numerous, never properly organised as a fighting force: the contest was unequal. By the later part of 1984, as the struggles on the picket lines during the surges back to work became increasingly bitter, both sides were brutalised: the police banged truncheons on riot shields as if auditioning for Zulu; the pickets strewed the roads with bunches of nails welded together to lame the police horses which charged them'[23]. This goes some way towards illuminating the conflict which took place.

Raphael Samuel *et al.*, in *The Enemy Within*, illustrate how the policing of the Strike was viewed in the mining communities. 'The police intervention was experienced - as it was in comparable cases in the nineteenth century - as an invasion, a violation of an almost private space - the colliery and the village which the miners and their families regarded as their own ('our pit', 'our village')'[24].

Various viewpoints have been put forward as to the role of the police during the miners' strike - in terms of what exactly were the police trying to do and whether or not their actions were justified. Some political observers believe that the police simply had to continue to attempt to maintain law and order, whereas others believe that the police went beyond what they, if not legally then at least morally, are empowered to do. This latter stance regards the police as having become almost an extra arm of the state.

Callinicos and Simons believe that the extent to which the policing of the miners' strike represented a change from previous tactics has been exaggerated (for example, see *State of Siege* by Coulter *et al.*). To them, 'The truth is more complex. Capital has ruled Britain ever since the defeat of Chartism in the 1840s through a combination of force and consent. The ruling class have, on the one hand, sought to incorporate the worker's movement within the existing order through the intermediary of the trade union bureaucracy. On the other hand, the repressive state apparatus - the police and sometimes the army - has regularly been used against sections of the working class whose struggles threaten this pattern'[25]. So, Callinicos and Simons are not blaming the failure of the Miners' Strike upon the extensive police tactics, rather they attach that blame to the T.U.C., the Labour Party and to the Left in general for failing to fully support the striking miners.

If the policing of the strike is regarded as a continuation of previous tactics then it is worth noting that in subsequent 'disputes', such as the handling of the Stonehenge Hippy Convoy, the Trafalgar Square anti-apartheid demonstrations, the anti-poll tax marches and the Tottenham riots, similar methods were used. This seems to indicate that the policing of the Strike *was* different.

Changed opinions?

The main way in which the policing of the 1984/5 Miners' Strike did have an effect is in the way in which many of the people in mining communities appear to have changed their opinions about the police. This seems to be as a direct result of the Strike.

This book seeks to show that in Hemsworth the majority of the people were deeply affected by police activities. The in-depth interviews indicate high levels of dissatisfaction with the policing of the strike. These attitudes will now be examined in detail.

This is what one interviewee (Number 4, a non-miner, politically active, house-husband) had to say about the policing of the Strike. 'I went on demos and stuff like that. I remember one at Blackpool in 1983, Conservative Party Conference. I went to concerts even in the 70s ... I wasn't really surprised how the police behaved during the Strike. The London police, I mean the police ... O.K. they've got the old S.S. excuse, they were just doing their job. But the thing that got me about the Strike was the sheer, the political will, that was willing to deploy police in such great numbers. They were at Orgreave the day Arthur Scargill got arrested (so you could tell it was going to be a violent day) and already there must have been about two or three thousand police. And I just looked at the motorway in the distance and it was a hot summer and there was a big long white line coming along this motorway and we couldn't see what it was and it turned off the junction and came towards us and we saw it was a convoy of white transit vans. Somebody counted sixty transit vans, 15 police in each van, just reinforcements! There were already a few thousand there and after that it was just haywire and they let the horses go and ... I only went to Orgreave once. I thought I'm not going again after that ... I think the violence was a mistake in terms of strategy but we can talk all day about tactical mistakes'.

The view expressed above is representative of a majority of the respondents. That is to say that most of the sixty interviewees felt that their attitudes towards the police had deteriorated since the 1984/5 Miners' Strike and they attributed that change directly to the policing of the Strike. Out of the sixty interviewees, 36 (60 per cent) stated that they had changed their opinions of the police. The remaining 24 (40 per cent) felt that they had not altered their opinion of the police due to the Miners' Strike. The majority of this 40 per cent were pro-police although one of the 24, (Interviewee number 16, Londoner married to a woman from Hemsworth, non-miner but politically active, unemployed) did say that he 'knew what they were like before' having lived in London prior to the Miners' Strike and having been 'involved' in race relations.

Clearly then, on the basis of the 60 in-depth interviews the policing of the Miners' Strike did appear to have an effect upon the majority of the people living in the community of Hemsworth. For most people their attitudes towards the police changed and what is more, these attitudes remain changed more than ten years after the end of the Strike.

It is worthwhile having a look in a little more detail at what the interviewees had to say about the policing of the Strike and their response to that policing: The interviewees represent a cross-section of the people of Hemsworth and, as stated, the majority changed their attitudes towards the police. As one former publican (Interviewee number 14, male, non-miner, politically involved) in Hemsworth stated, 'The local bobbies weren't too bad. It was the so-called police forces they brought from down South. I still say there were some out of the army in it. I'm still convinced of that me. I think she had some of the army involved with that. I didn't know we'd got that many police in this country anyway! Yes, I have changed my opinions. I'm very wary of the police now. I used to speak to them and that but we don't bother with them at all now'.

This viewpoint, that is to say making a distinction between 'local' and 'outside' police, was repeated many times. As a miner's wife (Interviewee number 11, active in support group) said, 'Local police - I've no problem but the policing during the Miners' Strike was disgusting. But they weren't our own local bobbies, you know and it put me off the police. It put me against the police actually because I saw such things and I heard such things about what happened. I mean it wasn't all hearsay, I saw a lot and I lost a lot of respect for the police during the Strike but not for our own local bobby'.

This theme of the local police behaving in a way that was more tolerant than those from outside the area was reiterated by a former striking miner (Interviewee number 10, politically involved) who has since become an insurance salesman; 'Well, my view of the police force is there's one good one and the rest are bastards. Ian Womersley's [Hemsworth's Community Constable] the only one that's any good. I used to get followed home by two of them during the Strike, same two. One of them promised he was going to get me like - but he isn't bright enough or crafty enough. .... They all made too much money out of it with doing overtime and strike-breaking. Blood money. They've all got posh cars and big houses out of it'.

A former Member of Parliament for Hemsworth was, on the whole, satisfied with the police performance but what qualms that he did have were levied against police from other areas (Interviewee number 5, Alec Woodall): Question: 'Have any of your views changed towards the police due to the Strike?' 'In West Yorkshire, No. I had full confidence in West Yorkshire Police. There was one incident that really upset me, so much that I went to see the Chief Constable. And that was an incident at Fitzwilliam. Now that was an isolated incident through one silly police sergeant (who I understand afterwards was moved). He really went over the top and got young constables there and what they did at Fitzwilliam was absolute mayhem. But if you look up in your records I think you'll find that in West Yorkshire there were no problems at all. All the problems were South Yorkshire and Nottingham and the other, course we had a riot at Frickley and the other one was at North Yorkshire at Kellingley. That was North Yorkshire. West Yorkshire - I understand there was also an incident on Crosshills at Hemsworth - one incident. And, I mean nowhere near the colliery premises, it was on Crosshills. And the Chief Constable himself came, full uniform, braid and the lot, walked amongst them. And I had a great admiration for Colin Sampson. I thought he was a first-class bobby and he'd come up through the ranks, from being a constable to being Chief Constable. So, in West Yorkshire, I'd no hesitation in saying that I fully support the police, except for that incident at Fitzwilliam. Now other parts of the country, I think, well, now we've got the report on the Wapping incident, it's quite obvious that the police went over the top in certain areas and were encouraged to do so. Now I don't think there's any doubt about that but I'd no qualms here'.

Andrew Taylor, a Lecturer in Politics at Huddersfield University who has written extensively on the miners, believes that this unwillingness to blame the local police in many mining communities is not fully justified. 'I think that has become part of the accepted mythology. It's also been one that the police in these areas have pushed. "We know what it's all about, don't worry". But I mean let's face it, the local police forces were just as active as the external ones'.

This 'accepted mythology' seems to be supported by majority opinion voiced about the policing of the miners' strike by the inhabitants of Hemsworth, that is to say the local police *are* regarded in a slightly more positive light than the 'outsiders'. The Metropolitan Police are singled out by many of the respondents as being the worst culprits. As a woman (Interviewee number 15, housewife) active in the Hemsworth Miners' Support Group says, 'Well, before the Miners' Strike I really considered the police to be a friendly force, always there if we needed them, you know P.C. Plod and things like that. Since the Miners' Strike my views have changed drastically but it's not only the Miners' Strike. I went down to the Wapping print-workers rally on the 3rd May [1986] and I was there when they charged us with batons and what have you. There were women with push-chairs and kids. Admittedly, they were the Metropolitan Police which is supposed to be the worst lot in the country but, even so, there was no need for the force that they used. Since then, I honestly, well I wouldn't pour a bucket of water on one if one were on fire. I know that for a fact. I just absolutely despise them and I would never ... don't get me wrong, I wouldn't do anything against them, if I was walking down the street I wouldn't throw a brick at them or anything like that but they would be the last person that I could help if I could possibly avoid it'. The Wapping dispute which this interviewee refers to concerns the 1986 dispute which occurred when Rupert Murdoch, owner of News International, moved production of his newspapers (*The Times*, *Sunday Times*, *News of the World*, *Sun*) to his new plant at Wapping with the ensuant loss of many jobs. The switch led to a bitter and protracted struggle by the former print-workers in an attempt to rescue their jobs. The scenes from the picket lines were reminiscent of scenes from the Miners' Strike.

This tendency to regard the Metropolitan Police as the worst force is reflected by Penny Green in her text *The Enemy Without*. She claims that 'Over 80 per cent of the picketing sample reported that certain forces were "worse" than others. Almost unanimously pickets cited the Metropolitan

Police and the Nottinghamshire Constabulary as being the most violent, the most unsympathetic and the most intimidating'[26]. So the perceptions of the majority of the people interviewed in Hemsworth seem to be in accordance with the pro-strikers living in other mining communities.

The impact upon the women is noted in greater depth in Chapter Five but, with respect to attitudes towards the police, perhaps the greatest change in opinion occurred in the women who worked for the miners' support group. Ten women who helped to run Hemsworth's Miners' Wives Support Group were interviewed. Out of these ten, eight (80 per cent) claimed that their attitudes towards the police had deteriorated as a direct result of the Strike. Only two (20 per cent) claimed that they had not changed their attitudes. This is what the two who differed had to say when asked whether their attitudes had changed (Interviewee number 15, housewife): 'Not really. I think they still do a really good job when you need them. I can't fault them that way. But after saying that, I didn't think they treated the miners with respect and when all said and done, they [the miners] were fighting for what they thought was right, they were fighting for their jobs'. So, even though this interviewee still supports the police, she does express her reservations. (Interviewee number 23, female, active in support group, works part-time) 'No, I've always been friendly with the police, never been in any trouble and, hopefully, never will be. It's just stories that you heard and things that you've seen on television. But I suppose there's good and bad on both sides - the miners' side and the police side'. This interviewee is prepared to concede that blame is to be attached to both sides in the dispute.

Apart from the two views cited above, by far the great majority of the women who were interviewed changed their views about the police due to the tactics employed during the strike. To quote Stead, the majority were 'Never the same again'[27]. Again, this accords with the research undertaken by Green, 'It was with the women of the strike, however, that the most dramatic changes in behaviour occurred and according to their reports it was the policing operation which largely determined these changes'[28]. 'Every woman active around the strike shared much the same experience of changed ideas and behaviour. All reported new levels of confidence and a new awareness of the police and politics'[29].

The policing of the Miners' Strike, according to the evidence gleaned from the in-depth interviews, does appear to have had a great politicising effect upon the inhabitants of the mining community of

Hemsworth. In Chapter Two, politicisation was defined, for the purposes of this research, as involving three factors. These factors being; political participation, political awareness and behavioural changes.

The way that the Strike was policed meant that, for many people, their political awareness was increased. They witnessed events on television regarding the policing of the Strike, they participated in the picketing themselves or they heard friends and relations recount tales of the activities of the police. Due to any one of these factors, or a combination of all three, the level of political awareness was heightened for a significant number of the inhabitants. Many, not just those who claim to have been politically aware prior to the Strike, emphasise the way in which they became much more aware and they attribute this to the policing.

The people who seem to have experienced the greatest change in their political attitudes were the ones who participated directly, be that on the picket lines or helping out with the miners' support groups. Direct involvement in the Strike resulted in a tendency towards a lasting change in opinion with regards to the police. For some, the policing of the Strike meant that they increased their level of political participation during and after the Strike in response to this. Membership of the Labour Party and participation on school governing bodies occurred in at least two cases.

Behavioural changes towards the police took place to the extent that many of those involved, and especially those who had direct contact with the police during the Strike, reported that they no longer felt the same towards the police. This manifested itself in some through such actions as crossing over the road when police approached and avoiding contacting the police even when a situation might necessitate it. It is debatable whether this constitutes politicisation but, nevertheless, it concerns action which the interviewees claim to have taken due to their experiences during the Strike.

The reasons why a great deal of attention has been focused upon the disturbance which took place on Crosshills on the night of the 13th July 1984 will now be explained. I believe that a detailed outline and comprehensive description of what happened that particular night is required precisely because of the impact which these events had upon the political consciousness of a significant proportion of the interviewees. All of those who were actually present at the time felt that the experience had changed them, in that it made them reassess and evaluate their previously held opinions and beliefs with regards to the police force. For others who were not actually present at the scene of the confrontation, they had a slightly less polarised viewpoint with regards to the police and the mining community. The majority of those interviewees were, nevertheless, still deeply affected by what friends and relations had recounted regarding the night in question. They too had to completely re-evaluate their perceptions of the police. So, in order to defend the detail given, in my opinion, this is necessary so that as full a picture as possible is painted. Otherwise the full extent of this politicising experience will not be appreciated.

Returning to the theme of a detailed analysis of what the interviewees had to say about the police, this is what one miner's wife (Interviewee number 41, works full-time, not politically involved) had to say; 'Well, I think they have changed. Yes, I always used to think that at one time the British police were very, very fair and above board and since the Miners' Strike my feelings have totally changed. I've seen some of the things that they've done, you know, which I've seen for myself. It's not what someone else has told me. I've seen it and yes I don't really trust them'. So, it appears then that this woman's perceptions were changed due to the fact that she participated directly in strike-associated activities, it was first-hand experience which fundamentally affected her attitudes towards the police and consequently her perception of politics.

This point about first-hand experience is repeated in the accounts of those who were involved in the 'riots' in and around the Hemsworth area. One woman who helped out with the Support Group (Interviewee number 21, divorcee, not politically active, works part-time) was also present on the 13th of July 1984 when there was the disturbance on Crosshills in the centre of Hemsworth. This major event was said to have deeply affected her opinion of the police. As she states; 'What I remember about the Miners' Strike is the police. That's what I do remember. I was once down in the Bell [Blue Bell Public House] and they came in. They walked straight through, straight to the back of the bar, straight through into the Lounge. And that was disgusting that ... It was either a Friday or Wednesday ... but I should imagine it was a Friday night and we were all having a drink, you know. I mean we weren't late or anything like that. And all of a sudden they came in. They marched straight behind the bar, I mean they were out of order doing that, and went into the Lounge. And there were young ones in the Lounge, you see. And they got anybody and everybody. They didn't care who they got. I mean they got a bloke across the road ... [name]. I mean he's as old as me and he'd nothing to do with anything. And it's not long since that he was up at court for it - that many years after. It [the police raid on the Blue Bell] affected me in a way that I would never trust, I don't think I'd trust a policeman again. But, I mean, you see they weren't from our area'.

A detached picture of the Crosshills disturbance is necessary for a proper apppreciation of its politicising impact. The events of that one night in July 1984 when the police did 'invade' the Blue Bell Public House constituted a flash-point with regards to the Strike and Hemsworth. This above all other events, save perhaps for the events at Orgreave, appears to have remained clearly in the minds of those who were directly involved as a turning point in their political attitudes and perceptions of the police. Another participant (Interviewee number 11, female, active in support group) helps to illuminate this impact; 'I mean I saw what happened on Crosshills that night. We'd come down home and we could hear all this noise and I said 'Come on, let's go up', because our Jeff [her son] was out see. Anyway, we went up and what the police were doing with them kids! I'm not kidding you, it was terrible. In fact my husband said to one of the policemen, "If that's the way you treat 'em then God help them kids." And then as we were walking further up Barnsley Road, we heard one policeman say to another one, "Corporal", and my husband said "I thought there were no corporals in the police force". He distinctly heard that. And he just said, "Get on, or else you'll be the next"'.

The above account constitutes yet another story of unpalatable contact with the police and, as such, fuelled the narrator with contempt for the police. Another woman (Interviewee number 12, active in support group, active in Labour politics) who had direct contact with the police, especially on the night in July, had this to say, 'There's good and bad in all but if I saw one on fire I wouldn't piddle on him. This is as a direct result of the Strike. Because, well, I've got to be honest, there are good and bad in all walks of life. The police force as we know it, as we *knew* it, was where you could say to your kids as they went out, "If you get lost you talk to a policeman". Now it's "If you get lost you don't say anything to the police" because they're being used by this Government as a paramilitary force. It's been proved beyond any doubt and nobody will ever convince me otherwise. Now, we had a rating system during the Strike. Metropolitan were the top for brutality - whatever they want to call it, "law and order"! Our lads were in plimsolls, trainers and sweat-shirts. They were in riot-shields, boots, knee-pads, helmets and batons. So, who were out for trouble?! The lads in running shoes and T-shirts in the sun for a day or them that came and opened the ranks and let the horses through at Orgreave such as that? Or, as [friend's name] said, her boy was out. She went to the 'Hill [Crosshills]. And then me, on my way up and ... I witnessed ... and I nearly got truncheoned. In fact, he did just tap me on the back of the neck, where they threw this one lad that had been to Wakefield for the night and he had nothing to do with what happened on the Hill and we saw eight of them jump on him and throw him in the van and put their boots on his head. Now they took my photograph because I said "I know his mother and I know you're not local coppers". So when you've experienced this, it's there, it stops there'.

Further detail regarding the event on Crosshill is necessary because it appears to have constituted a significant politicising incident. 'It reminded me of Ireland, you know. Oh, there were loads. In fact, it started from the Co-op, you can say and it went right up Barnsley Road. And the police were just dragging them kids down the middle of the road. They'd got a lad, 17, knelt him on his knees, put his arms behind his back, and put tie-wraps, not handcuffs, tie-wraps on him. And one bobby took a running kick between his legs and my daughter is five-foot in height and she tackled this bobby and she said "That lad's only a young lad and I've seen that" and he said "And you're the next if you don't get away" and he called her a ... choice names ... Then they got one lad and they pulled him up the police steps and they hit his head on every step up to the police station. That's true, that lad of ... [Cartwright's]' (Interviewee number 11, female, active in support group).

'But, I mean, Sampson, Police Inspector, he stood on the Hill just after that incident and he told the lads, my lad was one of them, he promised them that they'd withdraw the police from Hemsworth if they'd go home, disband ... and they were waiting down Robin Lane because I saw them and the vans were lined up down Robin Lane and he stood on the Hill and he told lies to them and what did they do? Within half an hour they were back again. And he stood there did Sampson, I'll never forget him' (Interviewee number 15, female, active in support group, housewife, not politically involved).

These recounted versions of the events on Crosshills bear a remarkable similarity; '[Betty] said these riot police just came in and they went straight behind the bar and nobody was doing anything wrong. Straight through the bar, straight through the lounge and out and they were just going for anybody and that's how the trouble started on Crosshills that night. That night the police provoked that' (Interviewee number 12, female, active in support group, politically active).

Still on the theme of the night in July 1984, 'They came out, split into groups and a man who was a councillor at the time, [name], he asked the police to give him two minutes to go and talk to the lads. They said 'Righto' and they waited thirty seconds and they charged. And that was a local councillor. They even got a lad kissing his girlfriend up side of the Chinese and battered. He hadn't even anything to do with the miners ... It was terrible. You know how the lads had studs on their jeans? This is true, they dragged this lad along Barnsley Road on Crosshills and there were sparks coming. And then they'd got another one, they were kicking his head' (Interviewee number 11, female, active in support group, not politically active).

Empathy with other oppressed groups

One other notable factor which emerged from the interviews was the fact that the Strike and in particular the way that the Strike was policed led many of those in the mining communities to make comparisons between themselves and what they saw as other oppressed groups. The most often cited links were with sectors of society such as ethnic minorities, homosexuals and the Catholics in Northern Ireland. This is an interesting development because previously, many of the interviewees claim, they had felt little for the plight of such groups whereas now they could identify with and appreciate the situations which many of these minorites had encountered. This ability to identify with other members of the working class (as the majority of these groups could be classified) could be seen as a step on the road to class consciousness.

The following comment illustrates this point: 'One of the things that got me is we used to watch the news and you'd see black people, Irish people and you'd think "No that can't be going on. Police wouldn't do that" and you'd look at it, listen and it'd go from your mind and we came to be aware that it did happen, it had happened and it was happening here. So that's stuck with you now, it's still there, you'll never forget. But what we never used to take any notice of we do now ... and you think "Ah, yes. It did happen!"' (Interviewee number 12, female, active in support group, politically active). For many of the interviewees the views expressed here fully accord with their own perceptions. But, as stated, those who were most affected were the people who had participated in key events themselves.

In *The Enemy Without*, Green appears to support the views expressed above. Many of the people whom she interviewed also were able to make this connection between 'oppressed groups', 'Certainly the links which many strikers and their wives made with the Catholics in Northern Ireland, Blacks in Britain, and workers in Poland indicates the development of an understood commonality in over half the sample. It seems that for some, the process of drawing links between themselves and other oppressed groups produced, for the first time, a sense of class consciousness, which linked them to other members of the working class'[30]. So, the interviewees in Hemsworth were undergoing similar changes in political awareness to those experienced by the people of Ollerton in Green's study. Rees reiterates Green's findings; 'Direct experience of police aggression generated a novel sense of identification with other oppressed and criminalised groups - Catholics in Northern Ireland, inner-city blacks - who previously were dismissed as merely "deviant". Moreover, this identification was a distinctively class-based phenomenon'[31].

Policing and Hemsworth

With regards specifically to the policing of the Strike in Hemsworth, a former member of the West Yorkshire Police Authority acknowledged that the policing of the Strike did give cause for concern. In response to this concern a special committee was set up mid-way through the Strike specifically to monitor police tactics in West Yorkshire. It is interesting to note that included in the list of those serving on this committee were Jack Taylor (at the time, the Yorkshire Area N.U.M. president), the N.C.B.'s Michael Eaton and the aforementioned Colin Sampson; quite a formidable gathering around the negotiating table. The former member of this committee claimed that one response to the events in and around Hemsworth (i.e. the disturbance on Crosshills on the 13th July 1984) was that the then Chief Constable of the West Yorkshire Police Force, Colin Sampson, decided that police forces from outside of West Yorkshire would no longer be allowed to operate within Sampson's domain. Andrew Taylor, of the former Huddersfield Polytechnic, highlights this, 'Funnily enough, it seems to me that relations in West Yorkshire recovered faster and further than in South Yorkshire, largely because perhaps West Yorkshire were responsible for most of their own policing ... And it [South Yorkshire] was largely seen, I think, as the battlefield to be won by the police'. So, perhaps Sampson's policy of using local police was a factor which served to modify local attitudes?

The special committee also fulfilled another useful role. It would send representatives, usually councillors on the now defunct West Yorkshire Metropolitan County Council, to be participant observers on the picket lines. They would then report their findings back to meetings of this 'special committee'. The former member of the West Yorkshire Police Authority found this to be a particularly useful procedure. The suggestion was that this practice of using observers might have had a moderating effect upon picket line activities - although this would be difficult to assert with any degree of accuracy.

Another question which needs to be examined in relation to the policing of the Strike is whether or not the action taken by the police in 1984/5 was just part of a wider general trend or whether it was something specific to the Miners' Strike. This is to say was the policing of the Strike just a continuation of a pattern *or* was it something new and specific to the coal dispute?

Was the Strike just part of the natural pattern of policing in this country or did it constitute the beginning of a much harsher, sinister even, form of police operations in the United Kingdom? A number of the respondents indicated that, yes, a general pattern of policing was emerging and that the Strike represented just another chapter in this particular aspect of social history, that is to say that it was not an entirely new phenomenon. It would be fair to say, however, that the majority of the interviewees did not hold this viewpoint. Most of those questioned believed that the police tactics during the Strike represented a marked departure from what had happened before. Road blocks, riot police, community sieges were all highlighted in order to illustrate the extent of these 'new style' operations. Those who espoused this viewpoint see the methods used by the police in 1984/5 as heralding a new genre of policing.

Those who support the 'just part of a wider phenomenon' argument (that is to say they did not really believe the policing of the Strike was that different or they believed that policing generally was changing) include the following, 'Well, I think the police have become more assertive now. And maybe that's been occasioned by the reaction to the police force in general now by the public. I think youngsters they live in a different environment now don't they? The police and young people ... So maybe the police have become a little more ... more young people are in trouble now than there have been before but some of those, I'm sure, have been occasioned by the changing attitude of the young people to the time of living. I don't think it's anything unique in Hemsworth ... I think that we suffer from what someone in the *Sunday Times* described as the "underclass attitude"' (Interviewee number 29, male, teacher). This interviewee does not regard the policing as vastly different from that which had gone before, simply a response to a decline in deferential attitudes in general terms and perhaps a growing disrespect for authority.

Another interviewee continues with this train of thought, 'Possibly it was the Miners' Strike when we heard the stories of them just going out and lashing out at people. But I mean that's happened since. There were student demonstrations, my daughters' friends were just walking peacefully down but because they'd been on the tail-end of a demonstration, the police just went in with their truncheons there as well. So my view, not necessarily the Miners' Strike, but that's the first time I became aware of it' (Interviewee number 32, female, teacher).

Andrew Taylor is another who questions whether police/community relations are bad everywhere 'to what extent is it the specific reflection of a general phenomenon?' He does not believe that poor community relations with the police is solely due to the Strike but 'I don't think that the Strike helped. Yes, they probably pushed it further and faster and that the relationship between the police and miners was much worse, obviously acute or stark as a result of the Strike'.

The conclusion of the Rees Report (written by Merlyn Rees, the Labour Party's former Home Secretary) is cited in Goodman's *The Miners' Strike* and that too regards the policing of the Strike and the breakdown of law and order as part of a wider general trend, 'There was some violence in some areas emanating sometimes from pickets, sometimes from the police, sometimes from both. It was not revolutionary but part of a broader general trend which can be seen more clearly since 1979 as more generally law and order in this country has steadily deteriorated. The miners' strike was not a thing apart'[32].

Basically, we are confronted by two questions in respect of the policing of the Strike. Firstly, was the pattern of policing in the Strike new? In other words, did it mark a break with previous methods of policing? Secondly, was the policing of the Miners' Strike representative of some more general pattern of policing evident in other cases? It is perfectly possible to answer 'No' to question one and 'Yes' to the second question. In response to these questions, it is necessary to be slightly wary in terms of laying too much emphasis upon what the interviewees actually say and to bear in mind that it is not necessary to attempt to answer these questions conclusively. Suffice to say, however, that we do need to look at the relationship between people's thinking about these topics and the Strike itself.

From the evidence gathered from both the in-depth interviews conducted in Hemsworth and from the research and examination made of the key texts which attempt to analyse the policing of the Strike, it would be a fair representation to say that most observers believe that the policing represented a departure from what had gone before. Certain commentators, however, point out that if the policing of the Strike was different, subsequent police tactics have often emulated what happened in 1984/85. Adeney and Lloyd help to buttress this argument; 'When West Country police later in the year [1985] sent in men with short shields and truncheons to smash the vehicles of the Stonehenge hippies' convoy; when the Metropolitan Police were seen to beat their long shields in the now familiar crescendo in the Tottenham riots; when demonstrators started to throw bricks and other missiles at police in Trafalgar Square anti-apartheid demonstrations; when Wapping seemed to re-enact scenes from the coal dispute - were these the signs of a new insensitivity and lack of inhibition bred by the miners' strike, or was there a wider explanation, a changing climate which itself had allowed such brutalism in the coal strike?'[33]. Thus Adeney and Lloyd leave open whether the Strike *caused* or *reflected* a change in policing.

Given that so many of the interviewees in Hemsworth, sixty per cent, claim that their opinions of the police had deteriorated due to their experiences during the Strike, it might be feasible to assume that the policing of the Strike was a departure from a previous 'softly, softly' approach. This would, however, be a spurious conclusion to draw from the fact that opinions regarding the police have changed. It might, for example, be the case that protracted industrial disputes are always accompanied by police brutality: it was just that none of the interviewees for this research had been through such an experience before.

Another interesting facet of the policing of the dispute is the level of blame which is attached to the police. Were the police simply used as pawns in the dispute? A number of interviewees seem to believe that they were. There is a school of thought which regards the police as political tools and mere 'victims of circumstances'. A number of the interviewees who did *not* report a deterioration in their attitudes towards the police espouse this particular point of view. One interviewee's perspective illustrates this point clearly; 'A general point is that I respect the police force. I think that we should all collectively support the police force. I think that the police acted very well during the Strike. I think the problem arose when politics entered into the situation and external forces were imported into the community. It was confrontational. And so, yes, my perception has changed due to the police. I think that I still support the police very much but I think that there should be some mechanism whereby they can't be used as a "political ping-pong", irrespective of which party is in power' (Interviewee number 6, male, former councillor, local doctor).

This view was re-iterated by others who claimed their opinion had not really deteriorated; 'I have always been in support of the police. I've found that they were ... that the actual footage of the miners' strike ... it proved that they were really, they were in a "no-win" situation' (Interviewee number 19, female shopkeeper, no personal connection with mining industry, not personally involved). The view that the police were 'just doing their job', even though it did constitute minority opinion, was more prevalent than might at first have been thought, especially given the fact that Hemsworth was a strong mining community, solidly pro-strike and which in the not too distant past had approximately 30 per cent of the local population employed in the mining industry. This view that the police were 'just doing their job' was espoused by 18 out of the 24 respondents who claimed that their attitudes towards the police had not changed. This constitutes 75 per cent of those interviewees who claim that their opinion of the police did not worsen during the Strike but only 30 per cent of the total number of people who were interviewed.

A number of factors relating to opinion and the policing of the 1984/5 Miners' Strike have been identified. These themes are relevant because, collectively, they help to illustrate how the policing of the Miners' Strike not only affected people's perceptions of the police but also had a fundamental impact upon the politicisation process. The policing was undoubtedly one of the most important aspects of the Strike in terms of the effect which it had upon people's political attitudes. Many of the interviewees believe that the police tactics heightened their political awareness, they became more questioning; for a few it meant that they were motivated enough to actually join a political party or to, as stated earlier, become a school governor.

The vast majority of the interviewees do claim that, for example, they became more interested in party politics as a result of the Strike. Others claim that their preferences with regards to the choice of early evening news on television altered with many coming to prefer the 'slightly more balanced approach' of the Channel Four News.

As stated previously, the majority of the interviewees do claim that their attitudes towards the police changed as a direct result of the police tactics used during the Strike. It is necessary, however, to examine whether this proportion of the respondents, 60 per cent, were interested in politics and political affairs prior to the Strike. If it is the case that the respondents were highly politicised anyway and therefore they might be predisposed, for example, to view the police as instruments of class oppression.

A statistical analysis of the respondents who claimed that their attitudes towards the police worsened produced some interesting results. Of these 36 respondents, 32 (89 per cent) claim to be interested, regardless of the depth of that interest, in politics. This leaves the remaining 4 out of the 36 (11 per cent) who claim that they have no real interest in political affairs. On a purely statistical level, it would seem that an interest in politics may lead to an increased awareness of police operations.

Of the 32 who say that their attitudes towards the police worsened and who also profess to having an interest in politics, 20 (62.5 per cent) claim to have become interested in politics during the Strike. They cite the Strike itself as being the motivating factor which produced their interest in politics. The remaining 12 out of the 32 (37.5 per cent) claim that they already had an interest in politics (again regardless of the depth of that interest) prior to the Strike.

So, an interest in politics does seem to increase the chances that an individual will perceive the policing of the Strike in a negative light but, of those who expressed an interest in politics, the majority were interested before the events of 1984/5.

Of the 24 respondents who said that they experienced no real change in their attitudes towards the police, 18 (75 per cent) claim to be interested in politics. The remaining 6 (25 per cent) said that they were not interested in politics. Of the 18 who did express an interest in politics 11 (61 per cent) claim to have been interested in politics prior to the Strike, six (33 per cent) claim to have become interested in politics as a direct result of the Strike and the final respondent (6 per cent) became interested in politics after the Strike but states that this interest had no real connection with the Strike.

Despite the fact that, as mentioned earlier, some people cited the policing of the Strike as a politicising factor others took an opposing view. The results constitute an interesting response to the policing of the Miners'

Strike. The method of policing affected attitudes towards the police in general terms and it seemed to have had a particularly significant impact upon whether or not people became interested in politics. It could be the case that the respondents had changed from having a very narrow definition of politics. If they perceived politics in parliamentary or institutional terms then maybe they felt excluded from this arena? If they changed and viewed 'politics' in a much broader sense then perhaps they saw its relevance to their lives. It was, however, the case that where the respondent did claim to be interested in politics then they were far more likely to condemn the police tactics used during the 1984/5 Miners' Strike.

Interview with Chief Constable Hellawell

Given that, albeit quite rightly, the bulk of this chapter is devoted to the perceptions of the interviewees with regards to the policing of the 1984/5 Miners' Strike, it is pertinent at this particular stage to attempt to redress the balance and reveal what the police have to say regarding the events of 1984/5. With this purpose in mind, the Chief Constable of West Yorkshire Police, Keith Hellawell was interviewed in August 1994. Hellawell was an apt choice of interviewee given that he was in charge of police operations in West Yorkshire during the Miners' Strike, even though he was not actually the Chief Constable at the time. This is what he had to say in response to a number of key questions: Regarding the current relationship between the police and the inhabitants of mining communities, Hellawell said, 'I think that we lost a lot of trust during the Miners' Strike and it will be difficult with this generation of people ever to return to the position prior to the Miners' Strike. I think the position is an improved one, the lack of co-operation and cold shoulders that we got immediately following the Miners' Strike is no longer there. But the people, if they sit down around a table and talk about it, there's a lot of bad feeling still there, and blame towards the police service. But we still get support with investigations and we do still have letters of appreciation from those communities about the police work. And there isn't any open hostility. So, I think, in short, the Miners' Strike did a great deal of damage, that damage will take some time to repair but it is being repaired'. Asked whether the police were scapegoats during the Strike, Hellawell replied; 'It's not a matter of scapegoats. We are the people that enforce the law and in a strike situation we can't win. And during the Miners' Strike, we were blamed by the right-wing of the Conservative Party for being too soft on the miners and we were blamed by the miners' unions for being too hard on the miners. In a way, we would have preferred that the Strike didn't occur and we weren't involved at all. We really didn't want it and we hate that sort of confrontation but ... we've got to be true to ourselves and keep law and order. In which case we really can't win'.

With respect to the debate surrounding local police versus police from outside the immediate area, the Chief Constable stated; 'I mean I don't know whether you know or not but I was in charge of policing here during the Miners' Strike. I adopted a strategy that was different to the strategy in other police areas. Firstly, we didn't allow the Met. to come in, so there is the myth, all sorts of stories about the Met. burning ten pound notes ... not true in this county. We did not allow the Metropolitan Police to come into this area. There was no Metropolitan police officer within this County. Because I'd heard the horror stories, whether they were true or not, I'd heard them ... I can't see any Metropolitan officer burning money, however well off they are. It's interesting, when I heard those stories ... I got all the myths then. But I never found someone who actually saw it. Nobody actually said, "I saw it". So we didn't have Metropolitan police officers within this County'.

In reply to a question about whether the police were justified in taking the action which they did, the Chief Constable gave the following response; 'No. I mean I don't think we'd any option but to do what we did. Can I say that here I will sing the praises of West Yorkshire. West Yorkshire Police Force took an approach that was not taken by other police forces. Our approach was that we would not take a confrontational stance until it was absolutely essential. And we put officers, we maintained officers on the streets in normal uniform and that made us the subject of extreme criticism by the Police Federation ... [for] putting police officers at risk of severe injury by putting them in situations without protective equipment. And we only put officers into protective equipment in West Yorkshire when the situation got such that leaving them without it would put them in extreme danger. And so we adopted a non-confrontational stance'. Hellawell proceeds to give further information regarding police tactics; 'We actually introduced the "Push" and I introduced it as a strategic move, to reduce pressure. Because when you have huge numbers of pickets and huge numbers of police officers ... there was so much tension building that we actually strategically introduced the push to get rid of the pressure. We pulled back from that because I was at the front on two occasions and lifted up with the strength of the force, two or three thousand to each side, it was very dangerous. So we pulled back from that but we did adopt it as a tactic to relieve pressure, both on the police side and on the miners' side - because there was all this locked up energy and stress'.

Hellawell also revealed how West Yorkshire was 'commended, if that's the right word, in a film done by Granada Television, who're usually not that favourable towards the police. They compared West Yorkshire tactics with South Yorkshire and showed that we'd far fewer injuries, far fewer arrests, no non-proceeded court cases. And so we were commended. It was showing West Yorkshire very, very positively'. He continues; 'I tried to stop the feeling that all miners were bad and the line we were pushing, which is the line I believe, that miners are generally good, and that there were a few renegades that were actually causing a lot of trouble. They were causing, they were agitating, within the picket lines. They were the ones that actually attacked the strike-breakers. They were the ones that were throwing the potatoes with razor blades in them and putting the spikes on the floor ... and what I said publicly was within the communities was that that doesn't do the miners' cause any good. They're as appalled by it as we are. They should help us stop these renegades, some of whom were not miners, some of them were subversives who were just causing trouble'.

When asked if he thought that the Strike was a great politicising event and what part, if any, the police played in this politicisation process, the Chief Constable said; 'To repeat myself, I would have preferred that it didn't happen at all. But as it did ... I don't know, I mean your research will tell you whether it is a politicising event. I think that any event that actually puts people on the spot ... then they do look at it to see "Well, who's got us into this situation", so it politicises them in that sort of sense. I think that the Miners' Strike was a blatant attempt, on behalf of the Conservative campaign, to show that they'd got a bloody nose in the previous ones and they weren't going to get it in this. And I saw that they supported the police service in terms of funding for the Strike in a way that they'd never done in the past which gave us the freedom to do things that we couldn't do before without the money. They paid 100 per cent of all policing costs after a certain date whereas in previous days, we'd had to take it out of our own budget. So, to that event, the Government of the day gave the police service the funding to police it and, this is the important point, in the way that *we* chose. There was no pressure and this might be difficult to believe but I can absolutely assure you there was no pressure from the Government to police it in a particular way because they were funding'. Hellawell then proceeded to dispute the notion that the police moved towards being a national force during 1984/5; 'It didn't. What I think that you've got to make clear is we do not have a national police force in this country. What we do have are national standards and we do also have national strategies'.

Asked whether the policing during the Miners' Strike was so different from what had gone before, the Chief Constable of West Yorkshire Police stated; 'Yes. Yes. My view was that the Miners' Strike was a disaster from the police's point of view. We were brought into an industrial dispute, and we'd no option, that was certainly the Government of the day taking on the unions. And the police had no option but to become involved and do their duty of maintaining law and order and they would be seen as the tools of the Government, tools of the employers'. He continues, 'In previous miners' strikes, we had failed and had been outnumbered and had to back off and from a professional point of view, we determined that we couldn't, we shouldn't be seen to lose. Now that didn't mean that we always won but it meant that if we were not going to win, we wouldn't endure a similar situation. So we actually had a much clearer picture of what was likely to occur and what the consequences of our actions were. There was a much more strategic approach to the dispute than there had been in previous instances'. Hellawell proceeds to outline how the 1984/5 Miners' Strike differed from previous disputes. 'The handling of the media and work within the community again was a stategic line that had never been operated before. We decided at the beginning to say that we could see the consequences of this. And the third thing was that we moved into what I would call quasi-military language that we'd never used before, like sterile ground and holding the ground, which was more military training than police training, became par for the course and I didn't like that ... but in order to deal with a situation like that professionally we had to understand and learn these sort of tactics in terms of policing the dispute. It was quite surprising the militaristic language which was used in our briefings. So that again was different'.

A fourth difference in terms of policing the dispute, states Hellawell, '... from a command point of view was that I'd never before literally sat on the top of a pit heap commanding two thousand police officers. I mean, it is more akin to battle. It wasn't a battle, as I've explained, our philosophy was not confrontation but in some situations you needed those numbers and that's not policing in Britain, commanding that sort of number of people was a change, it was something different'. A final change, believes Hellawell, was that 'it spawned, and we were conscious of this, that it spawned a number of police officers who were newly joined in the service who knew nothing else but this team policing, being with other police officers, working in a very tactical, militaristic-type situation where they weren't rubbing shoulders with the community, it was "them" and "us" ... and it was the daily war, the battle of "we won" and "they won" and that sort of thing, which is not the right grounding for police officers. We don't want that'.

On the positive side, from the police's point of view, the Chief Constable of West Yorkshire Police believes that 'from a professional point of view, we gained a substantial confidence at dealing with huge-scale public disorder and we came out of the Miners' Strike, and please this must be heavily loaded in terms of I wish this had never happened, it was an awful thing, but actually one of the positive things, we did come out of it with a great confidence knowing that we could deal with public disorder and a strike of that magnitude in a professional way and the unions ... I believe that there will never, ever be another miners' strike ever again because we beat the miners and I know it's awful to say it but we did. We were professional about it. And, therefore, it did give the police service confidence and it taught us a lot. We are professionally better for it ... Technically, we are better than we were before the Miners' Strike in dealing with those sorts of situations'.

When asked specifically about Orgreave, Hellawell said; 'No. I don't have any comments on the situation at Orgreave. It is our professional policy that we don't comment on situations in other police areas. I mean the argument is that unless you're actually there and face it, you would be wrong to comment on it. It's like the Yorkshire Ripper was an international case but you will not get other Chief Constables commenting on it ... there is an ethical side to it but it is more the practical side'. Thus the Chief Constable confined his comments specifically to West Yorkshire.

The Chief Constable, therefore revealed his views regarding the policing of the 1984/5 Miners' Strike. His comments are pertinent both from the point of view that he led police operations in West Yorkshire during the Miners' Strike even though, as stated earlier he was not the Chief Constable at the time and his opinions are also interesting because Hellawell is himself a former miner having worked at one time at Emley Colliery. His views regarding how different police tactics were during the Miners' Strike are illuminating and also the fact that he is prepared to accept that the Strike was a great politicising event. He adamantly disagrees with some of the interviewees in terms of this question of the involvement of the Metropolitan Police and he also believes that there were a number of outside infiltrators who saw the Miners' Strike as a vehicle for their 'cause'. Although it is inevitable that the Chief Constable has a vested interest and is obviously going to defend the tactics employed by police during the Strike, I did feel that Hellawell was keen to present a very balanced picture of the Miners' Strike and I must admit that some of his responses seemed more open and honest than perhaps I had anticipated he would be given his position. The interviewer had to reassess some of her previously held opinions.

Conclusion

The role fulfilled by the police during the 1984/5 Miners' Strike definitely had an effect upon the levels of politicisation of the inhabitants of Hemsworth. Evidence gleaned via the sixty in-depth interviews reveals that a significant proportion of those questioned felt that they had altered their opinions with regards to the police force. It is apparent that a majority of the interviewees were affected by police activities during the 1984/5 dispute. If the tripartite definition of politicisation, highlighted in Chapter Two, is examined in depth then the results are particularly interesting.

With respect to the first criterion, political participation, the research revealed that a number of interviewees were galvanised into political activity as a consequence of their perception of police activities during the 1984/5 dispute. The interviewees fitting this category are those who, for example, joined the Labour Party and those who became school governors. Whilst these did not constitute a majority of interviewees they were, nevertheless, people who felt that they wanted to become involved in the 'political' arena. They were affected and motivated into taking this action partly by what they had either experienced first-hand or what their friends and relations had told them about the activities of the police during the 1984/5 coal dispute. Obviously there are degrees of politicisation and some people will undoubtedly be more interested or committed to politics and the political arena than others. It is clear, however, that for these people who did increase their levels of political participation, either during or after the Strike, their comprehension of police activities and behaviour throughout 1984/5 had a marked effect upon their desire to participate in politics. The role fulfilled by the police meant that some of the interviewees felt almost compelled to become involved in the political arena in an attempt to redress the balance and to try to protect the interests of the working class in relation/opposition to the police which, for many of them, came to be seen as almost an additional arm of the state, enmeshed in the machinery of government. A point worthy of further reiteration is that those who had participated directly themselves in Strike activities, such as going onto the picket lines or collecting for Strike funds, were the ones who claimed to have experienced the greatest increase in their levels of political participation in the post-Strike period. The compulsion to participate was, for a significant number of the interviewees, the overriding legacy of the 1984/5 Miners' Strike.

The second criterion, namely that of political awareness, witnessed the greatest amount of change in relation to the levels of politicisation as experienced by the sixty interviewees. Whereas the interviewees might not necessarily have wanted to become involved in the political arena, a great many of them claimed that their personal level of political awareness had increased and they attributed this increase directly to the role fulfilled by the police during the 1984/5 coal dispute. The main claim was that because of what they had seen on the television, of what they had personally witnessed on the picket lines, because of local experiences such as the 'flashpoint' in Hemsworth on the night of the 13th July 1985 or because of what their friends and relations had recounted to them, they felt that this had led to them becoming more politically aware and having a perception of political events and of the political arena with a small p and a large P. It is perhaps the case that it takes more energy and more of a concerted effort to actually get up and do something and participate in politics, as the first criterion necessitates, whereas this second dimension requires less activity but, nevertheless, does still feature in the politicisation equation. It is perhaps for this reason too then that more people claimed to have increased their levels of political awareness than stated overtly that they increased their levels of political participation and that this was as a direct consequence of police activities throughout the course of 1984/5. Many of the interviewees claimed that they had found the police activities during the Strike to be almost a revelation in terms of what the police are capable of achieving. That is to say, in terms of the extent to which the police force is able to control aspects of individual behaviour such as the freedom of movement between counties or being able to impose curfews upon citizens. Police activities throughout the Strike, described in depth in the earlier part of this Chapter, had a profound and lasting impact upon the levels of political awareness of many of those questioned throughout the course of this research. The heightened political awareness which many of the interviewees referred to and which they directly attributed to the role fulfilled by the police should not be under-estimated.

Still focusing upon this criterion of political awareness, the impact which the interviewees perceptions of the policing had upon their levels of empathy with other oppressed groups is worthy of reiteration. This aspect, examined at length throughout the earlier part of this Chapter, was a significant legacy of the role fulfilled by the police during 1984/5. A significant proportion of the interviewees alluded to this increased awareness of the plight of, what they now came to regard as, other oppressed groups. This is an important factor to note in terms of the politicisation process.

A further dimension with respect to heightened political awareness is the significant impact which the policing of the Strike had upon the female interviewees. A brief statistical analysis is given earlier in this Chapter but it is necessary to reiterate that the impact upon the women, especially those who participated in the running of the Support Group, was considerable. The politicisation of the women is examined in detail in Chapter Five but it is necessary to, once again, highlight the fact that the policing of this particular industrial dispute had a significant and lasting effect on the levels of politicisation of the female interviewees.

Less dramatic perhaps but still deserving of a significant amount of attention and discussion is the impact which the role fulfilled by the police had upon the third element of the tripartite definition of politicisation, namely that of behavioural changes. Relatively few of the interviewees stated that they had actually undergone any behavioural changes as a direct response to the role undertaken by the police during the 1984/5 Miners' Strike. Nevertheless, some behavioural changes did actually take place and these were attributed, by those who cited them, to the police activities. Changes such as crossing over the street when a police officer was approaching or advising their children not to ask directions from a police officer when they are lost neatly fit into this category of behavioural changes. Again, if reference is made to what may be termed a continuum of politicisation then it is fair to say that, with respect to the role of the police during the 1984/5 Miners' Strike, behavioural changes are not necessarily the most important factor in this instance. Most of the interviewees claim not to have altered their behaviour or life-style in response to the activities undertaken by the police during 1984/5 but just because behavioural change was not an overriding feature of the post-Strike scenario does not mean that it is unworthy of a degree of discussion and debate. Behavioural change was evident, even if only in a small way, so it definitely deserves a mention. As to why behavioural change was less evident than heightened political awareness, again it is probably due to similar arguments as to why increased political participation was not as significant as heightened political awareness. Behavioural change involves a degree of action, no matter how small. Political awareness, as stated earlier, involves a change in consciousness and, as such, requires much less of a concerted effort on the part of the individual in question. Even though the numbers claiming to have undergone some behavioural change are relatively small, perhaps the significant point to note is that anyone should feel so affected by the activities of the police that they should actually want to consciously do something in response to the role fulfilled by the police. To clarify the argument being expounded here, is it the case that, precisely because behavioural change does involve a concerted effort on the part of the individual citizen, it is necessary to emphasise the impact which the role fulfilled by the police must have had if just one person has changed their behaviour? The point relating to a qualitative difference between the three components of politicisation is worthy of re-emphasis at this particular juncture.

To conclude, the policing of the 1984/5 Miners' Strike does appear to have been an important issue with regards to the politicisation process but the results are nowhere near as straightforward as might at first have been thought. An interest in politics, however, does appear to be linked to the way that the policing of the Strike was perceived.

As is highlighted by the depth of feeling inherent in the accounts given by many of the interviewees, the way that the 1984/5 Miners' Strike was policed remains for a majority of the inhabitants in the mining community of Hemsworth as the over-riding feature and the most enduring memory of the events of 1984/5. The results of this study do nothing to refute Goodman's warning that the 'relationship between police and mining communities may well have suffered for generations to come as a result'[34]. The effect of the policing lives on in the hearts and minds of this pro-Strike community.

Green sums up the effect of the policing, 'the uniformed policing of the strike was a crucial factor in the politicization of the striking community, sharpening class divisions, highlighting common class interests, and illustrating the role and partiality of the state in situations of class conflict'[35].

In this respect at least, there are marked similarities between Ollerton and Hemsworth. On the evidence unearthed through this research, the findings accord with those of Penny Green when she says that the policing was a 'crucial' factor in the politicisation of the striking community. In Hemsworth it certainly was an extremely important factor.

This book highlights the effect of the policing upon the attitudes of the people of the community under investigation. It illustrates the lasting impression which the police tactics had upon many inhabitants within that community and, therefore, it remains a central part of the politicisation process.

Notes:

[1] See Callinicos, A. and Simons, M. (1985) *The Great Strike*, (London: Socialist Worker), Chapter Four, pp. 82-119 for further details. Also, MacGregor, I. (1986) *The Enemies Within - the story of the Miners' Strike 1984-5* (London: Collins), pp. 205-208 and Winterton, J. and Winterton, R. (1989) *Coal, Crisis and Conflict*, (Manchester: Manchester University Press), pp. 87-9.

[2] Callinicos, A. and Simons, M., *Op. Cit.*, p. 101.

[3] McIlroy, J., in Beynon, H. (1985) *Digging Deeper - issues in the miners' strike*, (London: Verso), p. 101.

[4] Ibid., p. 102.

[5] See *The Economist*, May 27th 1978, pp. 21-22.

[6] See Callinicos, A. and Simons, M., *Op. Cit.*, p. 36. Also Winterton, J. and Winterton, R., *Op. Cit.*, p. 146 for further details.

[7] McIlroy, J., in Beynon, *Op. Cit.*, (1985), p. 103.

[8] Winterton, J. and Winterton, R., *Op. Cit.*, 1989, p. 160.

[9] Adeney, M. and Lloyd, J. (1986) *The Miners' Strike 1984-85 Loss Without Limit*, (London: Routledge and Kegan Paul), p. 102.

[10] Goodman, G. (1985) *The Miners' Strike*, (London: Pluto Press), p. 118.

[11] Ibid., p. 119.

[12] Ibid., p. 120.

[13] Thatcher, M. (1993) *The Downing Street Years*, (New York: Harper Collins), pp. 346-353.

[14] Ibid., p. 370.

[15] Ibid., p. 377.

[16] Hain, P. (1986) *Political Strikes*, (Harmondsworth: Penguin), p. 13.

[17] McIlroy, J., in Beynon, *Op. Cit.*, p. 104.

[18] Green, P. (1990) *The Enemy Without - Policing and Class Consciousness in the Miners' Strike*, (Milton Keynes: Open University Press), p. 51.

[19] Adeney, M. and Lloyd, J., *Op. Cit.*, p. 126.

[20] Winterton, J. and Winterton, R., *Op. Cit.*, p. 162.

[21] Goodman, G., *Op. Cit.*, p. 126.

[22] Winterton, J. (1987) 'The Miners' Strike: Lessons From the Literature', *Industrial Tutor*, (Volume 4, part 4/5, pp. 92-106), p. 102.

[23] Adeney, M. and Lloyd, J., *Op. Cit.*, p. 5.

[24] Samuel, R. *et al.* (Eds) (1986) *The Enemy Within. Pit Villages and the miners' strike of 1984-5*, (London: Routledge and Kegan Paul), p. 22.

[25] Callinicos, A. and Simons, M., *Op. Cit.*, p. 233.

[26] Green, P., *Op. Cit.*, pp. 72-3.

[27] Stead, J. (1987) *Never the Same Again*, (London: The Women's Press, 1987).

[28] Green, P., *Op. Cit.*, p. 74.

[29] Ibid.

[30] Ibid., pp. 75-6.

[31] Rees, G. (1993) 'Class, Community and the Miners: The 1984-1985 Miners' Strike and Its Aftermath', *Sociology*, (Vol. 27, part 2, pp. 307-12), p. 309.

[32] Goodman, G., *Op. Cit.*, p. 129.

[33] Adeney, M. and Lloyd, J., *Op. Cit.*, p. 128.

[34] Goodman, G., *Op. Cit.,* p. 117.

[35] Green, P., *Op. Cit.*, p. 82.

5 The Role of the Media

This chapter examines the interviewees' perceptions of the role played by the mass media during the 1984/5 Miners' Strike. The way in which the media portrayed the events of 1984/5 is cited by many political commentators as one of the most significant aspects of the Strike. As David Jones *et al.* say in *Media Hits the Pits*, 'Media coverage of the coal dispute has become almost as big an issue as the dispute itself'[1]. Rather than simply reflecting the key features of the dispute, some critics feel that particular sections of the media manipulated and shaped events. It is also said that partial images of the Strike were portrayed and in some cases blatant lies were conveyed to a largely unsuspecting public.

A number of issues will be examined throughout this discussion of the role played by the media during the 1984/5 Miners' Strike. One of the issues to be examined is whether the agenda under which the media operated was actually determined by the Thatcher Government/National Coal Board? Secondly, the conspiracy theory will be examined, that is to say, was there a determined plot by the media to participate in the downfall of the N.U.M.? Thirdly, media omission will be highlighted, i.e. that bias can occur in terms of what is not explicitly stated by the media. Fourthly, a more general political analysis will be examined, that is to say, is the media against *all* strikes? The crux of this chapter is, however, based upon the premise that media coverage of the Miners' Strike was an issue, purely and simply because the interviewees say that it was.

In their text, *Media Hits the Pits*, Jones *et al.*, writing for the Campaign for Press and Broadcasting Freedom, compare coverage of the 1984/5 Miners' Strike with that of 1974, 'The coverage was not pro-N.U.M., however the *Mirror* firmly blamed the Prime Minister, the *Express* ran sympathetic stories on the miners (if not on Strike), *The Times* announced that even the "moderates" and some Tory M.P.s backed the strike, and the *Sun* explained "the terrible danger of work underground"[2]. They go on to say that this contrasts sharply with media coverage in 1984/5, which 'was a far more hostile and polarised political situation for the miners'[3]. It appears then that the 'style' of media coverage given to the coal dispute represented a marked departure from that which had gone before.

Ownership and Control

It is necessary to examine the press and broadcasting separately as they operate quite differently. In terms of the press; newspapers are all privately owned and overtly partisan - usually favouring the Conservative Party. The ownership and control of newspapers is a matter of concern to many political commentators given that certain individuals, such as Rupert Murdoch, own huge media conglomerations. Observers, such as Bill Schwarz and Alan Fountain in Beynon's *Digging Deeper*, question how the press can be seen as a free institution given such a concentration of ownership and control.

In terms of the concentration of ownership and control, Tunstall, in his text *The Media In Britain*, cites a survey undertaken by Seaton and Curran. They 'published a series of tables ... One showed that around the late 1970s six media companies - Reed, Pearson, Thomson, News, Trafalgar and British Electric Traction - were also involved in a major way in other industries and other countries; a second table shows just three companies controlling well over half of all national newspaper circulation. Another table indicates that even the provincial press is highly concentrated - over half of all regional daily circulation being owned by five chains'[4]. This concentration of ownership in the hands of a few vast organisations remains the current state of affairs. In the opinion of the C.P.B.F., as depicted in *Media Hits The Pits*, 'for the majority of Fleet Street papers political considerations take precedence over news. Most newspapers are part of vast diversified industrial conglomerates and exist to serve the economic, ideological and political interest of their owners'[5]. Surely, questions arise concerning impartiality when power is concentrated in the hands of so few? Some observers, such as the Campaign for Press and Broadcasting Freedom and also the Glasgow University Media Group, believe that there is a definite relationship between the concentration of ownership in the hands of so few and media bias. Ownership is used, partly, to explain why the press is predominantly right-wing. Given that the majority of these owners are right-wing and inherently capitalist by nature it is hardly surprising that this should be reflected in their publications.

A distinction does need to be made between the tabloid or 'popular' press and the broadsheet or 'quality' press. The former, such as the *Sun*, places primary emphasis upon being entertaining whereas the latter, such as the *Independent*, aims primarily to inform. At first glance, one might regard the level of political content and analysis in the tabloids as, therefore, negligible. This is not the case. Even though the tabloids present the news in a more 'lightweight' fashion and couch their stories in less academic terminology than do the broadsheets, the extent of their political coverage is still quite significant. It can also be argued that, precisely because the tabloids appear to neglect politics, they are much more insidious and potentially more 'dangerous' in terms of the impact which they have upon the electorate. If people do not perceive political bias or propaganda they may accept certain contentious statements at face value and therefore cease to question and to seek a distinction between fact and mere opinion. Neil Kinnock, for instance, attributed part of Labour's failure to win the 1992 General Election to the negative campaign waged against the Labour Party by the tabloid press. Obviously, Kinnock's attribution of blame to the tabloid press does not represent academic evidence. Research[6] shows the reality to be far more complex than Kinnock's explanation allows. In Butler and Kavanagh's study, it is claimed that 'A case can certainly be made that newspapers altered the outcome of the election ... But there is a stronger case against allowing a decisive role for the press in 1992'[7]. The main arguments put forward are: Firstly, that the press had been just as biased in 1983 and in 1987. Secondly, the late swing to the Conservatives was a national phenomenon and not just based upon newspaper readership. Thirdly, press influence tends to be based on a long, rather than a short, campaign. In the light of these factors, we need to be wary of attaching too much blame to the tabloid press.

Paul Foot's former column in *The Mirror* was overtly political and Ken Livingstone obviously felt that there was more than financial benefit to be gained from writing for the *Sun*. So, the tabloids do serve an important political function. They are political but in a different way to the broadsheets.

Another angle is editorial control. Journalists may in fact exhibit a great deal of sympathy towards industrial disputes but, as Green states, militating factors include the 'economic interests of those who own and control the media, the hierarchical nature of media institutions (whereby critical journalism is generally edited at one of several stages in the hierarchy), the relationship between the media and the range of "official" and "acceptable" news sources and the internal constraints'[8].

In terms of television and radio, they are supposed to aim for impartiality and if this cannot be achieved then at least a sense of balance. The B.B.C. is bound by its Charter and I.T.V. by the I.B.A. Act to strive to achieve political neutrality. The rules governing Channel Four differ slightly. Here a sense of balance is still the ultimate goal but this may be achieved across programmes rather than within a programme. Thus Channel Four felt able to screen Ken Loach's *Which Side Are You On?* whereas I.T.V. regarded it as a political 'hot-potato'. Channel Four is also regarded as progressive by some political commentators because of the fact that they gave a camera crew to both Arthur Scargill and Ian MacGregor to enable them both to produce their perspectives on the Strike. This was regarded as a positive way to approach the dispute. Schwarz and Fountain believe that Channel Four News attempted 'to at least explore the issues with a modicum of journalistic seriousness and integrity'[9].

Main themes

As stated earlier, there are a number of themes which emerge during any examination of the media's role during the coal dispute. Winterton and Winterton, in 'Coal, Crisis and Conflict', regard the main themes as; the question of violence, the issue of democracy, the emphasis on the personality of Scargill. They also analyse the effect which media coverage had upon perceptions of the strike. Green echoes many of these sentiments, 'The vilification of Arthur Scargill, the unbalanced emphasis on picket line violence and intimidation, the failure to explain issues at the heart of the strike, the criminalization of striking miners, the unquestioned assumptions of police neutrality and the fundamental contradiction between the reality experienced by striking communities and the distorted presentation of that reality through the mass media - these were the key components of the media's ideological policing of the strike'[10].

In terms of the emphasis which the media placed upon Arthur Scargill himself, it is fair to say that the strike was regarded by many observers as 'Scargill's Strike' such was the extent of the high profile given to him by the press and broadcasting institutions. It is also fair to say, however, that Scargill has rather a love-hate relationship with the media to the extent that he appreciates the advantages which the media can have in conveying a message to a mass audience and he is is extremely adept at dealing with hostile interviewers. Nicholas Jones, in *Strikes and the Media*, emphasises Scargill's skill at dealing with the media; 'Mr Scargill's rise to power had been helped by his ability to increase his own newsworthiness by exciting the news media. He knew how to project himself on radio and television, he was not alarmed by the brightness of the lights or the confusion of the studio surroundings, as he had quickly learned to intimidate interviewers and take advantage of television and radio presenters'[11].

Ian MacGregor was no real match for Arthur Scargill in terms of effectiveness in using the media. Nicholas Jones questions MacGregor's motives; 'Why did he (MacGregor) personally try to take on Arthur Scargill in a media confrontation when he had been most successful when working as a team, and as at British Leyland, leaving the interviews to someone more capable like Michael Edwardes?'[12]. Jones goes on to postulate as to the reasons why this was the case. 'I think it was a combination of vanity, in the sense that Mr MacGregor believed mistakenly that he could out argue Mr Scargill, and irritation that all those jibes, about him being a butcher and an imported elderly American, had hit home'[13].

With regards to Scargill, Winterton and Winterton talk of the 'Personalisation of the miners' strike'[14]. They believe, however, that Scargill is able to resist Robert Michels 'Iron Law of Oligarchy' and that he is not a megalomaniac. 'Like A.J. Cook, Scargill is one of the few trade-union leaders to have defied the iron law'[15]. What they mean here is that Scargill maintains his radicalism and that he doesn't dilute his ideas in order to achieve success.

As stated, media coverage of the strike was a controversial issue. A number of political commentators believe that the media was used during the strike as a political tool by the Government. Winterton and Winterton express this clearly in *Coal, Crisis and Conflict*, 'The mass media should not be seen as autonomous from the activities of the Government, the N.C.B. and the police, since so much of their strategy for undermining the strike entailed the use of the media'[16]. Betty Heathfield, in her introduction to the C.P.B.F.'s *Media Hits The Pits*, echoes this view; 'Throughout the dispute we faced the onslaught of the combined efforts of the Tory government, the police and the judiciary with the overwhelming support of the British media. The commendable efforts of those sections of the press owned by the labour movement and a minority working within the media to counteract it could do little to prevent a remorseless campaign of prejudice, distortion and lies instigated by the Government and pushed relentlessly through the mass media'[17].

David Jones *et al.*, of the C.P.B.F., believe that the Government were able to use the media to serve their own ends. They state that the Government and National Coal Board's 'media interventions were as meticulously planned as were their policing operations and alternative energy deliveries'[18]. They go on to say that 'The press blatantly intervened on behalf of the Government, N.C.B. and working miners. At the same time broadcasting more subtly accepted the Government/N.C.B. "definition of the situation"'[19].

Nicholas Jones, in *The Media and Industrial Relations: The Changing Relationship*, highlights how the agenda under which the media operated was set by outside forces. 'Again it was the National Coal Board which had succeeded in dictating the agenda. What pre-occupied the news media every day for almost a year was: How many miners had defied Arthur Scargill and gone back to work?'[20].

Media bias

Besides the agenda-setting, another memory of the strike coverage was the stories which were printed in the press which were deliberately intended to portray the miners and their union in a particular and partial light. The C.P.B.F. mention a number of stories which they found especially harmful to the miners cause. They mention three stories which the *Daily Express* ran in April and May 1984. On the 9th May 1984 the *Express* had a lead story headlined 'The Truth That Scargill Dare Not Tell'. It was a 'spoof confession by Arthur Scargill that he had lied to his members and the public about the reasons for the strike'[21]. In the edition dated 19th April 1984 Professor Hans Eysenck 'warned of the similarities of propaganda technique between Arthur Scargill and Adolf Hitler!'[22]. Perhaps the most famous headline was the 15th May 1984 when the *Sun* attempted to print a picture of Arthur Scargill with his arm raised in an attempt to make him look like a Nazi. The headline 'Mine Fuhrer' was obviously intended to convey a particular and partial message.

In terms of media bias, it is fair to say that bias occurs in what is omitted just as much in what is included. The C.P.B.F. discovered a number of gaps, such as 'the conflicting claims and philosophies underlying the dispute; the government's constant behind the scenes management of the entire dispute ... the enormous support for the strike from the mining communities themselves, especially the women; the threat to civil liberties posed by the police role in the dispute'[23]. Besides these issues, the media, in the opinion of the C.P.B.F., failed to highlight the 'vast network of supporting organisations and groups throughout the country ... the extensive solidarity from sections of the international labour movement ... the quite sinister links between the working miners and organisations like the Freedom Association, the Aims of Industry and other right wing pressure groups'[24].

The lack of coverage given to the role of the women in the dispute is regarded by the C.P.B.F. as being due not just to a 'blinkered view of the dispute, but as also related to the "invisibility" of women within the media in general'[25]. As Betty Heathfield states, 'The role of the women's movement and its strength has been ignored and misrepresented by the media'[26].

One of the important aspects to emerge from the media coverage of the 1984/5 coal dispute was the way that the media, especially television, attempted to steer a middle path by aiming to support the so-called 'national interest' but in so doing it inevitably worked against the interests of the striking miners. This is not a phenomenon which is specific to the miners' strike, rather it is symptomatic of the media's difficulty in coping with strikes *per se*. The media is regarded by certain political commentators as being against strikes in general; as Green states, this is 'the product of structural anti-strike ideologies built into the media process which were disseminated to the general public in order to isolate the miners industrially, socially and politically'[27].

Green cites Downing ('The Media Machine', London, Pluto Press, 1980) who believes that there are seven key features of the way in which the media deals with strikes. These are: that the specifics of the strikes are ignored; a public voice is denied to the strikers; the causes of the strike are not fully explained yet the disruption which the strike causes is emphasised; the class significance of the strike is reduced; the strikers become isolated from their class and that elusive concept known as the national interest; the trade union is regarded as the only voice of the strikers and, finally, the state is seen as protecting the 'national interest' and being a 'benevolent neutral guardian'[28]. An examination of the media coverage of the 1984/5 Miners' Strike clearly highlights these seven features so perhaps it was the case that the media portrayal of the dispute was not unusual.

The Media and the Miners

In terms of the way the strike was portrayed by the media, it is necessary to examine people's perceptions of that coverage. What impact did the way that the 1984/5 Miners' Strike was represented on television and in the newspapers have upon those living in the mining communities?

An interesting point to note is that the numbers of those claiming that the media was biased against the miners corresponds exactly to the number of those interviewees who state that their attitudes towards the police changed during the 1984/5 Miners' Strike. Thirty six out of the total sixty (60 per cent) felt that media coverage was biased against the miners whereas twenty four (40 per cent) decided that it was not biased. The same interviewees were involved in both cases. How significant is this? Perhaps it is hardly surprising if these people hold a particular set of political opinions and beliefs. Surely, it is inevitable that they will think in a similar vein when questioned both in respect to the behaviour of the police and in relation to that of the media? An additional revelation was that twelve out of the sixty claimed that their level of participation increased, this constitutes 20 per cent of the interviewees. The remaining forty eight, 80 per cent, state that their level of participation did not increase. This is not, however, as significant as might be anticipated because a proportion of those who state that their level of participation did not increase as a direct result of the Strike were already heavily involved and participating in the political scenario prior to the Strike.

The interviewees who were questioned for this research were asked a number of questions about the media and about their perceptions of the media coverage during the strike. Firstly, they were asked whether or not they read a newspaper every day. Of the sixty interviews conducted, twenty six people claim to read the *Daily Mirror* on a daily basis, twelve claim to read the *Guardian*, five say that they read the *Independent*, four read the *Star*, three read the *Daily Mail*, two read the *Yorkshire Post*, one reads the *Yorkshire Evening Post*, two read the *Express* and five state that they do not read a newspaper.

Perhaps the most surprising aspect about choice of newspaper is the fact that no-one reads the *Sun* newspaper (or at least no-one admits to reading the *Sun*). This could be explained by a number of factors. Firstly, it could be that the interviewees, by their very nature, constitute an unrepresentative sample. This is to say that the 'type' of person who is likely to come forward for interview is perhaps unlikely to read the *Sun* in the first instance. Secondly, it could quite simply be that the interviewees are aware of the stigma attached to *Sun* readers in certain quarters (Jasper Carrott the popular comedian for one) so that they are reluctant to confess that they read the *Sun*, this is similar to the way in which many people, when questioned about race issues, do not own up to the fact that they are racially prejudiced. Finally, it could be that the interviewees are representative but representative of a community which has turned against the *Sun* due to the politicising effect of the Miners' Strike. It could be that the inhabitants of Hemsworth have undergone changes in their reading habits in the same way as many people in Liverpool turned against the *Sun* newspaper in protest at its coverage of the Sheffield Hillsborough Disaster. In retrospect, perhaps a question specifically relating to the *Sun* newspaper should have been levied at the interviewees. In an attempt to alleviate this problem, the local newsagents in Hemsworth were contacted in order to discover details relating to their circulation figures; in the belief that if 'x' per cent of the inhabitants read the *Sun* then this will determine how representative the sample is. By way of comparison, the average national daily circulation for the *Sun* newspaper was 4,007,520 during the first half of 1994 (Source: *The Guardian* 20/6/94) making it the most popular daily newspaper. Most of the newsagents in Hemsworth were reluctant to reveal this information regarding daily circulation but one did state that, on a daily basis, their circulation could be roughly broken down as follows; 40 per cent *Daily Mirror*, 20 per cent the *Sun* and 40 per cent 'others'. The *Mirror* remains, therefore, according to these figures, the most popular daily newspaper on a local basis but the figure of 20 per cent for the *Sun* newspaper means that although not as popular locally as it is nationally, the *Sun* is, nevertheless, more popular than reliance upon the interviewees alone would lead us to believe.

Comments on their choice of newspaper included the following; (Interviewee number 9, former miner, unemployed, not politically active), 'I've got mixed feelings about the *Daily Mirror* because so much contradictory evidence comes forward in that particular paper, especially of late [reference to the allegations of financial irregularities and Arthur Scargill's handling of the Union's funds]. But, having said that, that is a paper that probably my wife would pick up and bring home ... if any paper is available, from the *Times* down, now I don't fully understand everything that's in them but certainly I'll have a read in case there is any information that I can glean from them. So it's really any particular paper which tends to give you an unbiased view if I can get hold of one and the nearest one I've come to is the *Guardian'*.

Another interviewee had this to say about his choice of newspaper, (Interviewee number 10, former miner, now insurance collector, active during Strike), 'Always the *Daily Mirror*. I wouldn't touch the *Sun* with a twenty-foot barge pole. I don't even believe the date printed on that thing and the others are just so politically biased that I ... I mean the *Daily Mirror* it's supposed to be a Labour paper but if there's anything that's wrong about the Labour Party then they'll say it. Whereas the other papers just wouldn't dream of pulling the Conservatives to pieces. You know it's money, money, money all the time. I mean I'd like to have a million pounds but I'm dead certain that if I'd got a million pounds it wouldn't change my views one bit, on what we should do with the country'.

The role played by the media was commented upon by Andrew Taylor of Huddersfield University. When asked for his comments,Taylor had this to say 'You mean printable ones?! Yes, I mean clearly I think you have to distinguish between the electronic media and the print media. I think the print media were absolutely ... I'm not talking here about the *Sun* end I mean they're just beyond the pale ... although, having said that, clearly they were playing an important function in the sense of reproducing a particular image of the strike. The quality press, I suppose obviously, were anti-N.U.M., pro-Government; some attempts were made to put over the miners' case, the miners themselves didn't put over their case particularly well. It was picked up to some extent in the press and obviously the *Guardian* was the obvious one. The electronic media, I think, were particularly interesting. I spent some time with the Channel Four News team in Nottinghamshire and they were very anxious to do a good job, you know to put both sides. And I think that it is significant that of all the news gathering teams, it was Channel Four that had the best reputation for fairness amongst the miners and I think that was partly due to the fact that the items that the Channel Four did were longer because it's a longer news bulletin and I think that what the miners felt was that their case suffered not merely because of what they thought was political bias or, in the case of the press, that's obvious. But they felt that really they weren't given the opportunity to get their case over - with the possible exception of Channel Four. And Channel Four was seen as being the best of a bad bunch. So I think the media was crucial ... I've always thought the miners fought the media battle very badly. I'm not saying they could have won it. I don't think they could ... The media battle; I think they could have played it better than they actually did'.

When questioned as to whether there was a difference between the national and local coverage, Taylor had this to say 'Again, I got the impression that local television coverage, whilst it was reluctant to accept the miners' case, nonetheless, was willing to spend more time discussing both sides of the story for obvious reasons. Again, I had a little bit of involvement with *Look North* and *Calendar*. I thought that *Calendar* was probably more sympathetic. But that was just an impression and I couldn't document it or anything like that'. *Look North* and *Calendar* are the regional news programmes provided on a daily basis by B.B.C.1 and Yorkshire Television respectively.

Alec Woodall, the former Member of Parliament for Hemsworth, was questioned about his attitudes towards the role played by the media during the Strike. When asked which newspaper he reads, he replied, 'Crikey, I read two or three. The *Guardian* and the *Yorkshire Post* - and I only get the *Yorkshire Post* so I can see what the Tories are playing at and make comparisons. You know the way they dress up the head-lines'. In terms of the coverage during the Strike being biased, Woodall stated, 'I don't think there was any bias at all but I've always taken the *Guardian*, I've taken the *Guardian* for donkey's years and it's only these last few years that I've started taking the *Yorkshire Post*. But when I was in Parliament, of course, I read all the newspapers because they are provided there. I mean not just British newspapers but world newspapers. You could get the *New York Herald*, *New York Times*, they were all there in the House of Commons. You can get practically any newspaper you wish. All the dailies and provincial papers were provided in the House of Commons. Course, I used to read as many as I could'. In terms of news and current affairs programmes, Alec Woodall claims to watch them on a regular basis and he also watches 'the *Parliament Programme* now'. As to whether his views have changed, Woodall says yes in that he is disappointed with the N.U.M..

They are not, strictly speaking, a 'part' of the community [although Woodall, as a local man would probably wish to dispute this] yet both Woodall and Taylor had some very interesting comments to put forward regarding the impact of the media and they are, therefore, worthy of inclusion with respect to this Chapter on the media.

In answer to the question of whether or not they read a newspaper every day, two of the interviewees (numbers 16 and 17, both active during

Strike), husband and wife, claimed, 'We read everyday's newspapers but not on the same day! We can't afford to buy them so my mum saves all hers and we do get a daily newspaper but we get it two or three days late. The *Daily Mirror* usually, the *Sheffield Evening Star* and the Sunday papers and the local papers'. With regards to the news, 'I.T.N., usually, at 6 o'clock. And then, depending on what we're watching later, what fits in'. The interviewees felt that the Strike coverage was 'Very biased towards the Government and towards the police'. As to any difference between national and local coverage; 'Not a great deal. None of the television had much sympathy. We did have *Calendar* come to the kitchen [the "kitchen" being the communal kitchen which was organised by the Hemsworth Miners' Wives Support Group], it was summer, July/August maybe'. In terms of other current affairs programmes, they watch *Calendar Commentary* and the televising of the Commons during the day. If the subject matter interests them then they watch *Panorama* and *World in Action*.

The interviewee who was responsible for setting up a local branch of the Green Party (number 4, politically active, house-husband) was questioned about his perceptions of the media coverage of the Strike. In terms of reading a newspaper everyday, he had this to say; 'I can't afford it. I read the *Guardian* when I can afford it - and the *Observer*'. With regards to television; 'I watch *On the Record* (B.B.C.1). I watch the 6 o'clock News. I don't watch *Question-Time* because I get too frustrated. I tend to avoid a lot of political programmes now because I get frustrated. I don't watch the "Environment in Crisis" programmes which are going out now because I find that too depressing. I made the link between politics and the environment. I've always been interested in the environment but I only made the link in the middle of 1988. I thought the Green Party's the party for me. I was really depressed at that time. I think basically because of the television programmes'.

An elderly woman was questioned about her perceptions of the Strike coverage. She stated that she always watched the news; (Interviewee number 1, widow of a miner, pensioner), 'I did during the Strike. I didn't miss a session. I stick to Yorkshire most. You know to number three [that is to say I.T.V.] - because it's our area'. She went on to explain that she reads the *Daily Mirror* everyday but doesn't buy it, it is given to her by her neighbour. 'I don't have a Sunday Paper. I'm not bothered either because if I've had one given or lent, there's been nothing in it but filth'. The interviewee expressed a preference for *World in Action* provided that the subject matter interests her. In terms of the Strike coverage, she stated, 'Well, I think they portrayed it not quite as it was. You'd be sure that if there was anything the miners were doing on the picket-lines bad, they'd be on the telly. They didn't show you the police beating them up all the time and they didn't show you the police racing the horses down the road when the miners were picketing the early morning shifts ... When the Strike had been going a bit someone took a proper video of it and it was a different carry-on all together. The police were stood about waiting until someone shouted "Yes, Charge" and then they charged. And no-one was doing anything to them. It proved they were just doing it for practice. That's what I think about it'.

Another interviewee (number 27, female, active in support group, works part-time), claimed never to read a newspaper, nor to watch the news. She stated 'I don't watch it when they're on about politics because I don't understand it ... In the Strike I started listening a little bit to what they had got to say but I wouldn't say I was interested'. Another interviewee (number 19, female, shop-keeper, not politically active) who had no personal involvement in the Strike stated; 'I think probably on the whole they (the miners) didn't get a fair deal but, having said that, not being involved, I don't really know what went on. Do you know what I mean? All you can take it from is what you saw on the television'.

In reply to the question as to whether the media coverage was biased, one male interviewee (number 20, former miner, now school care-taker and governor), had this to say; 'It weren't true. It didn't give a true picture. A couple of years after the Strike there was a little, I don't know whether it was a documentary that was aimed at schools and colleges but I happened to have it on one day and I was watching this and what it was doing was showing you the difference between making a gathering look dangerous to making it look harmless and inconspicuous. What they did was they zeroed in on the trouble and there were just probably two or three people making a disturbance out of four or five thousand but when they panned out like that you couldn't see this trouble but when they zoomed in it just looked like everybody was fighting. And what it was saying was this is how (is it the directors or producers of these current affairs programmes?) make something bigger than it actually is. They were making news in a sense. You know like causing trouble at football matches is a minority but to hear the Government talk it's everybody who comes to a football match is out there to cause trouble'. According to this interviewee then, he has been made aware of how media manipulation can and does occur.

Another interviewee (number 10, former miner, now insurance collector, active during Strike) perceived this media bias against the miners but he also made a point of saying that the bias was present at local level too. 'During the Strike it was very biased against the miners. All they were showing was the occasional one or two throwing stones, breaking things. They never showed you ... well, one thing that we did we went off picketing one day - bearing in mind we'd been on strike for about nine months and everybody in the van was getting £1.50 a day that was to get us something to eat from maybe five in the morning while we got back to get to the soup kitchens at maybe two o'clock'. This financial detail is important given what happened next. 'In Kirkby [South Kirkby next to Hemsworth] coming back, near Kirkby Church, a car pulled out of the garage, a landrover I think it was, and a hand-bag fell off the bonnet or off the roof. I picked it up and obviously had a look to see if we could find out whose it was. There was a purse in it with about £300 in it, credit cards, cheque books. I took it up, found out where she lived, handed it to her. She was great. She lived on a farm. She sent no end of stuff down to the soup kitchen. She even reported it to the local paper and it was never, there was never a word printed'. There may have been 'genuine' reasons why this story did not appear but nevertheless it left its impression on this young miner. 'Even, well some of the local journalists were biased against us and they live in the area ... You did tend to get a little bit fairer treatment on your local news programmes, such as *Calendar*, but you never did on the national news. News at Ten and the Nine O'Clock News were ... well, Maggie's team were doing the interviews, weren't they?' It is important to note the reference to 'Maggie's team', this interviewee obviously perceiving a connection between the Government and the media. The media is not regarded as an entirely separate entity. The fact that the link is made is an important one.

This perception of bias against the miners was echoed in many of the interviewees' comments. One miner's wife (Interviewee number 13, active in support group) had this to say; 'I thought it was absolute rubbish! It seemed to be censored and some of the filming, we know what sort of filming was taken and hardly any of it was shown on the television. It was all in favour of the police and it was striking miners rioting and what have you. It was like at Orgreave. You notice on the news clips there was policemen in full riot-gear, there's miners in pumps and shorts and T-shirts.

Had they gone ... ? Now really ... anybody that's gone to do that are they going to go in pumps and T-shirts and shorts? You'd get ready, wouldn't you? Towards the back end of the Strike I think the national coverage it did show a little bit better view and some of the local programmes did but that's simply because they were coming round to the local groups trying to get stories and nobody would speak to them unless the true picture was shown. But we were sort of blackmailed really but we said "No way" would we be interviewed or anything because of the coverage that they'd shown us previously. They'd to make promises that it would be shown as we wanted it'.

A striking miner and his wife (Interviewees numbers 2 and 3, husband had relocated to the Selby Coalfield, wife is a clerical worker) also felt that media coverage of the Strike was biased against the miners. The husband had this to say 'Yes. I think there's no doubt about that but it was expected anyway. That's where we lost the Strike probably on a number of issues'. His wife continued, 'We do have relatives still in Cambridge and they say that people down there just don't understand'. The husband supported this view, 'Because the people were ignorant of what was going off, not by any fault of their own but by the media giving that sort of biased coverage but we knew when the Strike started that we'd have problems like that and in the end that could have been the lead up to the defeat that happened. It could have been that we didn't get public opinion on our side, not by a long way. It was biased, yes. Channel Four again was probably the exception. Channel Four probably gave the other view. I mean not extraordinarily biased but there were certain things said that they got away with. Unfortunately people take note of the media. They seem to believe everything what they read and that. We cancelled the papers during the Strike because we couldn't afford it. We used to get the *Mirror* but I wouldn't buy that now if you paid me. It's a tabloid newspaper. I'm not interested in who Elton John's carrying on with, and Boy George and that. If I had the money I would buy the serious ones *en bloc*, everyday like and read them but obviously I haven't got that money'.

This biased coverage was noted by a local doctor (Interviewee number 6, male, doctor and former councillor), 'Well, at the time, I thought that some of the national newspapers were more pro-Government and, for that matter, I think the whole country was pro-Government so maybe the newspapers were simply reflecting what people wanted. I think in a way the mining community was isolated at the time'.

A parish councillor (Interviewee number 14, male, former councillor who had been active in the support group) also recognised bias in the media coverage; 'It was very biased towards the Government. Even at the time, I wasn't in the Labour movement, I was a Liberal then but I still thought it was very biased towards them'.

A woman who was heavily involved with running the Miners' Wives Support Group in Hemsworth (Interviewee number 12, female, very interested in politics) had this to say about bias; 'Yes. Even the *Daily Mirror*. He is biased. He says he's a socialist but Maxwell's no socialist!' With regards to television, she continued, 'When they did that programme on *Calendar* up at our kitchen and we said, 'Yes, but you don't bring that Richard Whitely here'. So they brought Robert Hall, didn't they? We made arrangements for them to come and then early on the morning that they were supposed to come there'd been some trouble on the picket lines and, as usual, they'd turned their cameras away from our lads that were getting it and when it were the other way round, a police car had been tipped or something done to a television camera ... So, I rang them up and said "Don't bother coming. You're not coming in." I always remember this big bloke called Ronnie Mutch, can you remember he was a director or doing some directing freelance and he said could he come through and speak to me and I said I didn't believe in what, how they were portraying it here. They should have an unbiased programme on it. So, he said, "Well look, I've got my cameramen and all that waiting here and they've got Robert Hall, who you asked for as against Richard Whitely [Robert Hall and Richard Whitely are both reporters/presenters on Yorkshire Television's *Calendar* news programme], if I go and phone my producer and get permission for what you are demanding" (that we wanted to see it in full before it was shown on television and agree to any editing out, whatever, if one man objected they'd stop their cameras rolling, like that, different things that we put to him). So, I said "No, I don't mind" but I went down and I got in the phone box and I put my ear to the phone and he said I was very suspicious. I said "Yes, because we've had them from different newspapers and things have got twisted". But he did put a fair ... and he took us to Leeds to see it and that was put on the television while I was in Holland doing that tour'. She went on to say that coverage was very biased, 'I think sometimes on Channel Four, you might have got something a bit more nearer to the truth on Channel Four. But, other than that, I don't think there's a lot to choose between them'.

David Jones *et al.*, in *Media Hits the Pits*, echo the view that Channel Four News did portray the miners in a slightly more favourable light, 'During the coal dispute it was generally acknowledged by both miners and media-watchers that only Channel Four News gave the N.U.M. anything like a fair deal'[29]. Given that, as stated earlier, only Channel Four News gave Scargill and MacGregor the use of a camera crew to enable them to put their side of the argument perhaps this perception of fairness is not entirely without foundation.

Conclusion

Detailed examination of the role played by the mass media during the 1984/5 Miners' Strike reveals that newspapers, television, journalists in general, had a significant part to play in the politicisation of those interviewed throughout the course of this book. The effect of the media was not as prominent as the impact of the role fulfilled by the police during the Miners' Strike but it did, nevertheless, still have an important part to play in the politicisation process. Perceptions of the role undertaken by the media led many of the interviewees to claim that their attitudes and/or behaviour had altered. They, themselves, made a direct causal link between the media's coverage/non-coverage of events during the coal dispute and their own understanding of and interest in the political arena.

In order to produce a more detailed analysis of the impact of the media, it is necessary to employ the yardstick offered by the tripartite definition of politicisation. The three dimensions of politicisation, highlighted in Chapter Two, enable the impact of the role of the media to be assessed in some depth. As with the analysis of the role of the police, it is necessary to examine the three dimensions of politicisation separately.

With respect to the first criterion, political participation, the role fulfilled by the media during the 1984/5 Miners' Strike did not, of itself, galvanise many of the interviewees into participating in the political arena. They did not claim to have become so enraged or shocked by what they had witnessed on their television screens or by what they had read in their newspapers that they felt compelled to take action themselves. Rather, it appears to be the case, from what many of the interviewees said, that it was very much a cumulative situation. The effect of what was portrayed in the mass media, coupled with other aspects, such as the role fulfilled by the police force, combined to make some of them, albeit a minority of the interviewees, participate in politics. Participation meant, for example, that a few of the interviewees joined the Labour Party. For others, especially some of the female interviewees, participation meant such activities as collecting for Strike funds or engaging in, what for many of them was, the hitherto unthinkable task of giving speeches to often packed halls of interested observers and sympathisers. So, political participation did increase in some quarters and was, in part, affected by the role of the media but it is necessary to avoid over-emphasis of the impact which the role undertaken by the media had upon levels of political participation. Participation did not occur solely in response to media coverage but media portrayal was, nevertheless, a factor in the equation.

The second criterion, namely that of political awareness, witnessed increased levels and many of those interviewed directly attributed this to their perception of the part which the mass media played during the 1984/5 coal dispute. A significant number of the interviewees explicitly stated that because they had first-hand experience of events which took place during the Miners' Strike or because of the fact that close friends and colleagues had recounted their own versions of events to them, they were able to see that there was a discrepancy between their own interpretation and that portrayed in the media. Such a sharp delineation between what the interviewees perceived to be the truth and the 'official' account of proceedings had a marked effect upon politicisation levels. Again, as with those who claim to have directly experienced what they regarded as police brutality or harassment, those who had participated in many of the key events reported in the press and on television claimed to have experienced the greatest increase in the extent of their political awareness. The greater the degree of personal involvement the more the individual appears to have been affected by the role fulfilled by the media. Coverage of the picket lines, particularly of the mass picketing such as that which took place at Orgreave; coverage of local events such as the 'riot' or 'flashpoint' which took place in Hemsworth on the night of July the 13th 1985; coverage which portrayed the miners and their leaders in a negative light. Instances such as these served to fuel heightened levels of political awareness in many of the interviewees. They claimed that they came to realise that the media is able to portray a particular and partial version of events and that because they had first-hand experience they no longer accepted what they were told in the press and on television at face value. A majority of the interviewees felt that coverage of the Strike, in general terms, was biased against the miners. To reiterate a point made earlier, however, very few of them actually sought to analyse why the coverage should have been so biased and to question why the media should be so pro-establishment. Heightened political awareness meant that they developed a more questioning and sceptical response to what, many regarded, although not in so many words, as a Fourth Estate of the realm. The debate did not extend, however, towards an assessment of the existence of a Fourth Estate, regardless of the terminology employed.

Again, as with the role fulfilled by the police during the Miners' Strike, media coverage led to many of the interviewees citing an empathy with other 'oppressed' groups. According to a number of the interviewees, if miners could be portrayed in such a negative light, could it be the case that groups such as ethnic minorities, homosexuals, gypsies, etc... were also dealt a raw deal at the hands of those in the mass media? This aspect involving a more questioning and sceptical approach to those in positions of power was all part of these heightened levels of political awareness.

Moving on, it is necessary, at this particular juncture, to examine the third component in the tripartite definition of politicisation in an attempt to make a more explicit linkage between the empirical data and the theoretical debate surrounding the concept of politicisation as employed throughout the course of this book. With respect to the third dimension, behavioural changes, it is fair to say that a number of the interviewees did cite a change in their behaviour during and after the 1984/5 Miners' Strike and they attributed this change to their perceptions of the role fulfilled by the media in 1984/5. A number of examples will, hopefully, shed further light upon this claim. A couple of the interviewees claimed that they changed their daily newspaper in response to unfavourable or paucity of coverage which they felt was given to the striking miners by the some newspapers. They changed from reading tabloids to reading *The Guardian*. At least two other interviewees said that they changed from watching the news coverage on I.T.V. and on the B.B.C. to watching the Channel Four News. They felt that coverage on this Channel was, relatively speaking, impartial and was more likely to accord with their own version of events. It is worth noting that these behavioural changes were directly related to the media themselves (i.e., not taking the *Sun*, switching to Channel Four) rather than anything broader. So, media coverage of events during the 1984/5 Miners' Strike did induce a number of behavioural changes and, thereby, had a part to play in the politicisation process.

In conclusion then, the majority of those who were interviewed as part of this research state that they felt that media coverage of the 1984/5 Miners' Strike was biased against the striking miners. The results of this research accord with Winterton's view that 'The media came in for almost as much criticism as the police for their bias against the miners and distortion of events'[30]. It is fair to say, however, that the interviewees did not really proceed to analyse why the media behaved as it did. On reflection, the role of the media registered powerfully. The people were made aware but they did not appear to have gone a stage further to fully understand why. Green argues that 'the fundamental constituent of a class conscious position is the recognition that the mass media is structurally (and not by virtue of what government is in power or which individuals own particular newspapers) a medium for the dissemination of ideologies which support the existence of capitalism'[31]. She goes on to analyse her own findings and says, 'It is apparent from the data that the community, men and women, questioned far less why the media played the role of strike-breakers than how they carried out that role'[32]. Green firmly believes that 'the analysis of the media by the community is best described as conjunctural'[33]. So, although Green believes the media to be structurally biased against the miners few of the interviewees made that link.

This book supports Green's findings that only a very limited analysis of the role played by the media is undertaken by the interviewees. Nevertheless, a number of factors are worthy of amplification. Firstly, by far the greatest majority of those interviewed felt that the coverage of the 1984/5 Miners' Strike by the mass media was biased against the striking miners. Secondly, the local coverage was regarded as slightly less biased than that provided at national level, although even here there were problems in terms of it not always being regarded as impartial coverage. Thirdly, of the national channels, Channel Four News was regarded by many of the interviewees as providing the coverage which best approached neutrality. Finally, those who had actually participated in the Strike, be it on the picket lines, fund-raising or working in the kitchens, were more likely to claim media bias against the mining communities. Their first-hand experience meant that they were more likely to question the images which the media portrayed. Due to the fact that many of the interviewees were able to contrast their own experiences with other impressions, it appears that the media played a significant part in politicising the inhabitants of the community under scrutiny. As Douglass states in *Tell us lies about the miners*, 'A huge number of women, children and men living within the solidly pro-union mining communities, are today in possession of a radical new understanding of the nature of "the media", the press, radio and television'[34]. He continues, 'The degeneration of the British media has reached its lowest point. We in the pit communitities, have had the blinkers torn from our eyes. The real class nature of the media has revealed itself to us, we in turn must try and reveal it to the Labour movement, expose it, and tear the working classes from their transfixation to that screen'[35]. In terms of this book, it is not entirely feasible to declare that 'the real class nature of the media has revealed itself'. This is partly due to the interview questions which, on reflection, ought to have been more probing and to have demanded why the media is biased - if that was the conclusion which the interviewees reached. The conclusion of the interviewees in Hemsworth appears to be that the media is conjuncturally, as opposed to structurally, biased against the miners.

The role undertaken by the media in 1984/5 remains one of the most important aspects of the Miners' Strike. It is necessary, at this stage, to move on to another very important aspect of the 1984/5 Miners' Strike; the effect which those events had upon the women of the mining communities. This is examined in Chapter Six.

Notes:

---

[1] Jones, D. *et al.* (1985) *Media Hits the Pits*, (London: Campaign for Press and Broadcasting Freedom) p. 7.

[2] Ibid., p. 8.

[3] Ibid.

[4] Tunstall, J. (1983) *The Media in Britain*, (London: Constable), p. 173.

[5] Jones, D. *et al.*, *Op. Cit.*, p. 16.

[6] For a detailed analysis of this issue see Butler, D. and Kavanagh, D. (1992) *The British General Election of 1992*, (London: Macmillan), esp. Chapter Nine, pp. 180-210.

[7] Ibid., p. 208.

[8] Green, P. (1990) *The Enemy Without- Policing and Class Consciousness in the Miners' Strike*, (Milton Keynes: Open University Press) p. 158.

[9] Schwarz, B. and Fountain, A. 'The Role of the Media: Redefining the National Interest *and* The Miners and Television' in Beynon, H. (1985) *Digging Deeper - issues in the miners' strike*, (London: Verso) p. 126.

[10] Green, P., *Op. Cit.*, p. 157.

[11] Jones, N. (1986) *Strikes and the Media*, (Oxford: Basil Blackwell) p. 53.

[12] Ibid., p. 5.

[13] Ibid.

[14] Winterton, J. and Winterton, R. (1989) *Coal, Crisis and Conflict*, (Manchester: Manchester University Press) p. 166.

[15] Ibid.

[16] Ibid.

[17] Jones, D. *et al.*, *Op. Cit.*, introduction by Betty Heathfield p. 5.

[18] Ibid., p. 8.

[19] Ibid.

[20] Jones, N. (1987) *The Media and Industrial Relations: The Changing Relationship,* (Coventry: University of Warwick), p. 3.

[21] Jones, D. *et al.*, *Op. Cit.*, p. 9.

[22] Ibid.

[23] Ibid., p. 11.

[24] Ibid., p. 12.

[25] Ibid., p. 11.

[26] Ibid., p. 5.

[27] Green, P., *Op. Cit.*, p. 158.

[28] Ibid., p. 158.

[29] Jones, D., *et al.*, *Op. Cit.*, p. 21.

[30] Winterton, J. (1987) 'The Miners' Strike: Lessons from the Literature', *Industrial Tutor*, (Volume 4, part 4/5, pp. 92-106), p. 102.

[31] Green, P., *Op. Cit.*, p. 176.

[32] Ibid., p. 177.

[33] Ibid.

[34] Douglass, D. (1987) *Tell us lies about the miners*, second edition, (London: A.S.P.) p. 5.

[35] Ibid., p. 26.

6 The Role of the Women

'Brian made *my* snap for a change!'[1]

This chapter examines another equally important aspect of the 1984/5 Miners' Strike; the role played by the women of the mining communities. There are certain political commentators, amongst them Professor Vic Allen of Leeds University, who believe that the women were not just players in the events of 1984/5 but that they were central characters in terms of ensuring that the Strike lasted as long as it did.

Any pertinent analysis of the 1984/5 Miners' Strike must include discussion of the role played by the women during the Strike. It has been said, for example by Vic Allen[2], that many of the miners' wives were instrumental in ensuring that the strike lasted as long as it did. They not only encouraged their husbands to remain on strike but in many cases were openly warning their husbands not to return to work. The main issue of the strike was said to be, on the miners' side, the preservation of jobs and communities. So, in terms of the survival of the communities, it is perhaps not surprising that it was the women who were so vocal, forthright and politically active.

Certain political commentators, such as Geoffrey Goodman[3], believe that the role which the women fulfilled was unique in terms of the history of industrial relations in the United Kingdom. With regards to the 1984/5 Dispute the women were remarkably solid in terms of the support and encouragement, both practically and emotionally, which they gave to their menfolk. They were able to provide practical help for virtually a whole year via the vast support networks which were set up and through the many Miners' Wives Support Groups and 'Soup Kitchens' which they established.

In addition to the provision of at least one daily meal for striking miners, many of the women became involved in the political arena - if not at national level at least on a local basis. This, it is claimed, by commentators such as Jean Stead[4], was one of the most important outcomes of the 1984/5 Strike. The fact remains that the coal dispute galvanised many women, who previously had never considered politics to have any direct bearing upon their daily lives, to participate on a political level.

Women, who often had never had paid employment outside of the home or who had focused their energies upon raising their children, were suddenly thrust into the political limelight. For a great number of the women involved this meant taking part in such activities as fund-raising, making collections both in the U.K. and abroad in such places as Holland and Italy and also giving speeches about the plight of the mining communities to what were often huge gatherings of people.

Preliminary findings of a recent study into the effects of pit closures on mining communities in Yorkshire were first published in the *New Statesman and Society*[5]. The authors, Critcher, Dicks and Waddington, examined the employment status of ex-miners' wives in two former mining communities. Their ten per cent sample revealed that six months after the closure, 39.6 per cent of the women were housewives. Two years after the closure this had increased to 42 per cent. The second largest category was office/shop work; 14.6 per cent after six months and 16 per cent after two years. The third and fourth categories were titled, respectively, 'general labouring and manual' and 'caring'.

As Critcher *et al.* point out, 'women have to bear the brunt of family poverty and male despair. They have normally looked after shopping, cooking, organising the children and seeing that bills are paid. Now they have to manage this on a drastically reduced budget, and with the hourly presence of an often demoralised partner. Having or taking a part-time job can be double-edged, as the money is welcome, but may increase male resentment at this new form of dependency. Nor are miners adept at taking on many household chores, still less the role of homemaker'[6].

So, although this particular book is concerned with the politicising effects of the Miners' Strike, it is worthwhile analysing briefly the notion of women and employment. In Hemsworth, as in the communities analysed above, the majority of the women interviewed were housewives. Of those who worked outside the home, the majority were employed on a part-time basis. A significant employer of women in the Hemsworth area was the Hemsworth branch of Terry's Chocolate factory from York (which closed in early 1992 making approximately 90 women redundant). It is particularly interesting to note that Terry's, which employed a significant number of the wives of striking miners in 1984/5, contributed in no small way to the Conservative Party coffers via its parent company United Biscuits. (According to the Sunday Telegraph, 27th June 1993, United Biscuits is the 'number one' corporate donor to the Conservative Party, donations totalling £1,004,500 since 1979 were given to the Conservative Party and the company received one peerage and one knighthood.) It is a subtle irony perhaps that the wives of striking miners were inadvertently helping to finance the Conservative Government!

The sheer scale of the degree of politicisation involved on what is often regarded by many political observers, such as Vicky Seddon[7], as the most de-politicised sector of many communities (and here the reference is not solely to mining communities) - the women - are, it is claimed, one of, if not *the*, most important aspects of the Strike. If this research can isolate the factors which led to these high levels of politicisation taking place then, it is felt, this will have implications for other sectors in society. Are there lessons to be learnt from an examination of why the women were so determined not to give in and as to why many of them engaged in activities which previously they had never undertaken? What made women with negligible political experience in terms of campaigning, fund-raising, speech-making and generally organising themselves in a political manner, decide that they could take control and claim enough power in order to pose a substantial threat and challenge to those in positions of authority?

There have, as stated and referred to in previous chapters, been many books written about the events of 1984/5. A number of them make reference to the part undertaken by the women of the mining communities. Goodman, in his text 'The Miners' Strike', talks about the Women's Support Groups, 'The initials W.S.G. became synonymous during the strike with action, spirit and a remarkable endurance. It was the flowering of something quite unique to any industrial dispute. The miners' wives became a force in their own right and this may well have changed the course of the whole strike. It has certainly left a legacy which cannot be erased'[8]. Goodman certainly does not underestimate the role played by the women from the mining communities. He goes on to state that this role developed into something much more than perhaps they had originally intended, 'the miners' strike and the involvement of women from the mining communities developed into a far broader social and political movement'[9]. This is another important aspect of the strike, the extent to which it led women, in particular, to move into other areas of political concern and to develop an interest in politics *per se* which they had not had prior to 1984/5. Goodman quotes the wife of a South Wales miner to illustrate this point, 'Before the strike I was not interested in the union or politics. I am now'[10].

Goodman goes on to say that, 'The vast majority of wives, mothers, sisters, girlfriends and certainly grandmothers were not only anxious to support their men, but joined together to form the famous Women's Support Groups. Throughout the country they came together to establish this most extraordinary and spontaneous movement, and on a scale never before experienced in any industrial dispute'[11]. The speed and spontaneity with which the support groups were set up is certainly a factor worthy of emphasis. Goodman also states, 'One of the most powerful motivating impulses behind the remarkable involvement of the women was that they felt, as never before, that they too were on strike along with their men, to defend their homes and to fight for their children's future'[12]. The way in which the role played by the women differed from previous experience is emphasised, 'The uniqueness of the women's role throughout the strike has been remarked on many times. Some observers believe it was the most significant element in the whole dispute - possibly even a decisive one in helping to sustain the strike for so long. In all previous industrial disputes since the end of the Second World War the wives of strikers have generally been regarded, at best, as reluctant allies'[13].

This emphasis upon the role played by the women has been commented upon earlier. To reiterate, the key contention is that the role played by the women was one of the crucial aspects of the whole dispute. Goodman cites Vic Allen who has written on the role of the women in mining communities prior to the Strike; 'Professor V.L. Allen, in his book *The Militancy of British Miners* (The Moor Press, 1981) argues that "mining families, centred around women, have functioned as vital elements in the organization of mining". "The family", Allen claims, "has always been at the core of social relationships" in mining communities'[14].

Andrew Taylor[15], from the former Huddersfield Polytechnic, believes that because of the traditional gender roles, 'The men didn't want women on the picket lines. There was the feeling that it wasn't quite the place where women should be. There were men's roles and there were women's roles. And I think in bureaucratic institutional terms, there was a considerable amount of suspicion about the involvement of the support groups and the action groups in the organisation and management of the

Strike. And, that again, in the true sense of the word, the women's groups were seen as being auxiliaries. It's a nice parallel because in the mining communities as a whole the reproduction of labour simply could not take place without the unpaid domestic labour of women reproducing the labour force. Washing, cleaning, cooking, maintaining the workforce. Equally, the Strike could not have been sustained for so long as it was without the women doing that same sort of activity, albeit in a different sphere'. So, although the activities undertaken by the women were, in many respects, just a continuation of their 'normal' everyday domestic chores and duties, it is imperative to ensure that the extent of, the significance and importance of this work are neither underestimated nor devalued in any way so as not to detract from the part played by the women in the events of 1984/5.

It is necessary to ensure that the theory that the women were just doing very much what they had done before only this time on a collective scale is not over-emphasised. As Janet Hudson says in 'The Cutting Edge', 'even at that time it was recognised that this wasn't just a tea-and-biscuit exercise, but something important that women were doing that had never happened before'[16]. So, there are obviously two sides to the argument here.

Patriarchal communities?

The issue of gender relations and the sexual division of labour is an important one because of the particularly patriarchal nature of mining communities. As Sandra Taylor states in Seddon's *The Cutting Edge*, 'In mining communities women rarely have an identity that can be called their own, they are either miners' wives or miners' daughters'[17]. In many respects, mining communities remain as bastions of male dominance and female repression. If society at large retains a sexist outlook then mining communities are notably thus characterised.

Hebron and Wykes undertook an E.S.R.C. funded Project in 1987-88 entitled *Exploring Gender Differences in Mining Communities*. They examined three different mining communities in an attempt to discover 'the extent to which experiences and attitudes are differentiated by gender'[18]. They wanted to test their hypothesis that miners are 'a peculiarly enduring breed of male chauvinists'[19] and they wanted to assess 'how far women's - and men's - experiences during the strike have affected gender relations within each community'[20]. The researchers found 'clearly prescribed and demarcated gender roles[21]. They discovered that little had changed in terms of gender relations since the strike but they did highlight the 'conflict generated by women's questioning of their position in the light of their strike experiences'[22]. The Project ends on an optimistic note by quoting Joan Witham's 'Hearts and Minds' (Canary Press, 1986) - 'What is of fundamental importance is that they may do very much the same things as before the strike, but they will never again think in the same way'[23].

The findings of Hebron and Wykes are echoed by this book because, in terms of gender relations and the sexual division of labour in Hemsworth little has changed since the 1984/5 dispute. Many women did participate in activities, such as fund-raising and speech-giving, which were previously alien to them but the changes which occurred during the Strike have not continued post-84/5. Despite Beatrix Campbell's claim, in Seddon's *The Cutting Edge*, that 'the 1984-85 strike saw women transcending the political demarcations, the sexual division of labour'[24], it remains the case that primary responsibility for child-care and for domestic duties still rests with the women.

In terms of analysing the problems encountered whilst carrying out research in mining communities, other parallels exist with the Hebron and Wykes' Project. They note that 'there was surprise from some quarters that a woman should be carrying out research into a major industrial dispute'[25] a statement which this present author can relate to after being subjected to equally condescending comments, for example, her small car was dubbed by one miner as a 'suitable car for a woman'!

Allied to the debate about gender relations in mining communities is the notion that politics is a 'man's world'. This works to exclude many women from the political arena as the general perception is that politics is a domain which is alien to the female of the species. This perception is examined by Siltanen and Stanworth in *Women and the Public Sphere*. They argue that 'Accounts of the relation of gender to electoral and work-based politics are founded ... on the analytical separation of the public world of politics and employment from the private sphere of family and interpersonal relations'[26]. They go on to say that 'underlying many of the explanations of the relation between gender and politics there is an illegitimate superimposition of three dichotomies: political - apolitical, public - private, and male - female'[27]. It is Siltanen and Stanworth's contention that 'If politics is assumed to be the prerogative of the public sphere, and women are taken to be firmly located within the private domain, then the access of women to politics would appear to be understandably problematic[28]. The dilemma caused by this divide is one which had to be bridged by the women of the mining communities in 1984/5. As Sandra Taylor says in Seddon's *The Cutting Edge*, 'The strongest lesson has been that of solidarity and support, a practical recognition that patriarchy and class are intricately linked and a living example of how the "personal" may be brought into the political'[29].

The role played by the women is also examined by Loretta Loach in Beynon's *Digging Deeper*[30]. Loach argues that the miners' wives did not constitute a feminist movement as such but she believes that this is hardly surprising given that mining and the communities themselves suffer from an inherently 'macho' culture. Green in *The Enemy Without* also addresses this question of why feminism does not appear to have played a particularly significant role, 'The most important reason behind the non-penetration of feminist ideology was that the mining women did not see their own struggle as separate from their husbands, fathers or brothers'[31]. The class war is seen as more important than the sex war. One specific aspect of this was, as Green notes, the fact that 'It was the women of the sample who voiced most strongly a new awareness about their class in relation to the police'[32].

Loach highlights the fact that prior to the strike it was the women of Greenham Common who had attempted to challenge the Government. She believes that the important point about the miners' wives was that 'as women they were visible and active in their own right, separately and apart from men and not simply tagging along behind them'[33]. Loach appears optimistic with regards to the effect which the involvement of the women has had, 'Perhaps if their activity survives the strike, whatever the outcome, and feminist influence prevails these women may develop an explanation for their own specific world, relevant to their needs and aspirations, that will expand the scope and broaden the appeal of feminism and socialism alike, and provide the challenge to this government that is urgently required'[34].

Raphael Samuel *et al.*, in *The Enemy Within*, also refer to the impact of the women. In this text, Barbara Bloomfield quotes Mike Richards, a Maerdy miner, as saying 'In 1972 and 1974, we called them "the sandwich girls". The women started this dispute behind us, they came up alongside us and now they're in front of us'[35]. This illustrates the impact which the women had during 1984/5. In the same book, Christine Mahoney, who is described as a housewife from Doncaster, states, 'In my view, when all this is over, many attitudes will have been changed. I've been on picket lines with the other women and those women are never going to go back to the way they used to be. A lot of the men don't like it, and think a women's place is in the home but most of the women who had that old-fashioned attitude have changed now'[36].

The extent of gender divisions in mining communities is worthy of emphasis. One female interviewee (number 15, active in support group) illustrated this; 'I mean most miners' wives I know wouldn't dream of going out for the day and not having their husband's dinner ready. They'd have to leave something or come back early. It seems to go from father to son. My grandma did it with my grandad'. This interviewee did not feel that this aspect had really changed as a result of the events of 1984/5.

Andrew Taylor expands upon the point which he made about the existence of gender divisions; 'In fact ... what was so interesting about women's involvement in the miners' strike was the fact that, whilst there was women's organisation and women's involvement, the women were still doing very much "women's type" work. They were still feeding the kids, alright on a collective scale but they were still looking after the kids. They were still basically doing cooking, cleaning, that type of thing.' Taylor does have a point here in that the sexual division of labour, although, as he says, was 'on a collective scale', was still very much in evidence. This quotation from Taylor is still relevant because it underlines the public/private distinction and is, therefore, worthy of emphasis.

A break with tradition?

The fact that the women did not conform to the stereotypical role of being merely passive supporters of strikers is highlighted by Callinicos and Simons, 'From the very start of the strike the women of the mining communities have refused to play the role that the press usually ascribes to the wives and girlfriends of strikers'[37]. This is an important point because the women did not allow themselves to be portrayed by the media as only slightly more than impartial bystanders. 'In direct answer to the press and T.V., women's action groups sprang up in many pit villages in the first few weeks of the strike. They quickly got involved in all aspects of the strike, until they became the driving force behind much of the organisation which held the strike together on a day-to-day basis'[38]. Callinicos and Simons believe that the women's groups 'showed the depths of skill, talent, humour, guts and sheer organising ability that had lain untapped in the mining communities'[39].

Again the uniqueness of the role played by the women is referred to, 'The organisation and participation of women in the miners' strike was unique in recent British history. Without it, the miners would have been beaten long before the eventual return to work'[40]. It is also worth emphasising though that the women were not entirely unique; other women, as Callinicos and Simons point out by reference to the Barking hospital strikers, to the Ford sewing machinists, to women at Trico and also at Grunwick, had taken part in protracted and often acrimonious disputes but 'What makes the women's involvement in the miners' strike unique is both its sheer scale, and that it involved women outside the workforce in a prolonged war of attrition'[41]. This would appear to be an extremely important point, the fact that the women themselves were not directly employed in the industry. 'The involvement of the women in the Great Miners' Strike has broken down the idea that only those whose jobs are threatened can fight a strike. The women of the mining communities have proved that working-class women are as capable of fighting and leading a strike as their men. And in so doing, they have transformed their lives and their expectations'[42].

This way in which it was seen as a community struggle is echoed by Green in *The Enemy Without*, 'Certainly the role played by women in the strike was one of the most crucial aspects of the whole dispute. Their involvement not only broke down traditional notions of the "women's place" in a very traditional community, but also destroyed the idea that only those whose jobs were threatened could fight a strike. The Tory government's pit closure programme threatened the women directly - it was *their* livelihoods, *their* families and *their* communities that were under attack'[43].

This is obviously one of the effects of the process of politicisation. As Anne O'Donnel, from Bentley, said: 'There's no way I would return to the kitchen sink now. I'm not going back to how things were before. Both me and my husband were fairly unpolitical before the strike but now we've both changed!'[44]. It may be the case that the women did become politicised during the strike but this book also aims to discover whether the comments from women like Anne O'Donnel were indeed a prophecy of a lasting politicisation. To what extent has that politicising process endured over the twelve years since the end of the strike?

The role played by the women is assessed by the Wintertons in 'Coal, Crisis and Conflict'. They highlight the fact, however, that more women worked in the kitchens than went collecting and that more women went collecting than went picketing. They state that 'the pattern of women's involvement was nevertheless conditioned by traditional gender roles within coalfield communities'[45]. This is not, however, to detract from the importance of the role fulfilled by the women. 'The kitchens and food parcels organised by the women's groups probably sustained the strike more than any other factor'[46]. This point is made by a number of other commentators, such as Andrew Taylor, but it is worthy of emphasis because it highlights the gender divisions still prevalent in our society at large but especially noticeable in the machoistic mining communities.

The way that the women's involvement in the activities associated with the strike also brought them into contact with other oppressed groups is highlighted by the Wintertons. 'Their fund-raising activities took women beyond the parochialism of the coalfield communities to the large metropolitan areas and even abroad, bringing them into contact with radicals, blacks, gays, famous entertainers, and intellectuals'[47]. This aspect is emphasised by Beatrix Campbell in *The Cutting Edge*, 'The links between these profoundly and chauvinistically heterosexual communities and the lesbian and gay movement is a symbol of the cultural revolution born of the strike'[48].

How the men viewed the role fulfilled by the women is also an important factor, 'Some men saw the women as "morale-boosters", demonstrating that they were completely behind the strike and emphasising the unity of the communities against the employer, the Government and the police'[49].

It is also important to emphasise the fact that the role undertaken by the women was much more of a change from what they were used to than it was for the men. 'The extent of this departure from their normal lives was far greater for these women than for the men on strike who normally work and organize communally'[50]. Green expands upon this thesis 'while the men had always had the N.U.M. to encourage solidarity and collective sentiment, for the women this was a new experience. By contrast their previous lives were organized very much on an individual basis within the home. Even for those who did go out to work, employment was seen as being of secondary importance in defining their role as mining women'[51].

Politicisation and the women

The evidence unearthed by this book supports many of the viewpoints which have been expressed by the key commentators upon the events of 1984/5. The interviews illustrate the extent of female involvement in the industrial action and also highlight the significant degree of politicisation which appears to have taken place as a direct result of the coal dispute. The other surprising factor to have emerged as a result of this investigation is the lasting effect of that politicisation. Many of the women who were interviewed claim that they became more politically aware during the strike, that they participated in the 'political arena' and that they underwent behavioural changes. Not only this, they also state that many of these changes have been lasting ones.

One woman who was interviewed (number 17, active in the support group) claimed that the experience of the Miners' Strike changed her to the extent that she joined the Support Group and that she spent a lot of time in London collecting for the strike fund. She also met her husband in London whilst she was raising funds and he was helping the Labour movement so that had a radical effect upon her previously very parochial outlook upon life. She joined the Labour Party as a direct result of the strike and this was a lasting effect. 'We were involved last year [1990] when we were down at the Labour Party Conference ... We had a great time. That made it a lot more interesting'. When asked whether she intended to become more involved in politics the interviewee replied, 'Not more involved, no. More aware you become. I got progressively more involved from the start with the new school governors'. She had this to say in answer to the question as to why she joined the Labour Party, 'we joined the Labour Party because of the things that were happening in the Miners' Strike, not political ones as such. It was more the Labour Party councillors who came and offered us money to start the kitchen up, £100, and then said we want the items back when you've done with them. We said £100 for pots and pans isn't going to go far, they're going to get broken. They said "Oh, well we want 'em back" and the Labour Party councillors walked out of the meeting. So we thought the only way we can alter this is to join and to get something done ourselves. So that was one of the reasons we joined the Labour Party'. This woman and her husband whom she, as stated, had met whilst collecting in London both commented upon the gender divisions which exist in mining communities. In answer to a question about the key features of mining communities the husband replied, 'I think the biggest one as far as I can determine is the division between male and female ... It is very, very strong. That sort of division is prevalent in all communities to a greater or lesser extent but I'm finding it enormous here'. So from this respect it appears that the politicising effect upon the women has not fully penetrated the sexual division of labour.

The interviewee was keen to recount her experiences of collecting in the South of England. Fund-raising was something which she had never done before and it made her more politically aware, she claimed. 'We were collecting in East Ham High Street, I remember, and it went from being stood with a bucket and saying "Will you support the miners please" to a bus pulling up and me getting on and rattling a bucket to a bus full of Newcastle United supporters ... It took about half an hour but twenty pound notes were falling in. We were collecting on a Saturday about three weeks before Christmas when a police van pulled up full of policemen in riot gear. They all got ready to come out and they looked at us so we dived into a bread shop. We were carrying a big, red bucket that said "Support the Miners" on it. They gave us a carrier bag to put our bucket in. It had been the Salvation Army that had reported us because they thought that we were taking their Christmas money. So I don't go to the Salvation Army now'. This event had obviously has a lasting impact upon the interviewee.

One woman who was instrumental in setting up the Support Group in Hemsworth (Interviewee number 12) claimed that the strike also 'made me take an interest in foreign politics as well; the political scene in the world more than just my own community. It opened my mind towards politics'. Another interviewee (number 13, active in the support group) felt that her views had not really changed as a result of the strike; 'No, I don't think so really. I mean I thought before then that the rich get richer and the poor get trodden on. Probably though I was a bit more militant during the strike, a bit more involved'.

Having given a brief insight into what some of the interviewees said about the politicising impact upon the women, it is worthwhile at this stage analysing the results of the interviews in terms of what they reveal statistically.

This research involves a number of in-depth interviews which have been carried out over a three year period. As stated in previous chapters, sixty interviews were conducted. Of these, thirty-seven respondents are male and twenty-three are female. They include representatives from all sectors of the community of Hemsworth. If the responses are examined in terms of what the interviewees had to say about this question of politicisation, the results are particularly interesting.

Firstly, let us examine what the male respondents had to say about this question of politicisation. Of the thirty-seven, twelve claim to have become politicised (although one of the twelve claims that he has been politicised after the 1984/5 Miners' Strike), seven claim not to be politicised at all and, in terms of the tri-partite definition being employed by this research, this would appear to be the case. The remaining eighteen (49 per cent) interviewees assert that they were politicised prior to the events of 1984/5. If we put these figures into some sort of context; 32 per cent have become politicised, 19 per cent are non-politicised and 49 per cent were politicised before the Strike.

When these results are compared with those of the female respondents the distinction is marked. Of the twenty-three female interviewees, fifteen claim to have been politicised as a direct result of the 1984/5 Miners' Strike, three claim not to be politicised and five claim to have been politicised prior to the events of 1984/5. In percentage terms this represents; sixty-five per cent of the female respondents who claim to have been politicised as a result of the Strike, 13 per cent who claim to be non-political and 22 per cent who believe that they were already politicised before the outset of the 1984/5 Coal Dispute.

So, 65 per cent of the female respondents claim to have become politicised compared with only 32 per cent of the males who claim to have become politicised. On the basis of these crude statistics, it appears that one of, if not the, most remarkable aspects of the events of 1984/5 was the impact which the dispute had upon the lives of the women of this particular mining community. It seems to be the case that many of the men felt, prior to the Strike, that politics was already of some direct relevance to their lives and that they were able to participate in and take an interest in political affairs. For the women, however, it took an event like the 1984/5 Miners' Strike for them to appreciate that politics does have an impact upon their daily lives. It, many claimed, deeply affected their outlook upon life and they came to be much more questioning than they had hitherto been. No longer were they quite so willing to merely accept what those in so-called positions of authority were telling them. Alongside this, many women also claim, that because of their own personal experiences during the Strike, they developed more of an empathetic attitude towards other oppressed groups within our society at large. Beatrix Campbell sums this up in *The Cutting Edge*, 'The defenders of Labourist chauvinisms have always been able to turn to these outposts, the cradle of the authentic working class, and mobilise them against the queers, the blacks, the "middle class feminists" and the miscellany of modernisers. Not any more'[52].

It is necessary at this juncture to clarify what is meant by politicisation for the purposes of this research. The tripartite definition of political awareness, political participation and behavioural changes (as highlighted in Chapter Two) is the one being employed by this study. Briefly, in terms of the impact on the women, it appears that the most lasting effect has been in the arena of political awareness. Whilst heightened political participation and behavioural changes were more likely to have occurred during the Strike, it is increased political awareness which the majority of the interviewees claim as a lasting memento of the events of 1984/5. Their lives may proceed in much the same way as before but they have a more questioning approach. Stead, in *Never the Same Again*, states that 'The women who started to question the political system during the strike will continue to do so'[53], an assertion which, to a certain extent, is borne out by the evidence in this book.

The comments and experiences of many of the women will be examined in more detail in a short while but firstly, a number of academics have been questioned about their perceptions of the role of the women during the 1984/5 Miners' Strike. One of the more notable ones was Andrew Taylor of Huddersfield University. Taylor had this to say in answer to the question of whether or not he felt the Strike to be a great politicising event; 'Yes, at two levels'. He proceeds to highlight the impact which the dispute had upon young people and then he emphasises the effect on the women. In terms of the Strike, Taylor believes that 'the second area where it had a major consequence was, of course, on women'. He does not regard the politicisation of the women as the only factor involved but regards it as one of the major factors. He explains further, 'There's a huge body of material; oral evidence, video, print, which testifies basically to women saying it really brought us out. It brought us out of the home, it brought us into politics and this sort of stuff. It raised our consciousness and things will never be the same again. But what struck me forcibly, however, is how quickly not so much the attitude of the miners changed but how quickly the women reverted back to traditional roles'.

It is fair to say that Taylor in no way detracts from the part played by the women. He thinks that 'what was interesting was how speedily women took on board the case that this was a fight not just for jobs but also for the community as a whole and for their children and their families and so on and that they had a debt to past generations and future generations. That's true and I think the women did play a key support role in that sense. Whether or not that's lasted, of course, is a different question. I mean, it's the same sort of question as "How long did the miners' militancy last after their defeat"? Now, clearly the mining workforce is quiescent. Kellingley on Monday [January 1992], the management asked for 450 job losses, redundancies. I've heard that by lunch-time of the same day 500 men had put their names down. Again, from women I know and have talked to, there is no doubt there is a core of women still active, who've moved into things like the Labour Party and that, whose activism stems from the explosion of consciousness that took place as a result of 84/5 but the vast majority, I suppose, have faded away'. The issue which Taylor raises here, concerning the question of the permanence and or duration of this 'awareness' and political activity amongst the women is one which this book will address shortly.

In terms of the politicising impact upon the women, it is worthwhile examining what the women themselves have had to say on the issue. One woman (Interviewee number 12, active in the support group) felt able, as a result of the events of 1984/5, to draw parallels between the plight of the mining communities and other oppressed groups. 'One thing that hit me was that we used to watch newscasts and you'd see black people, Irish people, people in the inner cities and you'd say "Oh no. That can't be going on." Or you'd just look at it, listen and then it would go from your mind. But then you came to be aware that it did happen, it had happened and it was happening here. It's stuck with you now. It's still there, you'll never forget but what you didn't used to take notice of you do now and you know the other side of it. You can think "Ah, yes", plus the fact that you've got to stick together in anything, that's the main thing it's impressed on me'. This empathy with other oppressed groups was highlighted by a number of the female interviewees. Many interviewees stated that, prior to the Miners' Strike, they had perhaps been a little cynical in terms of attempting to understand the experiences of others in society at large. They now found themselves more willing to believe that perhaps there is an alternative viewpoint to that which is often propounded by the mainstream mass media.

This heightened awareness of the plight of others was cited by another miner's wife (Interviewee number 22, active in the support group, works part-time) who had worked in the kitchen right from the start; 'Yes, changed. More aware of what was going on around me, politically as well. It made me more aware of other people's problems as well. Before the Strike it was just a matter of living your own life, getting on with your own life and that was it but when the Strike happened it sort of brought the whole community together. I wouldn't say I've become more active in politics, the only thing is I've become more aware of it'.

One woman (Interviewee number 11, active in the support group), as already stated in Chapter Four which examines the role of the police, cited the Crosshills 'riot', the 13th July 1984, in Hemsworth, as being extremely influential upon her in terms of the politicisation process. 'I mean, I saw what happened on Crosshills that night. We weren't actually there, we'd come down home and we heard all this noise. And I said, "Come on let's go up" because our Jeff [her son] was out, you see. Anyway, we went up and what the police were doing with those kids ... I'm not kidding you ... In fact, my husband said to one of the policemen, "If that's the way you treat them, God help them kids". And then, as we were walking up Barnsley Road, we heard one policeman say to another, "Corporal". My husband said, "I thought there were no corporals in the police-force". He [her husband] distinctly heard that and he [a policeman] said "Get on or else you'll be the next"'. This interviewee claimed that this was a specific event which fundamentally affected her political perceptions.

Another woman (Interviewee number 45, full-time clerical worker, interested in politics) who said that her family had always had an active interest in politics nevertheless felt that the Strike was a significant event in terms of her own political awareness. 'It's something you never forget and it's something that I'd say I'd go through again. I'd still stick by my principles. My dad has always been an active councillor. I don't always believe everything that my dad believes in but I've always been brought up with politics. But you seem to take a lot more interest. Whereas before a lot used to ride over my head. I used to go and vote and that was it. But now you take note. I just take more note of what's going on. I don't really get involved still but my husband does'. So, although this woman has not really increased her level of political participation she, nevertheless, feels that she has undergone a significant change in terms of attitudes and awareness.

Another interviewee (number 24, female, housewife, active in support group) who claimed to have been politicised by the Strike had this to say in terms of her impressions of politics and whether her views had changed; 'This bloody awful Government! My views, in as much as for the police. I think it was really terrible. He [her husband] had also had a do with them in 1974. They were just as bad then and that was only a short strike'. She emphasised the fact that she felt it was imperative upon women in particular to ensure that they exercised their right to vote, 'Women tied themselves to fences for that vote and I'm having mine. And I get on to this lot [her family] if they say they're not voting. If I was younger I'd have joined the Labour Party. If I'd have only been in my twenties I'd have definitely become an active member of the Labour Party. I would have put up for the council. When you're getting older you don't remember things as much and you need to know what you're on about'. This interviewee had obviously enhanced her interest in politics as a result of the miners' strike but appeared to lack a little confidence in terms of her own political capabilities. Other women, however, went on to claim that the Strike had done precisely that, that is to say it had actually increased their levels of confidence in terms of their own capabilities outside of the domestic arena.

One of these women (Interviewee number 15, active in the support group) stated, 'Yes, it made me more aware of what was happening and what was going off. It also made me more confident in myself. I know it sounds daft like but just getting involved with other people and doing what we did. It gave me that bit of self-confidence'. Another interviewee (number 23, active in the support group, works part-time) echoed these views when she said, 'Yes, it made me a stronger person. You learn to fight against things, you don't sit back and let things happen. You learn to stand up'.

In terms of this emphasis on how it changed the women involved, a third interviewee (number 35, miner's wife, works full-time) had this to say, 'I worked on the miners' dinners every day, right from the beginning. I went to London once, fund-raising. I'd never done it before. I didn't like collecting but it certainly made me a lot tougher and gave me more confidence'. Another interviewee (number 21, divorcee, active in support group, works part-time) who was the family breadwinner throughout the strike said, 'It makes you a lot tougher and more conscious over money'.

With respect to the emphasis on a change, a young miner's wife (Interviewee number 41, miner's wife, works full-time) stated, 'We had a young family during the Strike. I didn't work then. I think it changed me completely. It changed my whole outlook on life. It was a shock because you thought it was all secure and your future was secure. Everything changed. For me this fear of not having any money, and for me it just came home to me how much a job means. We never thought it would have gone on that long. Since the Strike finished, I've worked ever since because we got that low on money. It's just changed every outlook, every aspect. When we first got married, we'd been married two years when the Strike started, he didn't want me ever to go back to work and everything changed. It was like a big shock'. This interviewee claimed to have become very interested in politics as a direct result of her experiences during 1984/5 but that she was particularly concerned about local politics; 'I'm very concerned with this area and how it concerns us as a family. I still feel that we're being punished for the Strike by this Government. I still feel they are punishing the miners of Yorkshire. Well, I keep feeling that Labour will come and save us but they don't. I keep banking on Labour getting in and saving the industry but we've realised that they're not going to. It's not as bad now as then because you have just got to accept it. Labour haven't a chance of getting back in soon enough to save the mining industry. When he [her husband] is still in the mining industry it's always on your mind because the problem never goes away'. This was interesting because here it was the wife who claimed to be much more interested in politics than her husband, usually the women who were politicised were as political or slightly less political than their partner; here the male expressed a genuine lack of interest in the political arena.

It is worthwhile examining the apparent levels of politicisation of the female interviewees and their spouses. Out of the twenty one women, eleven claim to be as politicised as their husband, four claim that their husband is more politicised whilst three claim that they are more politicised than their husband. Two of the female respondants were widowed and one was divorced. So, statistically speaking, it was unusual for a woman to claim to be more politicised than her partner.

Of the women who claim not to have been politicised, one (Interviewee number 32, teacher) stated; 'No, because none of our family were miners so other than me being at work [she is a school-teacher] it didn't really affect me directly'. What she meant was that the only connection which she had with the Strike was through teaching the children of striking miners. A second teacher (Interviewee number 31) claimed to be politicised but she stated that she had been interested and involved in politics prior to the events of 1984/5; 'At one time I was a member of the S.D.P. and I used to go around canvassing'.

Another interviewee (number 13, female, active in the support group) who had helped in the kitchen during the Strike said; 'I'm not overly politically minded. I was during the Strike. I think it was the Strike that sort of got everyone rallying around, the old "Dunkirk spirit". When you see riots on the television and things like Wapping it fetches it all back and you start thinking about all the pickets. It really put me against the police and I suppose it always will do. Yes, it changed me. Up to the Strike, I was going round, I suppose, with my eyes closed. I'd always been interested in things that were happening abroad, South Africa and stuff but I never really did much about it. And like Beirut, different people's struggles, and I sort of realised that there were struggles at home as well. We saw South Africa on television and we thought how horrible it was and everything but you forget that there's things happening in this country as well. And it brought me more aware of that, ... Shipworkers and the Silent Night dispute and things. So, I am interested in politics. I have my own views. I don't go to political meetings, unless it's someone that I really want to listen to speak. I try not to think about Mrs Thatcher. I think the working class will be the lower class, they'll be the downtrodden. I just don't think there's a chance for anybody since the Miners' Strike. It's made me more depressed ... We discuss politics with the kids as well. Andrew asks questions. They teach them politics at school, I think'.

A couple of the women emphasised the support which they received during the Strike, especially from people living in the South. This was, to a certain extent, a politicising experience because previously it was felt to be very much a divided country in terms of the north and the south. One (Interviewee number 12, active in the support group) said, 'I'll tell you another thing, it made you realise where your support came from. Even now in Hemsworth I've heard people say, "Oh people down the South don't know" and I pull them up and I pull them up very quickly. Because if it hadn't have been for the people down South and in London we could not have sustained the miners in Hemsworth. So, even some people here still aren't aware of where that support came from. Coloured people, old age pensioners, unemployed, lesbians and gays, the minority groups were all helping. It was so surprising where the support came from'.

These sentiments were echoed very closely by the wife of a miner (Interviewee number 35, miner's wife, works full-time). 'We're both interested in politics. We were brought up in a mining community and both my parents were Labour but I've obviously got my own views. Before the Strike I was politically aware but not as aware as I was after the Strike. It made me more politically aware. It opened my eyes to a lot of things that I wouldn't have considered before, like, people in the South of England, it seemed such a long way and I didn't realise that we would get the support in the south of England that we actually got. I mean when we first started collecting for the Strike obviously we went to Bradford. We had more abuse in Bradford than we actually got in London believe it or not. We were just so surprised at the support that we got in London as opposed to on our own doorstep if you like ... We went down to London most weekends collecting. We'd never done *anything* like that before. We had an office in London at Swiss Cottage from where we sent people off to do collections'. This support from other areas did have a profound impact upon many of the women.

The politicisation process is illustrated by Betty from Woolley who is cited in the North Yorkshire Women Against Pit Closures' *Strike 84-85*. She gave the following reply to a difficult question at a Miners' rally at the G.L.C.; 'Now flower, I'd like to get this straight. We're miners' wives. That doesn't mean that we're simple, only that we're not used to many of the phrases you used. I, for one, admit to not knowing a lot of the words and most of the concepts. But this I promise you: I've had three months up to now on the picket lines and my political education is being acquired at a gallop. Stick around and I'll come back in a year's time and answer all your questions'[54]. This is a useful quotation as it clearly depicts a woman who is gaining in confidence in the political arena.

Although not talking specifically about the impact upon the women, Andrew Taylor concludes his thoughts about the politicising nature of the Strike by saying; 'I think, clearly, going through an experience like that cannot but have a searing effect upon you. It was a major political struggle. A struggle that most people would never come within a million miles of. I don't know whether people think about it in those terms but what the miners were doing was taking on the State. There are few bigger political involvements than that and, yes, I think a lot of people who might not be active, nonetheless, it had a profound effect upon them. I don't see how it could not. Political struggle? Large P, small p, whatever P you want'.

Conclusion

Empirical evidence gleaned from the sixty in-depth interviews (male and female interviewees included) conducted for this book clearly indicates that one, if not the most, remarkable aspect of the 1984/5 Miners' Strike was the impact which the whole debacle had upon the women of mining communities. A majority of the interviewees referred to the impact of the 1984/5 Miners' Strike upon the women of Hemsworth and/or claimed that they too had been affected by the events of 1984/5. From what many of the women themselves claim, it can clearly be seen that the Strike was a great politicising experience. If the tripartite definition of politicisation is, once again, employed as a yardstick by which to measure any change, then a remarkable transformation took place in the hearts and minds of many of these women.

Using the definition of politicisation, as explained in Chapter Two, it has to be said that one of the most profound and lasting changes was the impact which the Strike had upon the women. As with the analysis of the role fulfilled by the police and the part played by the media, it is necessary to examine the three elements of politicisation in greater depth in order to ascertain the precise impact of the Strike upon the women. Regarding the first criterion, political participation, a significant number of the women claimed that their level of political participation increased either during or after the 1984/5 Miners' Strike. Some aspects of this participation was directly associated with the Strike itself and involved activities such as going on the picket lines, collecting for the Strike funds, giving speeches in order to rally support for the miners' cause and working for the Support Group. Other 'types' of participation was still political, both with a small p and a large P[55] but was less overtly connected to the Strike itself. Included in this category are activities such as, joining the Labour Party, joining the hunt saboteurs' movement, becoming a school governor and attending a 'women's group'. The Strike, for many of the women, led to increased levels of confidence and meant that they felt able to participate in the political arena. They worked on a collective basis during the Strike and moved out of the domestic sphere and into a more public domain. Helping with the Support Group, providing literally hundreds of meals on a daily basis, collecting funds and organising the distribution of food parcels; these were all tasks which the women proved that they could perform successfully. Achievement bred confidence. Evidence gleaned from the in-depth interviews reveals that it was precisely this success with the Support Group and its related activities which compelled them to want to participate in other 'political' spheres. They had already achieved a great deal of success outside of the domestic frontier, why should they stop now? Clearly then, the 1984/5 Miners' Strike galvanised many of the women of mining communities into political activity and participation on a scale which had, hitherto, been unheard of.

Moving on to the second dimension of politicisation, namely political awareness, it is fair to say that, on the basis of what they revealed in the in-depth interviews, many of the female inhabitants of Hemsworth experienced heightened levels of political awareness. As with the whole politicisation process in general terms, this second component witnessed by far the greatest amount of change. Political awareness meant, for example, that some of the women made a direct link between the actions of politicians, at both national and local level and the way that those actions impacted upon their daily lives. Other examples of change, with respect to this second dimension, included women who began to perceive that their own existence, centred around the domestic environment, could be equated with the political arena. There was a blurring of the distinction between the public and the private spheres, a dawning realisation that the personal could be regarded in political terms.

The point is made in Chapter Four, in an attempt to account for increased levels of political awareness and make comparisons with the two other criteria, that political awareness involves less of a concerted effort than either political participation or behavioural changes. Obviously, this point is applicable at this particular juncture too. Political awareness increased dramatically amongst the women, on the basis of what they revealed in the in-depth interviews but perhaps this is hardly surprising considering that they do not actually have physically to do anything in order to become more politically aware. This is not to decry the change in the women, for many of the women experienced a qualitative difference in terms of their general outlook on life and their perception of what exactly may be deemed to constitute the political arena.

Moving on to examine the third dimension, namely that of behavioural change, a significant proportion of the female interviewees reported that they had undergone a number of behavioural changes which they were able to connect directly with their personal experiences during the 1984/5 Miners' Strike. Examples of such behavioural changes included two women who divorced their husbands in the post-Strike period and who attributed their divorces, in no small way, to their experiences during the Strike. Attendance on Further and Higher Education courses (in this latter case the Open University) also exemplified the changes which some of the women underwent. Less dramatic perhaps but just as noteworthy, a couple of the women changed from reading the tabloid press to reading a broadsheet newspaper due to their dissatisfaction with tabloid coverage of the Miners' Strike. Clearly then, the third dimension of the tripartite definition of politicisation was also evidenced amongst the women of mining communities. The empirical data can be explicitly connected to the theoretical debate and illustrates that a significant amount of politicisation did take place amongst the women of Hemsworth.

As to why the 1984/5 Miners' Strike had such a profound and lasting impact upon one particular sector of the populace, that is to say the women; it is difficult to make confident assertions as to why, precisely, this should be the case. Certainly, the *extent* of the impact upon the women was one of the most surprising results unearthed throughout the course of the research for this book. A literature search, carried out prior to embarking upon the qualitative research, highlighted the fact that the gender dimension was certainly a factor in the equation. It remains the case, however, that until the in-depth interviews were conducted, the extent of the profound and lasting nature of the effect which the 1984/5 Miners' Strike had upon the women was not fully realised. It appears to be the case that the women were so deeply affected because here was a situation where, allied with their menfolk, their very existence and raison d'etre was threatened. Without being melodramatic, their communities were under siege and their way of life faced extinction. They had no option but to fight and, in so doing, many of the women found that they possessed hidden qualities which they never realised they held. In unearthing and utilising these qualities, surges of confidence befell the women and led to a dawning realisation that perhaps the political arena was not so threatening after all, perhaps the machismo associated with the world of politics was a whitewash and they too could contribute to and gain from political participation. Perhaps they too could change their lifestyles, could break out from the shackles of their oppressed existences and benefit from all that the politicisation process entails?

So, in conclusion then, it is fair to say that the 1984/5 Miners' Strike had a tremendous impact upon the levels of politicisation of the majority of the women interviewed. As stated earlier in statistical format, the majority of those interviewed expressed heightened levels of political awareness, a much greater than hitherto interest in political affairs, a change of attitude in terms of their own position within the domestic sphere (and for two of the women it actually led to divorce) and for a significant proportion of the women they actually became involved in political activity throughout the Strike - although only a very small minority have continued to have involvement in practical politics in the post-Strike era.

In his text, *The Miners' Strike*, Goodman refers to Arthur Scargill's relationship with the mining communities and states; 'It was an extraordinary relationship, romantic in sociological terms perhaps, but it did actually result in what Scargill later claimed to be a genuinely positive feature of the long and bitter strike: the politicization of mining communities'[56]. He reasserts this claim later in the book; 'Arthur Scargill's claim that the strike "politicized" people as had no previous postwar industrial event, was certainly correct. It could hardly have been otherwise'[57]. What this research seeks to prove is that, more than politicising whole communities, the most significant aspect of the strike was the effect which it had upon one particular section of the mining communities; the women. According to Lovenduski and Randall, 'even though the campaign inevitably ran out of steam after a while, many of those involved have testified to the lasting difference that it has made to their lives and to their view of themselves'. They continue, 'In Wales we were told: "Even though the battle was lost and the women returned to their kitchens - these were new women. Poems, songs and stories written by miners' wives and daughters as a result of the fearful events of the previous 12 months bear witness to their permanent politicisation"'[58]. As Seddon states; 'In the pit strike, it was they [the women] who broke new ground, who generated an alternative welfare system, who made the ideological leaps: women were the coalfields' cutting edge'[59]. As Hain and McCrindle state, 'It is increasingly said and believed that had it not been for the women's participation in this strike, the men would have been driven back to work months ago'[60].

It appears then that Beatrix Campbell issued a prophetic statement when she said in 1984 that 'In ten years time, the miners' strike will be remembered as one in which women emerged as an unprecedented force in the community'[61]. As Rees points out 'Although it is important not to lose sight of women's participation in earlier coalfield disputes ... it is certainly the case that women played a qualitatively different role during the 1984-1985 strike even as compared with the 1972 and 1974 strikes'[62]. This is the really important angle regarding the impact of the 1984/5 Strike; the impact upon the women is a remarkable dimension of the Strike as, in the words of Jean Stead, many of these women were 'Never the same again'![63]

Notes:

[1] Quote from a striking miner's wife.

[2] Interview conducted with Professor Vic Allen, the University of Leeds, Autumn 1989.

[3] See Goodman, G. (1985) *The Miners' Strike*, (London: Pluto), for further details.

[4] See Stead, J. (1987) *Never the Same Again*, (London: The Women's Press), for further details.

[5] Critcher, C., Dicks, B. and Waddington, D. 'Portrait of Despair', the *New Statesman and Society*, 23rd October 1992, pp. 16-17.

[6] Ibid., p. 17.

[7] See Seddon, V. (Ed.) (1986) *The Cutting Edge: Women and the Pit Strike*, (London: Lawrence and Wishart).

[8] Goodman, *Op. Cit.*, p. 89.

[9] Ibid., pp. 90/91.

[10] Ibid., p. 90.

[11] Ibid., p. 162.

[12] Ibid., pp. 161/2.

[13] Ibid., p. 162.

[14] Ibid., p. 164.

[15] Interview conducted with Andrew Taylor, Lecturer in Politics, University of Huddersfield, January 1992.

[16] Seddon, *Op. Cit.*, p. 64.

[17] Ibid., p. 85.

[18] Hebron, S. and Wykes, M., *Exploring Gender Differences in Mining Communities*, (E.S.R.C. funded project, 1987-88), p. 1.

[19] Ibid.

[20] Ibid.

[21] Ibid., p. 5.

[22] Ibid., p. 17.

[23] Ibid., p. 217.

[24] Seddon, *Op. Cit.*, p. 261.

[25] Hebron and Wykes, *Op. Cit.*, p. 4.

[26] Siltanen, J. and Stanworth, M. (Eds.) (1984) *Women and the Public Sphere*, (London: Hutchinson), p. 185.

[27] Ibid., p. 194.

[28] Ibid., p. 195.

[29] Seddon, *Op. Cit.*, p. 96.

[30] See Beynon, H. (Ed.) (1985) *Digging Deeper - issues in the miners' strike*, (London: Verso).

[31] Green, P. (1990) *The Enemy Without - Policing and Class Consciousness in the Miners' Strike*, (Milton Keynes: Open University Press), p. 190.

[32] Ibid., p. 76.

[33] Beynon, *Op. Cit.*, p. 171.

[34] Ibid., p. 178.

[35] Samuel, R., Bloomfield, B. and Boanas, G. (Eds.) (1986) *The Enemy Within. Pit Villages and the miners' strike of 1984-5*, (London: Routledge and Kegan Paul), p.163.

[36] Ibid., p. 178.

[37] Callinicos, A. and Simons, M. (1985) *The Great Strike*, (London: Socialist Worker), p. 178.

[38] Ibid., p. 178.

[39] Ibid., p. 182.

[40] Ibid.

[41] Ibid., p. 183.

[42] Ibid., p. 183. [It is worth highlighting that Alex Callinicos has modified his views with the benefit of hindsight and now points, for example, to what the wives of the South Wales miners did during the lock-out of 1926, in terms of being solidly and actively behind their menfolk.]

[43] Green, *Op. Cit.*, p. 189.

[44] Ibid., p. 183.

[45] Winterton, J. and Winterton, R. (1989) *Coal, Crisis and Conflict*, (Manchester: Manchester University Press), p. 122.

[46] Ibid., p. 123.

[47] Ibid., p. 125.

[48] Seddon, *Op. Cit.*, p. 281.

[49] Winterton and Winterton, *Op. Cit.*, p. 126.

[50] Green, *Op. Cit.*, p. 189.

[51] Ibid.

[52] Seddon, *Op. Cit.*, p. 281/2.

[53] Stead, *Op. Cit.*, p. 24.

[54] North Yorkshire Women Against Pit Closures, (1985) *Strike 84-85*, (Leeds: North Yorkshire Women Against Pit Closures), p. 56.

[55] See Chapter Two for further debate re- the whole notion of what exactly may be deemed to constitute political participation.

[56] Goodman, *Op. Cit.*, p. 92.

[57] Ibid., p. 168.

[58] Lovenduski, J. and Randall, V. (1993) *Contemporary Feminist Politics*, (Oxford: Oxford University Press), p. 124.

[59] Seddon, *Op. Cit.*, p. 15.

[60] Hain, P. and McCrindle, J., 'One and All: Labour's Response to the Miners', *New Socialist*, October 1984, No 20, pp. 44-46), p. 46.

[61] Campbell, B., 'The other miners' strike', *New Statesman*, 27 July 1984, p. 8.

[62] Rees, G. (1985) 'Regional restructuring, class change and political action: preliminary comments on the 1984-1985 miners' strike in South Wales', *Society and Space*, (Volume 3, pp. 389-406), p. 403.

[63] Stead, *Op. Cit.*, title page.

7   This particular study - Hemsworth

Introduction

Attention now turns in this, the seventh, chapter to address the question of Hemsworth and its politics. It is worth noting at this particular juncture that there is a change of emphasis in Chapter Seven. There is a movement away from the respondents themselves towards a study of the local political elite. The specific character of the political 'scene' in Hemsworth will be examined; in particular the de-selection, prior to the 1987 General Election, of the former M.P., Alec Woodall, will be investigated as will the controversial 1991 by-election regarding the election of the subsequent M.P., Derek Enright. It is necessary to try to define what the substance of local politics is in Hemsworth but it has to be remembered that the investigation is primarily about the 1984/5 Miners' Strike and its links with politics. In order to place the politics of Hemsworth into some kind of context, it is also necessary to give a little information regarding the role of the N.U.M. in Labour Party politics in Yorkshire.

The National Union of Mineworkers and the Labour Party

The significance of the N.U.M. in Yorkshire is highlighted by Andrew Taylor, in his seminal text, *The Politics of the Yorkshire Miners*. The Yorkshire Area, in particular, is credited with being responsible for pulling the N.U.M. to the left. Taylor argues that it 'was the political transformation of the Yorkshire Area (N.U.M.) as a result of the crisis of the 1960s which, in a large part, pulled the N.U.M. as a whole to the left, a movement which perhaps culminated with the election of Arthur Scargill as President of the N.U.M.'[1].

Taylor's work involves a detailed examination of how much influence the Yorkshire N.U.M. has had on the Labour Party and Labour Governments. The power of the N.U.M. is emphasised by Alec Woodall, the former Member of Parliament for Hemsworth (February 1974 to 1987), who believes that, due to the large numbers of mining M.P.s, the miners were, for most of the post-war period, in a relatively powerful position within the House of Commons. Taylor does not accord the N.U.M. with as much power and influence as Woodall believes they had.

Taylor also examines the role played by the N.U.M in terms of the 'coalfield Constituency Labour Parties (C.L.P.s) and in the recruitment of M.P.s'. Traditionally, the Yorkshire N.U.M. has been regarded as the home of the militants yet this was not really the situation until the 1960s and the strikes of the early 1970s. Taylor highlights the fact that the Yorkshire miners were 'the largest group in the N.U.M.'. The change which occurred in the Yorkshire Area N.U.M. during the thirty years between 1944 and 1974 is described as moving it 'from the political and industrial right to being the leading left-wing Area in the N.U.M., a transformation symbolised by the rise of Arthur Scargill'[2].

The relationship between the N.U.M. and the Labour Party is examined in detail by Taylor, who states that 'Theoretically, affiliation to the Party subordinated the miners' political activity to the Party Conference, but the local dominance of the miners led some Party leaders to fear that the Party would become the tool of the unions'. He believes that this was not the case because 'the miners accepted the leading role of the Party in politics and because the miners' M.P.s rapidly assimilated the Party's role as a national integrative party as opposed to a trade union or working class party'. Taylor emphasises the fact that the mining M.P.s' primary objective was to represent 'the constituency for which they sat in the interests of the Labour Party, not the Y.M.A. [Yorkshire Miners' Association] or the M.F.G.B. [Miners Federation of Great Britain]'[3].

The Hemsworth constituency is specifically highlighted by Taylor as providing a classic example of the linkage between the miners' union and the Labour Party - even as far back as 1918. 'The Labour candidate, John Guest, M.P. since 1918, was a miner from Hemsworth enjoying wide support not only from the miners but from other trade unionists'. [Guest was the Labour Member of Parliament for Hemsworth from 1918 until his death prior to the General Election of 1931 when the seat was vacant at the time of dissolution.] He states that Guest's 'party label was important, but it was part of a wider appeal based on work and community, party ideology was woven into the mining electorate's everyday experience at work and in the pit villages'. He goes on to highlight the fact that 'Hemsworth enjoyed the reputation of being the best organised of all Yorkshire mining seats'[4].

Taylor traces Labour's 'electoral dominance in the Yorkshire coalfield' as having been 'established between 1918 and 1924'. He states that 'Labour voting in mining constituencies is a complex mixture of class consciousness, rational calculation, and habit'. In support of this, he cites higher than average turnout figures as indicating 'that voting is an act of collective affirmation which has a symbolic import beyond that of merely endorsing a political party'[5].

One of the reasons given for the N.U.M. moving to the left was frustrastion felt towards the Labour Party. As Taylor emphasised, 'The miners were to be frustrated by their reliance on the Labour Party (in and out of office) and these frustrations were to contribute to the resurgence of industrial militancy in the early-1970s'. With regards to how much actual influence the miners have held over the Labour Party, Taylor believes that the amount of influence has been greatly exaggerated in the past; 'the miners have not enjoyed a high degree of influence largely because of their acceptance of Labour's electoral strategy and their unwillingness to take sanctions against "their" party or "their" government'. This unwillingness persisted throughout the 1970s and 1980s. Did Neil Kinnock feed upon this acceptance and unwillingness when the Labour National Executive Committee imposed their candidate on the Hemsworth by-election? This by-election, held in November 1991, is dealt with in greater depth later in this Chapter.

So, because the Labour Party is a catch-all, pragmatic party it has been able to 'ignore or reject demands felt to be "sectional" or inimical to the electoral and political interests of Government or Party'[6]. The N.U.M., regarding the Labour Party, to a certain extent, as the lesser of two evils has felt it necessary to defer to Labour. It might be pertinent at this stage to give examples of the N.U.M. leadership's loyalty to Labour - for example, going along with the National Power-loading Agreement and the rundown of the workforce in the 1960s; accepting the pay incentive scheme in 1977-78.

The extent to which the N.U.M. is influential in the C.L.P.s and in terms of the selection of M.Ps is also examined. Taylor believes that the extent of this influence is a myth due to a number of factors, notably, 'the decline of the industry, changes in party rules, problems of participation by miners, defects in political organisation and social change in the coalfield'[7]. The role of the N.U.M. in terms of the sponsorship of M.P.s is also regarded as being greatly exaggerated; 'These are not miners' M.P.s in any proprietorial sense, and sponsorship cannot be used as a means of political influence: he who pays the piper does not call the tune. Sponsored M.P.s are expected to hold a "watching brief" over the industry, the miners and mining communities, but the Union rarely intervenes in their Parliamentary activities'[8].

The Yorkshire N.U.M. moved to the left and this is cited by Taylor as being due to a perception amongst certain members of the N.U.M. that '"moderation and reasonableness" had failed' and also he feels that this was 'vindicated by the 1972 strike'. This is to say that the N.U.M. moved to the left of the political spectrum and achieved a certain amount of success in so doing. The Yorkshire N.U.M. is regarded in 1972 as having gained the 'self-confidence lost as a consequence of 1926' and their 'contribution to victory' is regarded as 'considerable' especially through the way in which 'they perfected the devastatingly effective tactic of the mass, mobile picket which won the crucial battles before the power stations'. Both 1972 and 1974 are regarded by Taylor as producing 'an aura of invincibility'[9]. The rise of OPEC and the resulting energy crisis are also seen as factors which enabled the Yorkshire N.U.M. to become increasingly militant - although OPEC was not a factor in 1972 it did help the miners' victory in 1974.

The Labour Party, the N.U.M. and Hemsworth

With regards to the relationship between the Labour Party and the N.U.M. in Hemsworth, perhaps the main feature worthy of reporting is the fact that Hemsworth is a safe Labour seat and this has meant that the Labour Party is in a very powerful position in Hemsworth. Likewise, the strong links with the mining industry and the extent to which Hemsworth has, in the past, been a coalfield constituency mean that the N.U.M. has had a tremendous amount of influence over this particular area. At first glance, this appears to contradict Taylor's claim that the N.U.M.'s influence has been exaggerated but it is fair to say that, once elected, mining M.P.s from Hemsworth have had a degree of autonomy from the Union.

All the Parliamentary representatives for the Hemsworth Constituency have, in fact, been N.U.M. candidates. The (s)election of Derek Enright in November 1991 broke with that tradition. According to the interviews conducted after the by-election, opinion was very mixed as to whether this is regarded as being a positive or negative feature of the local political scenario. It is fair to say that a number of the respondents definitely regard this weakening of the link between the N.U.M. and the Labour Party in Hemsworth, the break with tradition, as a positive development. One of the interviewees (Number 39; Hemsworth resident, no personal connection with the mining industry, currently a joiner) said 'We might have better M.P.s in the future. Why should the N.U.M.'s man always get the job?'. Taylor highlights the traditional image of the mining M.P.; 'There is a tendency to see miners' M.P.s as a stereotype - old, solid, unimaginative and with little talent, forming the ballast of the P.L.P.'[10]. It is clear that Enright and now Jon Trickett provide a stark contrast to this caricature. Does the fact that the Member of Parliament is no longer sponsored by the N.U.M. mean that the latter is losing its grip upon this particular constituency? The evidence would appear to support this view. Ken Capstick, the N.U.M.'s choice in 1991 and its vice-chairman in Yorkshire, was regarded by the Labour Party at national level as a political, if not an electoral liability. Added to this is the fact that Frickley Colliery was, at the time of the by-election, the only colliery still in production in the area and even this was one of the original thirty one pits on Michael Heseltine's so-called 'hit-list' [that is to say, pits which were ear-marked for closure]. It closed on the 26th November 1993.

The level of influence of the Labour Party in Hemsworth is extensive. They occupy the majority of the seats on the local council. Yet this degree of representation does not satisfy all the inhabitants of Hemsworth. As one interviewee (Number 48; male, ex-paratrooper, very interested in politics but not aligned to any particular party) said; 'It's almost like the Hemsworth Mafia'. Evidence suggests that to achieve any kind of political power in the Hemsworth area the ambitious must ally themselves with the Labour Party. It has also been highlighted that during the Miners' Strike people could join the Labour Party with a reduced fee; in fact they did not pay anything because they were on strike. Observers have pointed out that many of those who joined during the Strike have since left the Party. The former M.P., Alec Woodall, claims that at one time the constituency had almost a thousand members and that when they had a

General Management Committee [this is the ruling body of the local Constituency Labour Party machinery] they would have almost two hundred delegates whereas, as his wife pointed out, nowadays (1990) they can hardly manage forty five.

Hemsworth's Politics

A certain amount of detailed information was given in Chapter Three regarding the constituency of Hemsworth so it is not necessary at this particular point to give an historical outline and other 'scene-setting' data. Suffice to reiterate, however, that as quoted in Robert Waller's *The Almanac of British Politics*[11] and referred to in Chapter Three, 'Hemsworth is a famous name, in electoral history at least. This is the seat which has produced the largest Labour majority in so many general elections, remaining over 30,000 from 1950 to 1974. This is where it is said that the Labour votes are weighed and not counted'. He continues in a manner which, with the benefit of hindsight, now has a somewhat hollow ring to it; 'Hemsworth is a mining seat. Together with Bolsover in Derbyshire, a higher proportion of its population is employed in the coal industry than any other constituency in the U.K. - 30%'[12].

In terms of the Parliamentary representation which Hemsworth has received over the last decade or so, the Member of Parliament for Hemsworth between February 1974 and 1987 was Alec Woodall. He was succeeded, after a controversial de-selection row, by George Buckley. Buckley was the M.P. for Hemsworth between 1987 and 1991, when his untimely death from cancer led to the Hemsworth by-election which was held on the 7th November 1991. The victor at this by-election was Derek Enright, who despite being the official Labour Party candidate, it would be fair to say, did not enjoy the unanimous backing of all of the local Labour Party members. In order to throw a certain amount of light upon both the de-selection of Woodall and the Enright by-election, it is necessary that these two events are examined in detail.

Before examining the de-selection row, it is necessary to give a certain amount of statistical information relating to the results of general elections and Hemsworth. These are presented, taking 1950 as the starting point, in tabular format[13].

Going back into the annals of history, in 1970, according to 'The British General Election of 1970' by David Butler and Michael Pinto-

Duschinsky, Hemsworth was ranked number one in terms of the numbers employed in the mining industry - with 40.7 per cent employed in the mines, narrowly beating Bolsover with 40.3 per cent[14]. At the General Election of 1970, 71.8 per cent of the electorate turned out to vote. This was down 4.3 per cent on the 1966 figure. 80.8 per cent voted for the Labour candidate with 19.2 per cent voting for the Conservative candidate. The swing was 4.6 per cent between 1966 and 1970 and the swing had been 2.5 per cent between 1955 and 1970.

By the time of the General Election of October 1974, according to Butler and Kavanagh, 'the percentage employed in the mining industry had fallen to 32.4%, a close second to Bolsover which now stood at 32.9%'[15]. Hemsworth is cited as 'the extreme case of a very safe seat in which the Liberal vote was taken more in numbers from the dominant party and more in proportion from the minority party and different measures of swing simply reflect this'[16].

According to Crewe and Fox, *British Parliamentary Constituencies*[17], in 1983 Hemsworth was the seventeenth safest Labour seat. It was ranked eighteenth in terms of constituencies with the highest proportion of manual workers - with 64.6 per cent employed in manual occupations. It was ranked nineteenth out of the constituencies which contain the highest proportion of *skilled* manual workers - 41.4 per cent. With respect to the constituencies which had the highest Labour share of the vote, it was ranked fourteenth - with 59.3 per cent. In terms of the constituencies which have the lowest Conservative share of the two-party vote, it was classified as number 26 with 24.8 per cent. From the constituencies with the highest proportion employed in manufacturing, Hemsworth was ranked 26 with 53.9 per cent deemed to be employed in manufacturing.

The Parliamentary constituency of Hemsworth comprises the wards of Crofton and Ackworth, Featherstone, Hemsworth, South Elmsall and South Kirkby. In terms of the social composition of the constituency, in 1984 only 10.4 per cent of the population were categorised as professional and managerial, 41.4 per cent were deemed to be skilled, 64.6 per cent manual workers, 10.6 per cent unemployed, 8.5 per cent had professional qualifications, 53.9 per cent were employed in manufacturing, 44.5 per cent employed in the service industries, 46.5 per cent of householders were owner-occupiers and 41.2 per cent were council tenants. The 16-24 year old age category made up 14.3 per cent of the total population and pensioners comprised 14.9 per cent of the total population. As Crewe and Fox state; 'A constituency based on scattered mining towns south-east of Wakefield. Working-class and rock-solid Labour'[18].

It is worthy of reiterating, at this stage, the point that was made in Chapter Three regarding turnout in mining constituencies; according to *The British General Election of 1987* by Butler and Kavanagh, one of the most important effects in 1987 was increased turnout. They state that 'Increased political awareness also produced higher turn-out. The clearest example is in mining constituencies which used, in the 1950s, to have the highest turnout in the country but where, from 1966 onwards, turnout has been declining at an above-average rate'[19]. They go on to say, 'In 1987 the passions felt on both sides of the dispute amongst the miners over the 1984-5 strike was evident. In the 18 constituencies with over 15% employment in mining, turnout rose 4.4% on average and in the nine with over 20% employment it jumped 5.2%. As a result, turnout in mining seats is now once again higher than the national average, even though most are safe seats; turnout in 1987 averaged 76.5% in the 33 constituencies with most mining. It is noteworthy that the rise in voting occurred in both Arthur Scargill's Yorkshire bastion and in the Nottinghamshire stronghold of opposition to his leadership of the strike. Mansfield, the headquarters of the Notts miners, had the third biggest rise in Britain, whilst Hemsworth and Barnsley East, the two most solidly mining Yorkshire constituencies, lay seventh and fifteeth in that league table'[20].

As stated in Chapter Three, however, by 1992 this increased turnout was no longer evident. Butler is quoted in Chapter Three as saying that, it was 'no longer the case' that there was an increase in turnout in mining constituencies. It is fair to say that, by 1992, any impact of the Miners' Strike upon turnout in mining constituencies appears to have subsided.

The de-selection of Alec Woodall

So, turnout rose at the 1987 General Election in the constituency of Hemsworth. It is difficult to determine whether the de-selection of the former M.P., Alec Woodall, had any impact whatsoever upon the '87 result[21], but, as stated previously, it does appear to be the case that the Strike itself did have an impact upon turnout. Alec Woodall held the seat of Hemsworth from February 1974 until his de-selection in 1987 when he was replaced by George Buckley.

Mandatory reselection was a policy which was agreed by the Labour Party at a special conference held at Wembley in January 1981. Here it was decided that a sitting M.P. had to be re-selected by his/her local constituency party in order to enable them to fight the following General Election as the official Labour Party candidate. It was felt by many in the Labour Party that this would eradicate the 'jobs for life' syndrome and that, in so doing, it would automatically improve the calibre of incumbent M.P.s. It is perhaps inevitable, therefore, that this form of 'political tacograph' would lead to a certain amount of ill-feeling within the Party.

Alec Woodall, the incumbent Member of Parliament for Hemsworth, was de-selected in 1987. It was felt, in certain quarters, that he had failed to support the miners enough during the 1984/5 Miners' Dispute. This is an accusation which Woodall hotly denies. It is relevant at the particular point to examine in close detail precisely what Woodall had to say, in hindsight, about the affair.

When asked whether any of his views had changed as a result of the Strike, Woodall replied; 'Yes. In as much, I'm very, very disappointed in the N.U.M. In 1945 there were 38 miners in the House of Commons, 38, it was the strongest single group from a trade union in the whole of the House of Commons and they had terrific power. They could tell the Prime Minister that they wanted to see him and the Prime Minister had to go'. This is an interesting comment from Woodall because it appears to contradict what Taylor claims earlier. According to Woodall's evidence then, mining M.P.'s *did* represent a force to be reckoned with. Woodall goes on to explain why he feels that mining M.P.s lost their power. 'They had 38, now the N.U.M. is down to 14, for the simple reason through the abandonment of the Parliamentary panel. [This was a short-list of (potentially) sponsored candidates.] They don't have it any longer, Arthur Scargill did away with it. And he only did away with it, in my opinion, because he couldn't get the people he wanted to onto the Parliamentary panel ... his left-wing friends or extreme left-wing friends. So, very quietly, in its stocking feet, it went through the Yorkshire Area Council, while he was President, to do away with the Parliamentary panel and instead the whole of the Yorkshire Council (that's delegates from every branch of the N.U.M. in Yorkshire) would meet and would decide on who would be a candidate if there was a vacancy'.

Labour's policy of mandatory re-selection of M.P.s is cited by Woodall as 'the worse thing the Labour Party's ever done. Which has caused a lot of upset. They've lost many good M.P.s for no reason whatsoever other than the cliques that were formed in different constituencies, including this one, and people were ousted'.

In defence of his stance during the Miners' Strike, Woodall goes on to say, 'I was ousted for no reason whatsoever. They started a rumour that I wasn't seen on the picket lines and I wasn't fully supporting the strike. Completely ignoring the fact that we had nine miners' wives support groups in the Hemsworth constituency who I visited and donated to. Every one of them had a hundred pounds off me. Nine miners' wives support groups during the strike and each one told that they had not to be without money so that they couldn't provide the meals every day. And that was my contribution to the constituency. The picket lines I did go on were in Nottingham, not in Hemsworth. They didn't need pickets here, you see'.

Woodall's actions during the Strike are mentioned in   the Wintertons' *Coal, Crisis and Conflict*; 'moderate Labour M.P.s from mining constituencies, like Roy Mason, Allen Mckay and Alec Woodhall, also showed their support by visiting strike centres, kitchens and picket lines, and by taking up individual cases involving police harrassment or denial of social security benefits'[22]. So, the Wintertons appear to vindicate Woodall's claims.

Woodall gives a little more detail about his de-selection, in particular, concerning the way in which he felt that his accusers failed to confront him directly; 'Never a word to me! I was never accused by ANYBODY! It was all done underneath. That's what happened and then, of course, I got de-selected. I got de-selected *massively'*. He continues 'they tried to do the ultimate dirty trick. They put three candidates in; one from U.C.A.T.T. and they even tried to force me to the bottom of the poll, you know, so they could then go to the press and say "Well, we've lost complete confidence"'.

When asked whether he felt that there were any similarities between his situation and that of Frank Field, who at the time the interview was conducted (January 1990) was the Member of Parliament for Birkenhead and had been de-selected by his local constituency party, Woodall replied thus; 'Probably that's due to a different element in the Militant Tendency. I'm not saying that the Hemsworth constituency is infiltrated by a militant tendency because I don't think that it is. There might be some who think that they are extreme left-wingers but they are young people who don't know what the hell it is all about. So, I think it is a completely different picture'.

Woodall does go on to illustrate similarities between his de-selection and others; he highlights the de-selections of Michael McGuire, M.P. for Ince; Sid Vincent, the General Secretary; Reg Freeson, the former Housing Minister; Ron Atkinson, the former Labour Party Treasurer; and also the Labour Chief Whip, amongst others. 'There were seven in total for the Labour Party for the 1987 General Election. People who hadn't put a foot wrong, hadn't done anything, done their job in Parliament and, in Michael McGuire's case and my case, did our duty by the N.U.M. during the Strike. And neither of us were accused by anybody, it was all done underneath, behind our backs'.

When asked whether the de-selection had a lot to do with Arthur Scargill, Alec Woodall felt that Scargill was, at least partly, to blame because he got rid of the Parliamentary Panel. The Panel meant that, 'by and large, always the local man got the job. Now I was number seven out of eight on the Parliamentary panel in 1973. There were six of us appeared before the selection meeting at Barnsley. That's, as I say, with delegates of the N.U.M. branches affiliated to the Hemsworth constituency. And I romped home'. Again, Woodall emphasises the fact that his case was not unique; 'And, of course, this happened at all the other miners' constituencies as well - like Pontefract and Castleford. Now Arthur Scargill got that one thrown away. That, Pontefract and Castleford, was a miners' seat for donkeys' years, right up to Joe Harper dying in 1978. Then after that they lost it - through Scargill interfering again'.

The extent of the decline in terms of the sheer numbers of mining M.P.s and the influence which their numerical strength gave them in the past is clearly illustrated by Woodall. 'Yorkshire, at one time, had nine, I think, or ten, mining M.P.s. Now they're down to six, down to six! And they've only got six by virtue of boundary changes - which gave South Yorkshire two extra constituencies. Otherwise they would have a handful in Yorkshire. Of course, we lost Makerfield. We also lost Mansfield. The miners' panel now ... the miners' group in the House of Commons is down to fourteen. And in 1945 it was 38! Alright, I mean collieries have closed and different unions have come into more prominence in mining areas but we should never be down to fourteen because six have been thrown away'.

Again, Woodall has no hesitation in deciding where the blame lies; 'Scargill was instrumental in throwing Chesterfield away. We'd three Labour M.P.s in Derbyshire, all good M.P.s, including Eric Varley, who was a cabinet minister, Secretary of State for Energy. He decided to leave politics to go into industry and instead of a miner getting it, Tony Benn got it. Don Concannon, he was Minister of State for Northern Ireland, from Mansfield. He retired from Parliament after he had a serious road accident coming back from the Labour Party Conference. That seat was thrown away. A chap, not from the area, an extreme left-winger, not a miner, it's now gone. So, at the moment, we've got two M.P.s in Derbyshire, two miners in Derbyshire. One in Nottingham, six in Yorkshire, one in Lancashire - where we used to have three. None in Durham, one in Northumberland and one in Scotland'. Woodall ends on a pessimistic note with regards to the N.U.M., 'the N.U.M.'s influence in Parliament is gone, just as it has in the industry and in the country'.

It is interesting, therefore, to be able to see the de-selection from the point of view of the person on the receiving end of this, relatively speaking, new piece of Labour Party policy. A good few years after the event the 'victim' stills feels deeply hurt by what he regards as a miscarriage of justice and the work of a few, unrepresentative, left-wingers who, through their actions, have deprived the Party of a number of hard-working and loyal M.P.s. He adamantly refutes the main charge against him, that he did not support and espouse the miners' cause enough during 1984/5, claiming this accusation to be patently without foundation and, what is more, he highlights the way in which he says that he was denied the opportunity of being able to defend himself against the charges which were levied against him.

It is fair to say that a number of the interviewees felt that the Labour Party was correct to oust Alec Woodall as they did and indeed feel that he had failed to support the miners during 1984/5. Whether this was influenced by the portrayal of Woodall in the media is open to question; one respondent mentioned a local newspaper headline to the effect that 'local M.P. "threatens" to ask questions in the Commons', the interviewee said 'What was he supposed to be doing!'. This illustrates a lack of confidence in Woodall amongst some of those questioned.

An attempt was made to interview Woodall's successor but at the time the request was made Buckley replied that he was too busy dealing with constituency business to be able to assist with this research. Sadly, it will be difficult to assess whether this was the reply of a conscientious Parliamentary representative or whether the de-selection furore meant that inquisitive authors are best avoided?

Before moving on to examine the by-election controversy, it is necessary to give more detail regarding the opposing viewpoint with respect to Woodall's de-selection. A couple of additional interviewees were questioned precisely because of their involvement in the de-selection. A local councillor who was closely involved with the de-selection stated that, as far as he was concerned, the de-selection was 'done procedurally correct'. He went on to reiterate that re-selection was 'an integral part of the Labour Party's constitution', the implication being that it was natural and correct that Woodall had to be put forward for re-selection. He continued, 'The guy who's got it now, Derek Enright, he'll face re-selection'. He went on to describe the hostility which certain members of the local Labour Party felt towards Alec Woodall; 'They thought that his ways were flamboyant, gesticulating when making a point. A right of centre man'. He proceeds to illuminate how this contrasted with the local Constituency Party which was left of centre, especially at the time that the Strike broke out. 'There was a mood for wanting a change throughout the Party [locally], the N.U.M. group had made up its mind that it would seek someone who would represent mining interests more fully. I believe that Woodall could have done so but the general mood was that he was not militant enough'. He goes on to say that 'The Strike made people more militant. If the Strike hadn't happened there's a possibility that he would not have been opposed'. This is an interesting point to note, if it had not been for the Strike perhaps Woodall would have survived attempts to oust him or perhaps those attempts would not have materialised in the first instance? Obviously, the Strike did take place and so at this moment in time we can but speculate as to an alternative outcome.

The councillor involved in Woodall's de-selection continued; 'Men living on food parcels and picketing money expected Alec arm-in-arm on the battle-front'. He goes on to describe how George Buckley was the Chairman of the local Labour Party and how Alec felt that he did not always get a fair hearing and protection from George as the Chairman; 'George was left of centre, he was a supporter of Arthur Scargill'. With regards to the relationship between Woodall and Buckley, he states, 'There was no love lost between the two'. This interviewee felt that 'Buckley reflected the mood of the constituency more accurately' but he refused to be drawn on the question of who made the better Member of Parliament.

Another interviewee (Number 58; male, union activist, Labour supporter, politically active) who was involved with de-selection of Alec Woodall had this to say: 'If I remember discussions about it he wanted to go to seventy and then you know to the next general election which would have been the '87 and run that which obviously meant to '92. In that period he would have been seventy, he wouldn't have finished at seventy, he could have been seventy two or three. Now that was his feelings, that was his intimations'. He continues; 'But I think the trigger for Alec Woodall was his actions during the Strike because he lived in Hemsworth at Market Street and less than a mile away was a picket line at Kirkby Lane End. It was the morning ritual of the scabs going in and the lads battling with police to get at the van, etc. Five o'clock, six o'clock, within an hour it was deserted again but there was a constant vigil on at the end of the lane until they came out again. And his appearances there, just to observe, not to push or get physically involved, were very minimal. In fact, I think virtually nil but I couldn't be sure on that. And that produced, in my opinion, the President of South Kirkby N.U.M., Frank Clarke, to make it his crusade to get rid of Alec Woodall as the M.P. for Hemsworth'.

When pursued on this point about it being a personal crusade, the interviewee said; 'No, I think the feeling was maybe not quite as intense at Frickley but it was a consensus. But it was stronger with Frank Clarke and Frank Clarke was the motivator within the N.U.M. delegation which, at that time, had a very big influence within the C.L.P., I'm talking about numerically, with delegates'. [Attempts to contact Frank Clarke about an interview were unsuccessful.] The interviewee continued to assess the reasons behind the demise of Woodall; 'It was his performance in the Strike that really, in my opinion ... O.K. he visited the various kitchens but he could never picket the picket lines at the pit. And there was a lot of violence, give and take on both sides but he didn't condemn any of the police brutality similar to what old mining M.P.s did'. He sums up; 'It was just his general approach to the political situation and the battle that was going on for that year that I agreed, personally, myself that he should go and that influenced my vote'.

When questioned about the procedures undertaken to get rid of Woodall, this second interviewee said, 'we proceeded through the general course of the rule book to get rid of him and obviously used our vote within the selection conference which was 48 nearly 50 delegates at that time. And we had been recruiting obviously because there was a surge during the Strike and after it dropped off'.

Derek Enright was also questioned about the de-selection of Alec Woodall and, although, as he states, he was not around at the time, he had this to say; 'I think it was a very complicated de-selection. I know Alec doesn't feel this but I don't think George Buckley went out of his way to get rid of Alec. Though Alec certainly had his problems with Arthur at the time [Arthur Scargill] and I think, although I don't really know because I was in Africa at the time, it's just what I've been told, I think that Alec had his problems during the Strike. I mean he didn't agree with certain things that were done during the Strike and one of Alec's great virtues is that he always says exactly what he thinks at any given time. I'm also given to believe that people thought that Alec was leaving anyway and that he was going to retire then. All those things got meshed together so it all became very unclear. And it was only well afterwards that somebody said to me that he was de-selected. That is a very murky view of what happened because I wasn't here, I didn't see it clearly. But that is the best I can tell you, the post-impressionist view really'.

So, the three views expressed above provide a counter-balance to the views expressed by Woodall and enable us to have more of a holistic view of the de-selection saga.

The interviewees themselves expressed mixed views regarding the de-selection. It is a fair assertion to make that few of the interviewees had more than a shady recollection of the Woodall saga. Most felt, however, that it was a just dessert if he had not supported the miners enough but some did feel that, this aside, he had a legacy of being a hard working, 'local', Member of Parliament. As one said, (Number 36; former miner, currently self-employed), 'I once went to his surgery with a problem about my daughter getting a council house and he was great. I couldn't fault the chap'.

Clearly, the de-selection of Alec Woodall constitutes an important political event in Hemsworth's history. Views have been expressed both commending and criticising the de-selection. Given that Woodall's behaviour, or perceived behaviour, during the 1984/5 Miners' Strike has evidently had a part to play in his downfall, the linkage between the Miners' Strike and the de-selection is apparent. Social scientists ought, perhaps, to avoid hypothetical dilemmas but it is probably true to claim that had the 1984/5 Miners' Strike not taken place then Woodall would have been able to serve his time as the Member for Hemsworth until old age necessitated retirement. The Miners' Strike was a central component in the de-selection saga. Local events, such as Woodall's lack of attendance on the picket lines, were of central importance but, with the benefit of hindsight, it is evident that the significance of the local in comparison with national factors declined over time. National factors, such as the role undertaken by Neil Kinnock in his attempts to modernise the labour Party, had a more lasting impression upon the interviewees and, it is fair to say that the de-selection row now remains as rather a hazy memory in the minds of most of those questioned. As one interviewee (Number 50; unemployed former mineworker) said, 'It [the de-selection] was obviously important at the time but, looking back, we had other important things to worry about'.

The 1991 Hemsworth by-election

Following on from the controversial de-selection the next time that Hemsworth hit the headlines was in late 1991 with the debacle concerning the by-election. As stated, the by-election was held on the 7th November and arose due to the death of the former M.P., George Buckley. The candidates were Derek Enright for the Labour Party, Garnet Harrison for the Conservative Party, Valerie Megson for the Liberal Democrats, Paul Ablett standing as Independent Labour and Tim Smith representing the Corrective Party.

The Liberal Democratic candidate, Valerie Megson, obtained some adverse publicity following revelations of a cheque which bounced and non-payment of the poll tax. The *Hemsworth and South Elmsall Express* reported on polling day that 'some who had previously decided to vote for her have said they will now not bother voting at all'. Valerie Megson attempted to clarify the matter by saying, 'I had no intention of evading the poll tax' she blamed it on an oversight as she was in the process of leaving her husband. Megson believed that 'The trouble is that Labour have never been threatened before as this has always been a safe Labour seat. Now they are threatened and it's no longer a safe Labour seat'[23].

The other controversial aspect of the by-election, which in terms of media coverage made the Megson revelations pale into insignificance, was the selection of Derek Enright as the Labour Party candidate. As stated in the *Hemsworth and South Elmsall Express*, Thursday October 24, 1991, controversy surrounded 'Scargillite Ken Capstick's rejection - despite overwhelming grassroots support'. As stated earlier, Ken Capstick was the N.U.M.'s choice of candidate. It goes on to say that 'The N.U.M. nominee was black-balled before a shortlist of four was drawn up which included Wakefield planning committee chairman Norman Kennedy, district councillor for Hemsworth ward 20 Cr Wayne Jenkins of East Hardwick, and Ackworth School old girl Gaye Johnson'. The *Express* highlights the furore which Enright's selection caused by saying, 'The row over Mr Capstick's exclusion sent shock waves through the party, prompting leader Neil Kinnock to deny "stitch-up" accusations'. A local councillor and constituency party chairman, Henry Daley, is quoted as saying, 'We have been left with a candidate we do not want'.

It is necessary to highlight the alternative side of the coin. Enright was a politician with impressive credentials. A former Euro M.P. for a Leeds constituency, He had been an E.C. West African delegate and also a representative for the Commonwealth Institute. Enright asserted that he 'was chosen according to party rules'[24].

The by-election is cited in *Politics Review*, February 1992. It states 'Of the three seats up for election, [Kincardine and Deeside and also Langbaurgh were held on the same day] in only one was the result a foregone conclusion. At the 1987 general election, the Labour candidate received a majority of 20,700 in the Yorkshire seat of Hemsworth and, although the turnout of 42.8% was very low, Labour achieved a comfortable majority of 11,087 in the by-election. The Liberals increased their share of the vote by 4.2% to push the Conservatives into third place'[25]. It might be argued by certain commentators that, because of the selection procedure, this by-election in Hemsworth was not quite so routine as it at first appeared.

An EXIT poll was conducted, specifically for this book, on the 7th November 1991 at a number of polling stations in the Hemsworth constituency (permission was obtained from the Electoral Office in Wakefield). The voters were asked a number of questions relating to their political preferences. They were, first of all, categorised according to gender and the age group into which they fitted. They were then asked their answers to the following questions; Who did you vote for? Have you changed your vote from the last General Election? Were you voting for the party or the candidate today? Will you vote the same way in the next General Election? If no, how will you vote? Do you always vote? On a scale of 1-10, how interested are you in politics? 1=low, 10=high. Do you agree with the Labour Party's decision to impose its own candidate, Derek Enright? Did that decision affect the way that you voted today? Would you have voted for Ken Capstick? The final question was, Did the 1984/5 Miners' Strike have any influence upon the way that you voted today?

Tensions were obviously running high as far as the Labour Party was concerned. The local Labour Party Campaign Headquarters felt nervous enough to be able to place political pressure upon the author's employer, with the effect that the employer, who had previously given permission for the research to be undertaken, was forced to capitulate and recall the author from outside of the polling stations.

As stated, the research was being carried out outside of the polling stations, not on their land (that is to say, outside the boundaries of the polling station) and questions were only asked as electors returned after having cast their vote. The main objection was to question seven 'Do you agree with the Labour Party's decision to impose its own candidate, Derek Enright?' Yet this was a question which the media had found perfectly acceptable and which really was the crux of the whole controversy. This was the key issue which transformed this by-election in a 'rock-solid' Labour seat into a much more exciting political occasion. If the word 'impose' had been removed from the question it would have meant ignoring the real facts involved in this particular episode.

As events transpired, it was not particularly important that the research was brought to a halt during polling hours. This is due to the fact that it could be claimed that perhaps a certain section of the electorate voted with their feet. Turnout was down considerably on the figure for 1987 (where it was 75.7 per cent) and even down in comparison with what has been stated as the average turnout figure for a by-election (sixty three per cent according to the television programme *Is Democracy Working?*)[26]. As stated in *Politics Review*, February 1992, 'At the 1987 general election, the Labour candidate received a majority of 20,000 in the Yorkshire seat of Hemsworth and, although the turnout of 42.8% was very low, Labour achieved a comfortable majority of 11,087 in the by-election. The Liberals increased their share of the vote by 4.2% to push the Conservatives into third place'[27].

In terms of what the respondents who were questioned in the Exit poll had to say; 77 people were questioned before the author was forced to abandon her inquiries. In terms of the by-election questionnaire, however, this is what the seventy seven respondents had to say: In answer to the first question which asked who the elector had voted for (electors were told that they, obviously, could refuse to answer this question if they so wished) 40 out of the total 77 claimed that they had voted for the Labour Party candidate, Derek Enright. Twenty three refused to reveal who they had voted for. Seven claimed that they had voted for the Conservative Party candidate, Garnet Harrison and seven claimed that they had voted for the Liberal Democratic Party candidate, Val Megson. In percentage terms this works out at 52 per cent voting Labour, 30 per cent refusing to reveal how they voted, 9 per cent voting for the Conservative Party and 9 per cent voting for the Liberal Democratic Party.

In terms of question three, which asked the electors whether they voted for the party or the candidate, the replies were as follows; 54 out of the 77 claimed that they voted on the basis of the party, ten claimed that they voted for the candidate, 12 said that they voted on the basis of both the party and the candidate and one refused to say. In percentage terms, this works out as follows; 70 per cent voted on the basis of the party, thirteen per cent voted on the basis of the candidate, 16 per cent voted for both and one per cent would not say.

With regards to question seven, as stated earlier, perhaps the most controversial question (which asked the electors whether they agreed with the Labour Party's decision to impose its own candidate, Derek Enright) the replies were as follows; 32 people said that they disagreed with that decision, indeed one of the 32 said that he felt that 'the people should pick the candidate'. Thirty four people said that they agreed with the Labour Party's decision. Of those 34, four people made comments. One said 'He's [Derek Enright] better than the normal Labour candidate', a second said, 'He's [Derek Enright] the best man for the job' and a third comment was made that they agreed with the decision because, 'it's more democratic', one said he was sceptical but still felt that 'Enright's the best man for the job'. Eleven respondents stated that they did not know whether they agreed or disagreed with the Labour Party's decision, this included one voter who said that he was not bothered because he 'would vote for the Party regardless'. [The author was unable to obtain a great deal of information about the political attitudes and behaviour of these particular interviewees as they were questioned as part of the EXIT poll and time was limited in order to question as many people as possible.]

In percentage terms, this works out as follows; 42 per cent of those questioned disagreed with the choice of Derek Enright as the Labour Party candidate in the Hemsworth by-election, 44 per cent of those questioned agreed with the choice of candidate and 14 per cent neither agreed nor disagreed.

So, effectively then, a majority of those who were questioned in the Exit poll which was conducted for this research felt, by a very slender margin, that the Labour Party *was* correct to impose its own candidate, Derek Enright, to stand in the Hemsworth by-election. It is necessary, however, to reiterate the comment which was propounded earlier that perhaps the majority of those who were disgruntled at the Labour Party's decision had 'voted with their feet'. If this was indeed the case, then those questioned would tend to be electors who either agreed with the decision or who were unsure as to whether they agreed or disagree. It would be extremely difficult to conduct research which would provide a conclusive answer to this particular question.

In the event, Labour's Derek Enright was elected as the Member of Parliament for Hemsworth on the 7th November 1991. He obtained 15,895 votes, a majority of 11,087. He retained Labour's share of the vote despite a low turnout - in 1987 George Buckley obtained 67 per cent of the total vote whereas Derek Enright was just one per cent behind with 66 per cent. In his victory speech, as reported in the *Hemsworth and South Elmsall Express* 14th November 1991, he stated 'This result gives notice to the Government that they are running scared. They are running out of excuses and running out of time'. He went on to say, 'The people of this constituency want a government that will bring jobs. They want a government that cherishes the health service'. He highlighted Hemsworth's problems by stating, 'One in eight people in this constituency have lost their jobs. Isn't it time this Government lost its job?'. As the *Express* reported, Enright 'dismissed the "row" over his selection as candidate rather than that of N.U.M.-sponsored Ken Capstick. "The row was in the papers and the media. On the doorsteps the concerns were about jobs and the health service", he added'[28].

The by-election result: Val Megson came second with 4,808 votes; Garnet Harrison, the Conservative candidate, polled 2,512 votes. Paul Ablett, the Independent Labour candidate, polled 648 votes. Tim Smith, who stood as the candidate for the Corrective Party, obtained 108 votes.

Analysis of the Hemsworth by-election result then appears to indicate that the imposition of a candidate by the Labour Party's National Executive Committee did have an impact upon the election result. Whilst the impact was not as dramatic as certain political commentators might have predicted or anticipated, the choice of candidate does, nevertheless, appear to have affected the outcome of the by-election in no small way. Although there was never any real doubt that such a safe Labour seat would fall to an opposing party, it does indeed appear to be the case that a significant proportion of the electorate in Hemsworth felt significantly perturbed by the N.E.C.'s decision that they made their annoyance known by, as stated earlier, 'voting with their feet' and not voting at all. A turnout figure of 42.8

per cent is low even by 'normal' by-election standards and this remains so even when allowance is made for the complacency factor which inevitably affects safe seats. Hemsworth is a safe Labour seat and, therefore, complacency might lead to a low turnout figure but, nevertheless, 42.8 per cent was particularly low (as stated earlier, average turnout in by-elections is estimated at approximately 63 per cent). Although it is diificult to prove that there is a conclusive link between candidate selection and low turnout, the results of the EXIT poll lead to the belief that it is necessary to be wary of totally discounting any direct linkage.

Both Derek Enright and Ken Capstick were interviewed for their views on the by-election saga. This is what they had to say; firstly, Derek Enright, 'I mean it was quite interesting because, of course, Ken got the majority of nominations and it was just left the same. Ken got the nominations which indeed he did but they were all N.U.M. nominations and strangely enough, in fact there were, I think two or three people that they could have chosen from within the constituency to be the official N.U.M. rep ... but Ken was chosen and that caused enormous problems. It was seen on the one hand as Arthur Scargill's bid to get back at Neil Kinnock and it was also seen as the N.U.M. imposing a candidate once again. My nomination was from the Co-op and from the Electrician's Union and from one branch - which was actually a broader spread in a way than Ken's and it certainly wasn't a central spread. Nobody made them move me in any way'. Enright then proceeds to lists all the other candidates. He continues; 'It was an extraordinary day. The day of the choosing. I mean we all went in and we all got flogged and flayed and all the rest of it. And the National Executive Committee did their short-list and there was much shouting which I didn't see but which I certainly heard from outside and rude words were said and then the short-list was finally imposed and a candidate, i.e. myself was imposed if you like. I'm putting it in that way. In a way I was almost quite sorry it didn't go to a vote because I think I would have had a very good chance in the vote because I would have picked up some of the other candidates' votes in the end. I mean, Ken would clearly have been in the lead on the first vote. I don't think there's any doubt about that whatsoever. But I was fairly confident that I would pick up the others. I'd done a lot in this area. I'd been Chairman of the Community Health Council ... I mean all the papers portrayed me as if I'd been bombed in from London, of course when I was just living right on the edge of the constituency. I was Deputy Head of Saint Wilfred's [a local Catholic School] which covered all this area and many of the people in there were parents that I'd worked well with before. I mean quite apart from our political affiliations. And, of course, I'd been Chairman of Planning for West Yorkshire ... and I knew the churches in this area, with another ecumenical hat on'.

So, Enright gave his version of events, for the record what did Capstick have to say? Capstick stated; 'I almost became the M.P. for Hemsworth a few years ago and perhaps many people think that I should have been if it hadn't have been for some manoeuvring by the Labour Party National Executive Committee'. When asked whether he feels bitter, Capstick replied; 'I didn't feel bitter and I don't feel bitter now. That's not a politician's answer, it's a truthful answer because at the time I expected it because it was always a possibility that the Labour Party National Executive Committee, at the end of the day, could do what they did. My task was to try and make it as difficult for them as possible. And the way I did that was to try and get as many nominations as possible and as much support in the constituency as I could. If I had a groundswell of opinion behind me then perhaps they wouldn't dare. I thought I'd achieved that but they still did what they did. So, in a way I didn't feel bitter about it because I was able to rationalise it'. Capstick was rather philosophical about the defeat, 'I mean politics you have your successes and you have your setbacks and it's always like that'. He also emphasised how, following the by-election episode he was able to get really involved in campaigning against the October 1992 pit closure announcement. He did feel, however, that the by-election didn't do the Labour Party any good, in terms of the national leadership asserting its authority, 'We certainly didn't go on to win the General Election'.

The two main participants in the by-election controversy were thus able to put forward their interpretation of events. They obviously disagreed with regards to what happened but it is interesting, nevertheless, to hear their versions.

The interviewees were, generally speaking, critical of the selection procedure undertaken for the 1991 by-election but most, in retrospect, conceded that Enright had proven himself to be a worthy Member of Parliament. One interviewee (Number 53; unemployed former mineworker) stated; 'I've seen him [Enright] on telly quite a few times and he seems to be doing a grand job. He seems to be "for us"'. Another respondent (Number 55; unemployed former mineworker) was less enthusiastic but still conceded, 'He wouldn't have been my choice and I still think it was wrong the way they did it. But to give the man his due, he works hard and he's always in the local rag'.

It is not quite so easy to link the by-election to the Miners' Strike as it was with the de-selection but, nevertheless, the Strike still had a part to play in the Enright debacle. It could be said that the Strike had led to a scenario where the N.U.M. could be overruled in the selection of a candidate in this, at one time one of the most prominent mining constituencies. Surely, if the events of 1984/5 had not taken place then this situation would have been unheard of? The National Executive Committee would not have 'dared' to impose its own candidate in lieu of the N.U.M.'s choice. Whilst not as self-evident as in the de-selection furore, a connection between the Miners' Strike and the by-election can definitely be made.

In terms of an evaluation of the importance of national and local factors, it is fair to say that national factors had a tremendous impact on the by-election. Indeed, it was the action undertaken by the Labour Party's National Executive Committee that made the election of such political significance in the first place. Local factors certainly played a part in terms of the strength of the opposition to Ken Capstick's fate but, as with the de-selection furore, the significance of these local factors appears to have faded over time. In retrospect too, Enright's reputation as an erudite and articulate Member of Parliament appeared to have all but quelled the dissenting voices.

The 1991 by-election has an important part to play in terms of the politicisation question. To a certain extent, it enhanced politicisation from the point of view of focusing attention, especially media attention, on Hemsworth and thereby heightening political awareness. It also forced the inhabitants of Hemsworth to focus upon the relationship between the Labour Party and the N.U.M. and, if turn-out is taken into consideration, it does seem that the links with the N.U.M. were the stronger factor - even though we must not lose sight of the fact that the Labour Party did still win the by-election. The 1992 result (whereby turnout was 75.9 per cent and Enright received 70.8 per cent of the total vote) illustrates that perhaps the annoyance over Labour's choice of candidate has waned and/or that constituents are pleased with the way that Enright performed as an M.P.

Prior to the by-election taking place, Sarah Baxter of the *New Statesman/New Society* had investigated the controversy. She began, 'Hands up all those Labour M.P.s who owe their seats in parliament to a trade union fix ... No one is going to admit it, but there are plenty of older members at Westminster who would never have been selected as candidates had friendly unions not flooded their constituencies with delegates in good time to sway the vote. In the postwar period, this was normal practice. It was a case of who pays wins, and trade union money kept the local parties afloat'[29]. Baxter goes on to say, 'The longer Labour has been in opposition, the more the party has felt obliged to interfere in the selection process. The political fixes engendered by Walworth Road are no more frequent than those brought about by trade unions with a nod and a wink from above in the good old days. But in our more democratic times, the party is less able to call in favours and more reliant on the rule book. As a result, its involvement looks much more obvious'. Baxter continues, 'Three factors are likely to trigger Walworth Road's attentions: a by-election, the removal of a sitting M.P., or the presence of Trotskyists. There is a fourth factor: union corruption, but the Labour Party is often willing to overlook irregularities so long as nobody complains too loudly'. Attention then turns specifically to the Hemsworth by-election: 'In Hemsworth, in Yorkshire, where a by-election takes place on 7 November, the miner's union thought that, as ever, it could pick - and pay for - its own sponsored candidate. But Ken Capstick, who moved a motion of censure against Neil Kinnock at the N.U.M.'s summer conference, was a provocative choice. The local party could have helped itself to virtually any other mining candidate, but it has instead been landed by the national executive with a teacher, Derek Enright'.

Sarah Baxter then proceeds to explain why Capstick would have been the wrong choice: '"What's wrong with Ken Capstick?", asked the Tory deputy chairman, Sir John Cope, kicking off his party's by-election campaign this week. The answer is simple. Capstick would certainly have won Hemsworth, where he is a popular local figure, but he might well have spoiled Labour's chances of victory in the marginal seat of Langbaurgh in Teesside, which goes to the polls on the same day. This is known in Labour circles as the "Lambeth effect". This supposedly loony London borough somehow manages to get its councillors re-elected, but at the price of a Labour wipe-out in neighbouring Wandsworth'. The explanation given by Baxter is that, 'However aggrieved the N.U.M. feels, the rule change enabling the national executive committee to impose a shortlist of one on a recalcitrant constituency was not drawn up lightly, but was born of defeat'[30].

A New Model Labour Party?

It is worthwhile highlighting the extent to which the media was able to weaken the N.U.M. during the Strike, the conflicts between the N.U.M. and the Labour leadership, Kinnock's refusal to speak out in favour of the pickets and his condemnation of the violence. All of this means that part of the project involved in constructing a New Model Labour Party would inevitably involve Walworth Road wanting to distance itself from the N.U.M. This is, effectively, what happened during the 1991 Hemsworth by-election and hence the relevance of Baxter's Lambeth analogy can be seen: the Strike associated the miners apparently irrevocably with the loony left with whom Kinnock wanted to break ties.

This particular debate - about the strategic importance of distancing Labour from the miners for Kinnock's strategy - is worthy of further expansion given that it is one of the areas of key importance. The relationship between the Labour Party and the N.U.M. has been de-stabilised by the behaviour of the N.U.M. If the N.U.M. had stayed on the right then it is unlikely that Walworth Road would have intervened in the affairs of local Constituency Labour Parties to the extent that it has felt necessary.

As stated, it is no secret that Neil Kinnock had been attempting to produce a new model Labour Party and, that, really, this process had started as far back as October 1983 when Kinnock was first elected to the Party Leadership. A relatively young politician, determined to stamp his mark upon the Party and wanting to ensure that by the time of the next General Election the Party was in a much better position and able to present a more threatening challenge to the incumbent Conservative Government. Relatively recently, there has been much talk of the so-called 'Clintonisation' of the Labour Party but, upon closer inspection, political observers will note that really this process began, to a certain extent, with the election of Neil Kinnock. The process of change gathered momentum after 1987 and the loss of a third general election in a row. A thorough policy review was instigated by Neil Kinnock, a procedure that was to require two years before completion. The late John Smith attempted to continue in the same vein with regards to this attempt to create a new model Labour Party and, although Smith's efforts were short-lived, it appears that Tony Blair seeks to maintain the momentum which Kinnock and Smith established. The landslide Labour victory in the 1997 General Election indicates that Blair has been successful in his efforts.

Returning to the impact of the N.U.M. on this process of modernisation within the Labour Party, it is a fair judgement to say that the 1984/5 Miners' Strike posed serious problems for Kinnock because it presented a flagrant contradiction of what he was trying to do. Kinnock was under a great deal of political pressure with respect to the Miners' Strike. The wave of public sympathy such as existed for the miners, their communities and their families, meant that Neil Kinnock was severely constrained with regards to the extent that he could criticise the actions of miners and their leaders. Indeed, it is fair comment to say that after the Strike it was easier for Kinnock to criticise the actions of Liverpool councillors [as he did at the 1985 Labour Party Conference] than it was for him to verbally attack the miners.

Undoubtedly then, the miners were a problem for Kinnock. It is worth highlighting, however, it is not just mining M.P.'s *per se* who appear to be the problem. Rather, it is the (potential) left-wingers who cause the greater anxiety amongst Party selectors. Indeed, the ex-N.U.M. official, Kim Howells is illustrative of the fact that the Labour Party is able to 'tolerate' the right-wing N.U.M. fraternity. The N.U.M. was heavily involved in the selection of Howells for the constituency of Pontypridd and his candidacy was not seen as a threat to the image of the new model Labour Party. Howells was an N.U.M. official for the South Wales Area between 1982 and 1989 and he has been the Member of Parliament for Pontypridd since February 1989. It is possibly the case that Howells proved more acceptable to the Labour leadership because, by the mid-1980s, the South Wales miners were part of a faction that was very much anti-Scargill. On a relatively minor point, perhaps Howells' academic background means that his strong links with the N.U.M., even bearing in mind his criticisms of some of their tactics and leadership styles in 1984/5, are seen as less of a problem?

With reference to this idea of the new model Labour Party, it is apparent that this is an ongoing debate. Indeed, the issue was raised before the Newbury by-election, held on the 6th May 1993. As stated in *The Guardian*, 'A by-election focuses media attention upon a single constituency and gives John Smith, for the first time since he became leader, the chance to present his new model Labour Party to the country. His message, which should be of a revived, confident, conviction-politics Labour Party, is unlikely to commend itself to a majority of Newbury's voters, but this is relatively unimportant. It is the uncommitted in less blue-rinse areas that Labour needs to reach. So Labour should not go through the motions at Newbury. It should fight positively to show the country that the political agenda in Britain is once again being set by the left'[31]. Likewise, the Rotherham and the Bradford South by-elections, held on the 5th May 1994 and the 9th June 1994 respectively, have witnessed successful attempts by the Labour Party at national level to impose its will over the local constituency party's selection of candidates.

It is necessary to determine the extent to which the decline in terms of the significance of the N.U.M. on the Labour Party is due to longer-term factors or whether it is due to more overtly political factors. On one level, the power and influence of the N.U.M. is declining anyway. It is, therefore, inevitable that the number of N.U.M. sponsored M.P.s will fall correspondingly. Union funds are declining; it is fair to say, therefore, that the financial aspects need highlighting let alone the political aspects.

Baxter highlights the potential problem of 'non-Labour party members in local trade unions' being able to have a 'decisive say' in terms of candidate selection. She goes on to say, 'Unless Labour breaks its links with the trade unions (and financially and emotionally, it is unable to do so), this problem will be difficult to solve ... neither the new methods nor the old have proved adequate to ensure a proper mix of candidates according to race, sex and class. The only answer may be to abandon open-ended selection contests and introduce an approved list'[32].

Baxter's solution may indeed be the only option open to the Labour Party if it wishes to be a pragmatic party and to avoid being in perpetual opposition. The result of the 1997 General Election could be cited as a vindication of this approach. It remains the case, however, that constituencies with a strong history and links with the mining industry will not give up these ties without a vocal and perhaps acrimonious struggle. The depth of the ties are aptly illustrated by Andrew Taylor in his text *The Politics of the Yorkshire Miners*. Parallels can be drawn between the strength of feeling regarding the choice of the candidate for the 1991 Hemsworth by-election and the manner in which that selection was made and the feeling, for example, that an N.U.M. man and a local man should represent mining constituencies. Taylor cites the example of Roy Mason who was selected to fight the Barnsley constituency in 1953. As Taylor says, 'Support for Mason was immediate. A miner from Cudworth argued it was essential that a miner represent Barnsley, and that he be a local man; Mason met both criteria'[33]. So, obviously the N.U.M.'s dissatisfaction over the fact that Capstick was not chosen to fight the by-election has its roots in history. It is fair to say, however, that the Mason case suggests that the issue is not just a matter of left-right politics, since Mason (and the Yorkshire Area at that time) were right-wing.

Conclusion

The politics of Hemsworth then, whilst remaining mundane in comparison with other constituencies, has been sparked by two major events which occurred in the post-Strike scenario. The first being the de-selection of the former Member of Parliament, Alec Woodall and the second being the furore relating to the selection by the national executive committee's choice of candidate, Derek Enright, to fight the 1991 by-election in preference to the N.U.M.'s choice, Ken Capstick. The question remains as to whether or not these two episodes would have occurred if the 1984/5 Miners' Strike had not occurred? Undoubtedly, the first event, the de-selection, can be directly related to the events of 1984/5 given that, rightly or wrongly, accusations were made that Woodall had failed to support the miners enough.

With regards to the second major political event in the constituency of Hemsworth, the by-election controversy, it is slightly more difficult to ascertain whether there exists a direct causal relationship between the occurrance and the Miners' Strike. Did the defeat of the Miners in 1985 mean that the National Executive Committee was empowered to challenge the monopoly of influence which the National Union of Mineworkers had, hitherto, been able to exert over the constituency of Hemsworth and others like it? Or, was it part of a much wider phenomenon relating to Walworth Road's desire to modernise itself and create almost a 'New Model' Labour Party, an enabling device which would move the Party from a position of seemingly never-ending opposition? Evidence suggests that the latter viewpoint is probably the more accurate, that the events which related to Hemsworth were just part of a general trend, but it remains to be said that the N.E.C.'s ability to achieve its goal was undoubtedly facilitated by the defeat of the miners in 1984/5. The 1984/5 Miners' Strike and the subsequent defeat of the N.U.M. meant that the Labour Party was able to weaken its links with the N.U.M. In terms of the power relationship, the 'ball' was clearly located in the Labour Party's 'court' - with the Party being able to dictate terms to the N.U.M., especially, as has been noted, with regards to candidate selection. The impact of the Strike upon the Labour Party should not be under-estimated.

Notes:

[1] Taylor, A. (1984) *The Politics of the Yorkshire Miners*, (London: Croom Helm), p. xi.

[2] Ibid., p. 1.

[3] Ibid., p. 103.

[4] Ibid., p. 106.

[5] Ibid., p. 107.

[6] Ibid., p. 4.

[7] Ibid., p. 5.

[8] Ibid., p. 6.

[9] Ibid., p. 7.

[10] Ibid., p. 121.

[11] Waller, R. (1991) *The Almanac of British Politics*, (London: Routledge), p. 229.

[12] Ibid., p. 230.

[13] See Appendix Two for further details.

[14] Butler, D. and Pinto-Duschinsky, M., (1971) *The British General Election of 1970*, (London: Macmillan), p. 381.

[15] Butler, D. and Kavanagh, D. (1975) *The British General Election of October 1974*, (London: Macmillan), p. 327.

[16] Ibid., p. 332.

[17] Crewe, I. (1984) *British Parliamentary Constituencies - a statistical compendium*, (London: Faber and Faber).

[18] Ibid., p. 182.

[19] Butler, D. and Kavanagh, D. (1988) *The British General Election of 1987*, (London: Macmillan), p. 345.

[20] Ibid., p. 345.

[21] See Appendix Two for further details.

[22] Winterton, J. and Winterton, R. (1989) *Coal, Crisis and Conflict*, (Manchester: Manchester University Press), p. 113.

[23] *The Hemsworth and South Elmsall Express*, 7th November 1991, p. 1.

[24] *The Hemsworth and South Elmsall Express*, 24th October 1991, p. 1.

[25] Benyon, J., 'Two More Conservative By-election Defeats', *Politics Review*, (Volume 1, number 3, February 1992), reverse side of front cover.

[26] *Is Democracy Working?*, Seven part television series produced by Tyne Tees Television, first transmitted August 1986. Produced by David Jones.

[27] Benyon, *Op. Cit.*, reverse side of front cover.

[28] *The Hemsworth and South Elmsall Express*, 14th November 1991, p. 1.

[29] Baxter, S., *New Statesman/New Society*, (25th October 1991), p. 23.

[30] Ibid.

[31] *The Guardian*, Letters Page, 8th March, 1993.

[32] Baxter, *Op. Cit.*, p. 23.

[33] Taylor, *Op. Cit.*, p. 136.

8 Conclusion

What has this research unearthed? In what ways does it add to the sum of knowledge? Does it have a practical application? These are all questions which this chapter will attempt to answer. It is worthwhile stating that the mining industry remains an important issue given the recent coal dispute and also because of the sale of the Yorkshire coalfields. Michael Heseltine's announcement that 31 collieries would be closed has ensured that the results of this research have added interest and pertinence. Heseltine, as President of the Board of Trade, instigated a furore with the statement issued in October 1992 and placed the mining industry, once again, firmly on the policy-making agenda.

The 1992/3 Coal Dispute

The recent coal dispute is mentioned briefly in Chapter One but it is worthwhile giving slightly more detail at this particular stage. The coal closures were actually announced on the 13th October 1992. It was stated that 31 out of the total 50 pits would close by March 1993. The closures were criticised by Labour, the unions, some senior Conservative M.P.s (such as Elizabeth Peacock the M.P. for Batley and Spen, dismissed in October 1992 as parliamentary private secretary to Nicholas Scott the Social Security Minister) and ex-ministers and church leaders (amongst them the Rt. Rev. Nigel McCulloch, Bishop of Wakefield) and community leaders. Scargill dubbed the closures 'the most savage, brutal act of vandalism in modern times'[1]. In defence of his plans for coal Heseltine said, 'B.C. cannot go on producing coal which cannot be sold. These decisions have been taken only after the most careful consideration. They are painful, but they are essential to secure the industry's future and cannot be postponed'[2].

The October announcement prompted a great many miners and their supporters to march on Parliament in the autumn of 1992. As James states, 'The rationale for the decision was a familiar one, and driven by powerful logic: the market for coal was simply too small for the volume of fuel being produced by the mines. Even so, the violence and breadth of the public reaction to the announcement evidently surprised the government'[3]. The effect of the closures upon the mining communities is worthy of emphasis. As Huw Richards says in the *Times Higher Educational Supplement*[4], 'The impact of the closures is accentuated by the nature of mining communities - often isolated and with the pit as their sole reason for existence'. The loss of mining communities is very significant. Ruth Winterton reiterates this impact, 'The mining community, like the miner as a traditional proletarian, is rapidly becoming an historical phenomenon'[5].

In terms of what has happened to the mining industry over recent decades, it is relevant simply to look at the scale of the decline in sheer numerical terms. After the Second World War there were 750,000 people employed at almost 1,000 pits. At the beginning of the 1984/5 Strike there were 184,000 miners, by the end of the year-long Strike this had declined to 171,000 miners in 169 pits. By October 1992, when the closures were announced, there were 41,000 miners employed at 50 pits. To repeat the figure that is mentioned in Chapter Three, in September 1994 there were only 8,000 miners left in the coal industry[6] and in October 1995 there were no miners employed by British Coal given that the industry has been privatised. The main successor companies to British Coal are listed in Appendix Five.

It is fair to say that Heseltine miscalculated the impact of his announcement. The furore caused by Heseltine's disclosure prompted an investigation into the mining industry. This was carried out by the American consultancy firm John T. Boyd - based in Philadelphia and resulted in a White Paper being published at the end of March 1993. The White Paper, carried by 319 to 297 - a Government majority of 22, stated that 12 pits would survive, 12 would close, six would be mothballed and one, Maltby, would be used for research and development purposes. With regards to the area covered by this research, of the local pits affected, nearby Frickley would be one of the 12 survivors but Grimethorpe Colliery would close even though Derek Enright, the M.P. for Hemsworth, said that it makes a profit and has a market for its coal. It was said that even the 12 pits which would be reprieved would only have a two-year stay of execution. The White Paper estimated the potential job losses at between 13,000 and 18,000.

The White Paper was dubbed a 'politically expedient package' whose aim is to save 'the Conservative Party from humiliation at the hands of its own M.P.s'[7]. Furthermore, it was criticised by a number of commentators for failing to offer a long-term solution to the energy problem. Simon Beavis, in February 1993, had already highlighted the fact that Heseltine has 'rejected action to halt gas projects, delay introduction of competition in the electricity market, and close nuclear power stations early'[8]. The White Paper appears to affirm this viewpoint. According to Michael Smith, industrial editor at the *Observer*, 'the Government is neither prepared to protect the market for coal nor devise a coherent long-term energy policy based on the balanced use of Britain's oil, coal, gas, nuclear and other, alternative resources'[9]. The move towards gas will still continue and the pits will be privatised at the earliest opportunity. As Stephen Bates and Simon Beavis state[10], Heseltine 'repeatedly declined to give guarantees about the pits' long-term future'. This lack of foresight is reiterated by John Meads, General Secretary of the British Association of Colliery Management. He believes that a long-term energy strategy is needed which looks at the problem of cheap French electricity coming through the cross-channel interconnector and also the so-called 'dash for gas' where gas-fired power stations are pushing out 'perfectly good coal-fired stations which have lower costs'[11].

Besides the immediate costs of closing the collieries, the wider social costs of running down the coal industry need to be highlighted. The absence of tax revenues from displaced workers is significant as it is estimated that each unemployed person costs the D.S.S. £9,000 per year in social security payments. One scenario forecasts the loss of 18,000 jobs directly and up to 50,000 jobs indirectly - a cost of more than £600 million to the taxpayer each year[12]. As B. Robinson says[13], 'is the real cost of coal not the production cost but the difference between that and the cost of paying redundancy and unemployment pay, with nothing produced but poverty, poor health and misery for the miners and their families, together with a further decline in the economy?'

Again, one interesting phenomenon of the most recent (and continuing) coal dispute is the role undertaken by the women of mining communities. It is debatable whether such activities as the underground sit-ins staged by the women and the women's pit camps would have occurred had it not been for the events which took place in 1984/5. An example of such a sit-in is the one staged over Easter 1993 at Parkside Colliery by four women. The sit-in took place 500 metres (1,600 feet) down the mine and included Anne Scargill, the wife of the N.U.M. President. Like many women, she 'came to politics fairly late, joined the Labour Party after he became N.U.M. President in 1984, and taking no part in the 1972 and 1974 strikes'. It is said that 'She changed in the same way as many other miners' wives who made the tea and sandwiches in 1972 and 1974, went on the picket lines in 1984 and are now more interested in direct action'[14]. Alongside other women, in December 1992, Anne Scargill occupied the offices of Markham Main, in February 1993 she chained herself to the railings outside the Department of Trade and Industry and, as stated, took part in the sit-in at Parkside over the Easter period, 1993. She has also taken part in a number of 'Greenham Common-style', pit-camps.

A Wider Application?

Given the continuing saga of the coal dispute, it is fair comment that the coal industry retains its topicality. In terms of the relevance and practical applicability of research such as this, it is fair to say that, if reasons for and factors behind politicisation can be identified then perhaps various political organisations and parties will be able to draw lessons from the information and personal accounts given here. Given that even major political parties, such as the Labour Party, are suffering a loss of membership and that recent recruitment drives have failed to procure an increase in numbers then perhaps they may be able to take heed of this research. Having said this, however, it is relevant to question whether political parties do actually want a politicised electorate? As has already been stated in previous chapters, a politically illiterate and extensively apathetic populace may serve the interests of politicians. This is to say, it might be much easier for politicos to 'get on with the job' unhindered by questioning and demanding voters.

An attempt is made throughout the course of this book to define the potentially woolly concept of politicisation. It is a concept which people define differently and which may change over time. For the purposes of this study a tri-partite definition is employed. As stated in Chapter Two, this includes political awareness, political participation and behavioural changes. This complicated and detailed definition is utilised precisely because of the necessity of pinpointing whether the changes which did occur in certain members of mining communities deserve to be regarded as monumentous and extraordinary ones and, as such, worthy of note. Having said this, however, a case can also be made for saying that any change, no matter how small, ought to be regarded as note-worthy if it is traced to the events of 1984/5.

The wider scenario is dealt with later on in this Chapter but it is worthwhile looking at the wider applicability of this study in slightly greater depth at this particular juncture. It is necessary to analyse whether or not there are actually any wider lessons which can be learnt from this book. Are there lessons which can be learnt from the study of this one particular mining community which are applicable to other areas of investigation? Or, is it the case that this particular study is unique and does not necessarily have, nor need to have, a wider application? In addition, could a claim be made that this study is now redundant given the closure of the majority of the coal-mines and the way in which coal mining has ceased to be a major industry in the United Kingdom? Clearly, these are all issues which need to be addressed in any analysis of the overall impact and importance of this study.

Firstly, it is appropriate to examine the wider lessons emanating from this particular research. The basic aim of the book is to investigate whether the 1984/5 Miners' Strike was a major politicising event. Utilising the tripartite definition of politicisation (political participation, political awareness and behavioural changes) it is apparent that the events of 1984/5 did indeed prove to have an impact upon levels of politicisation. The specific findings are examined in detail in preceding chapters and in the earlier part of this concluding chapter and, it is clearly shown that, this major industrial dispute definitely had an impact upon the politicisation process. It appears, therefore, that the main lessons to be learnt are as follows; it can be proven that a major industrial dispute does have an impact upon politicisation, the research has illustrated that industrial disputes, more specifically, strike activity does have an impact upon levels of politicisation, strike activity can galvanise normally apathetic people into political activity, the strike situation can enhance levels of political awareness and can lead to individuals altering their behaviour. Given that it has been determined that these changes can occur as a result of strike activity, it is likely that an investigation could be made into all strikes in an attempt to ascertain the exact nature of any changes which take place. There may be lessons to be learnt by psephologists and others who analyse political behaviour. If a political event can be isolated and shown to have an impact upon political behaviour maybe there are lessons which can be learnt by those who seek a more informed electorate and participatory society? Questions such as how can we get more people to participate in the democratic process, how can we raise levels of political awareness and even how can we challenge patterns of individual behaviour such as the predominance of the sexual division of labour, may all benefit through the analysis given to the politicisation process in this book.

It is pertinent to respond to the claim that the research is unique and, in the light of recent events, possibly also redundant. It is fair to say that this particular study, because of its precise and narrow focus, is unique. Concentrating, as it does, upon one specific (former) mining community this inevitably leads to discussion of whether or not it does in fact have a wider application. The first major point to note at this particular juncture is whether or not it does in fact need to have wider applicability? Quite clearly it is not a requirement of investigative research that it needs to offer a blue-print or a yardstick for use in other investigations. As stated above, the research may prove useful and to be of interest to other political scientists but it does not necessarily have to feed into other related works.

As to the question of whether or not the whole issue of mining communities and the investigation of those communities is now redundant, it would be premature to dismiss the study of these communities as irrelevant and redundant. The inhabitants of former mining communities may not now be employed in the coal industry, indeed they may not be employed at all, this does not mean to say, however, that their experiences ought to be neglected. They have little voice in the political scenario as it is. Surely, a failure to investigate their lives and their experiences would sideline and silence them even further. In addition, whilst the coal industry appears to have been decimated during the Thatcher and Major governments, who knows what the future scenario will look like now that there is a change of governing party? Finally, the current state of affairs in industrialised West Yorkshire is very different from, for example, the 1950s when the 'Coal Is Our Life' study by Dennis *et al.* was produced but that does not, necessarily, mean that their work is redundant.

Further discussion of the wider implications of the study leads to an analysis of whether or not the way in which industrial disputes and other forms of mass protest were policed in the 1980s and 1990s has implications for the politicisation process. Firstly, was the policing of the 1984/5 Miners'

Strike used as a model for the policing of other disputes? Secondly, can it be claimed that this policing also had an impact upon levels of politicisation?

One of the main findings unearthed by this research is the impact which the policing of the 1984/5 Miners' Strike had upon the interviewees and, if wider implications are to be considered, it appears reasonable to assume that the policing of similar disputes would have similar effects upon the participants. It is outside of the scope of this particular research to move on to an analysis of other disputes as having politicising effects but, it is necessary, at this particular point, to draw attention to the fact that there is an area here worthy of further investigation. It is apparent that similar police tactics were used in the policing of disputes such as the anti-poll tax demonstrations in 1990 and against those protesting over the exportation of veal cattle to Europe in 1995. These are not industrial disputes but, in these examples, the police employed the same hands-on approach as they had during the Miners' Strike; that is in terms of the sheer scale of the numbers utilised and the way in which the police appeared prepared, willing and fully ready to take on these political protesters. It appears that the policing of the 1984/5 Miners' Strike did leave a legacy relating to the way in which disputes were to be policed. There are, therefore, wider implications to be drawn from this study of one particular dispute and its impact upon one particular community. As stated earlier, explaining and accounting for heightened levels of politicisation in response to other disputes and mass protests is outwith the remit of this research but, given the parallels between the policing of these other disputes and the way in which the 1984/5 Miners' Strike was policed, it can reasonably be assumed that other similarities, notably in terms of politicisation, could reasonably be anticipated.

Further exploration of the wider issues arising from the book leads to consideration of whether it matters that a strike takes place in the public or the private sector with respect to raising levels of politicisation. In the case of the 1984/5 Miners' Strike the Government was clearly the strikers' opponent but what if the employer had been, for example, a private chemical company? Would the outcome, in terms of politicisation, have been very different? Without undertaking a detailed analysis of the politicising effects of other industrial disputes (again, an area of investigation deemed to be outwith the scope of this book - although texts such as Beynon's *Working for Ford* and Lane and Roberts' *Strike at Pilkingtons* do shed some light upon this topic), it is reasonable to assume that a strike in private industry would be unlikely to lead to the same levels of politicisation as the Miners'

Strike. It is obviously difficult to make the connection with other industries but it is reasonable to assume that levels of politicisation would not be as high as those which occurred during the Miners' Strike precisely because the coal dispute was not simply about working conditions or rates of pay. It concerned an issue that struck at the very heart of mining communities; it actually related to the very survival of those jobs and communities themselves. In addition, it could be argued that the Strike was, to a certain extent, a last ditch stance, not just of an industry but almost of a tradition in trade unionism. The 1984/5 Miners' Strike built upon the legacy of previous miners' strikes and the long history of the miners' Union. Presumably, most private sector disputes would not have such a tradition or legacy and this may affect levels of politicisation. A related area of concern is whether it is necessary to distinguish between a traditional heavy industry, as in the case of mining, and the newer high tech industries? The evidence unearthed via this study suggests that it is likely that there is a difference here in terms of the politicisation process. A degree of caution is necessary at this particular juncture, however, given the emphasis which has been placed upon the politicising impact of the policing of the Strike. This is obviously a variable which needs to be considered with respect to private sector strikes too. A detailed analysis of the policing of private sector disputes is outside the remit of this research but, nevertheless, it will be examined briefly later on in this Chapter particularly with respect to the Timex dispute. It is worth raising as a factor affecting the politicising process.

This is not to say that a dispute in private industry does not have the potential to be politicising but there are a number of key differences between this and the Miners' Strike. Firstly, would the private dispute affect a whole community or is the work-force geographically dispersed? Secondly, how much media coverage is given to the dispute? Is this coverage supportive or critical of the strike? Thirdly, does the employer have a predominantly male workforce and, if so, are the employees' spouses and partners fully supportive of the strike? Fourthly, is there a perception of it being a 'Them and Us' confrontational situation? Is the strike perceived in terms of it being a direct confrontation between the employer and employee? Fifthly, does the actual duration of the dispute have a part to play? Has it been ongoing for a significant period of time? Sixthly, is there any perception whatsoever that the employers are being advised/manipulated by the government, even though it is a private industry? What is the extent of any government intervention? Finally, what about the sheer scale of numbers involved in the

Miners' Strike? Surely, the numerical aspect was significant in 1984/5 (even bearing in mind the breakaway Union of Democratic Mineworkers and those who returned to work before the end of the Strike) and private industry would not be able to match the numbers involved in the 1984/5 Miners' Strike?

The main point to note is not that a strike in the private sector cannot be politicising but that there are significant key differences between the 1984/5 Miners' Strike and other industrial disputes. In addition, bearing in mind the tripartite definition of politicisation adopted by this research, any analysis of disputes in the private sector would then need to proceed to investigate the extent to which it made people participate in politics, the extent to which it raised political awareness and the extent to which the dispute led to individuals altering their behaviour. Clearly, there is potential here for further research to be undertaken by scholars who are keen to analyse the parallels between the politicising effects of the 1984/5 Miners' Strike and strikes which occur in the private sector.

The Results

After examining the wider applicability of this research, it is necessary to look in more detail at the overall findings. On a basic level, it can be seen that politicisation does appear to have taken place and this can be directly attributed to the events surrounding the 1984/5 Miners' Strike. As stated, the roles undertaken by the police and the media do seem to have been instrumental in heightening political awareness and leading many of the interviewees to question previously held ideas and opinions. A key factor affecting attitudinal change appears to be whether the interviewees were themselves involved or whether close friends and relations had direct involvement - especially so in the cases of the police and the media.

Given that since the end of the 1984/5 Miners' Strike, Hemsworth has become a virtual ghost town, it is worth emphasising the effect which the loss of a colliery can have upon a community. According to Warwick and Littlejohn, 'Closure of a local pit, which makes up much if not all of the local labour market, almost certainly deprives a mining town or village of its chief source of income. It will also have several knock-on effects in the whole local economy, in the infrastructural provision of goods and services to the mining enterprise and in the distributive and service trades linked to the mining locality'[15]. The effects of closure then can be seen to permeate the whole society. Warwick and Littlejohn continue to assess the peculiar nature of mining communities, 'The class character of such localities, the local social institutions and their separateness from other not dissimilar places, tend to lead to frequently repeated claims of a dual experience, hardness, ugliness and danger on one side, and friendliness, closeness and solidarity on the other'[16]. Mining communities appear, therefore, to possess a number of unique qualities. It is necessary, however, to examine the findings of this book in more detail to discover the extent to which these unique qualities have contributed to the politicising effect.

Comments from the interviewees, given in Chapter One, illustrate the extent to which a number of those questioned do appear to have become much more politicised. The community of Hemsworth is outlined in detail in Chapters One and Three. Chapter One mainly sets out the scope of this research and brings into the discussion the concept of politicisation. It also analyses the methodology and how the primary data was obtained. The level of interest in the coal industry is also referred to in Chapter One although it is fair to say that, given the recent coal dispute, interest does appear to have increased. Plans to privatise the coal industry are also mentioned.

It is necessary to analyse whether Hemsworth can be regarded as a valid case study in terms of 'lessons' which other areas can learn. Chapter One highlights how the book will attempt to define politicisation and how specific examples will be given. It emphasises that defining politicisation is vitally important as it really forms the crux of the thesis. In terms of politicisation; psychological factors such as beliefs and attitudes are regarded as of equal importance to the more tangible factors such as participation in various political organisations. Thus, politicisation is highlighted and then an attempt is made to analyse the extent to which this is as a direct result of the 1984/5 Miners' Strike and also, of course, the extent to which this occurred specifically in Hemsworth. This thesis also deals heavily with the *processes* of change - looking at how and why such changes took place in the inhabitants of Hemsworth. It is for this reason that a number of specific events, such as Orgreave and, as stated before, the roles played by the police and the media, are examined.

Chapter Three analyses the community of Hemsworth in terms of how it has changed since the Strike. It traces the history and origins of the community of Hemsworth and how it has grown since the pits were sunk. The politics of Hemsworth are also referred to. The Miners' Strike is examined as is its impact specifically upon the community of Hemsworth.

The Strike does appear to have motivated people who had never before had an interest in politics into political action. One tangible factor, which is highlighted in Chapter Three, is the increased turnout in mining constituencies at the 1987 General Election. Noteworthy events in Hemsworth were the setting up of the Miners' Wives Support Group and the 'riot' in the centre of Hemsworth. There was also the setting up of a local branch of the Green Party. The Greens are mentioned in Chapter Seven but it is necessary to go into slightly more detail at this stage in order to give the complete picture and enable a full summary to be given regarding the events in Hemsworth. The local branch was set up in Hemsworth in 1989 following the Greens' national success in the European Elections of June 1989. Here they obtained 15 per cent of the total vote but, due to the electoral system, they did not obtain any seats. The Green Party did not, however, stand a candidate in either the 1991 Hemsworth by-election nor the 1992 General Election. Perhaps their apparent decline has more to do with a national (or even international) trend rather than a phenomenon which is specific to Hemsworth. It is worth stating that there is little evidence linking the rise of the Greens in Hemsworth specifically to local issues. There is a school of thought[17] which espouses the viewpoint that environmental politics are a luxury which can only be afforded in times of relative affluence and prosperity so in view of the economic recession perhaps it is hardly surprising that their electoral fortunes appear to have dwindled. Another school of thought looks to Anthony Downs' 'Issue-attention' cycle[18] for explanation. The viewpoint held here is that environmental concerns have had their heyday as far as the policy-making agenda is concerned but now they have, quite naturally, given way to other issues. A further reason could be that the mainstream political parties, given that they aim to be 'catch-all' parties have, to a certain extent, stolen the Green Party's 'clothes' and have, thereby, crowded out the Green Party from the political scenario. Finally, it is fair comment to say that David Icke's claims that he was the Son of God did not really help the Green Party's quest to be regarded as a serious political alternative to the mainstream parties.

With specific respect to the community of Hemsworth, an attempt was made to ascertain whether changes occurred in the socio-economic profile of the community either during or as a direct result of the Strike in terms of divorce rates, increase in benefit claimants and also in terms of the numbers of repossessions of homes by building societies. With regard to the first criterion, divorce rates, the Lord Chancellor's Department does not keep any specific data which refers to the Hemsworth area but it did provide statistical data relating to the number of petitions filed for divorce, nullity, and judicial separation, decrees nisi and decrees absolute, and judicial separation decrees granted in Pontefract County Court, which covers Hemsworth. Unfortunately, the only information available was for the years 1987 until May 1994 (See Appendix Six). These statistics did, however, indicate that the highest number of petitions filed and decrees nisi and decrees absolute granted was in 1987. It might be the case that these higher figures in the immediate aftermath of the 1984/5 Miners' Strike indicate that there is a causal link and that the stresses and strains imposed upon many relationships due to the impact of the Strike is the reason behind the breakdown of so many marriages.

With respect to the second criterion, increase in benefit claimants, the Benefits Agency in Hemsworth stated that 'concerning the 1984/5 Miners' Strike. I can confirm that the number of claims to benefit increased during this period but unfortunately, all statistics relating to this period are long since destroyed'. Further investigations led to a discussion with an employee who was in charge of dealing with claims from strikers and their families during the Strike. He stated that during the Strike approximately 2,000 payments a week were being made by Giro. The main qualifiers were men whose wives did not work. Single miners did not receive anything and married men whose wives worked were lucky if they obtained any financial support from the state. The employee also stated that many women became eligible to claim income support because they left their husband. The claims from separated women did increase and although his office was conscious of the fact that there is always an element of what he termed 'fictitious separation', the stresses of the Strike did mean that many of these separations eventually led to divorce. In addition, the benefits office was also aware that many miners were, understandably, experiencing difficulties with their mortgages and whilst lenders were relatively lenient during the Strike, the pressure was applied in many cases as soon as they returned to work. The man from the Benefits Agency also highlighted the fact that 44 additional staff were brought in to Hemsworth at the start of the Strike to deal with the increased numbers of claimants. This figure dropped to between 20-25 additional employees after a couple of months once the initial claims had been dealt with but these 20-25 remained for the duration of the Strike. He said that the bulk of these extra staff came from the Hull area and, interestingly enough, some of these actually lodged with striking miners families.

It was more difficult to obtain information relating to the number of homes which were repossessed in the Hemsworth area in the period following the 1984/5 Miners' Strike. The Halifax Building Society was approached (given that it is Britain's largest building society), they were unable to provide the required statistics but suggested the Council of Mortgage Lenders might be of help. In the event, the Council of Mortgage Lenders were only able to provide figures relating to the national scenario but they did reveal a sharp increase in the number of repossessions from 1988 to 1991. Given that a detailed break-down was not obtained regarding the number of repossessions in mining communitiies, it would be difficult to put forward confident assertions with respect to the number of repossessions in mining communities. The financial hardship endured by many families during the Miners' Strike leads to speculation that there must have been an increase in repossessions but the building societies were not able to furnish statistical data which would buttress this claim.

Returning to the overview of the book as a whole; the chapter on politicisation, Chapter Two, is perhaps the most important chapter as it is here that it adds to the theoretical debate. The definition which this research employs is a tri-partite definition incorporating political awareness, behavioural changes and political participation. This three-way definition was felt to offer the most comprehensive framework for analysis. As far as possible, a water-tight definition was desired. Having said this, however, (as Chapter Two illustrates) there are degrees of politicisation.

With respect to the findings of this book the overall level of politicisation was high. A majority of the interviewees acknowledged that the extent of their politicisation had increased. Analysis of the model of politicisation employed by this research is given at the end of this section on the actual results. It is fair to say, however, that levels of political participation, political awareness and behavioural change were affected to differing degrees. It is appropriate to focus at this stage, therefore, upon the overall findings.

Key aspects of politicisation which this research unearthed was the impact upon the women of this particular community. For many of the women of Hemsworth, the Strike had a profound influence upon their political actions and also upon their thoughts, i.e. they do appear to have undergone increased political awareness. Many of those interviewed also came to have a much more critical approach to both the media and to the police. In terms of the media, many came to be distrustful of all forms of political information becoming cynical and disbelieving. One very politicising factor was the way in which many of those in the mining community perceived the Strike as an overtly political dispute - as opposed to an economic dispute which was the Government's viewpoint, perhaps not the Government's entire impression of the dispute but certainly a substantial part of it. There was a kind of duality in the Government's treatment of the Strike - both treating it as an economic dispute which Scargill was illegitimately politicising *and* playing it politically (not just in terms of the tactics used but, for example, Thatcher's denunciation of the miners as 'the Enemy Within').

With regards specifically to politicisation and Hemsworth only 17 per cent of those interviewed claimed that their level of politicisation had remained static and none claimed that it had actually decreased (although only perhaps political participation could actually decrease). Everyone else claimed that their level of politicisation had increased. A significant proportion of those interviewed joined a political party, in all but one case this was the Labour Party. The one exception was actually instrumental in setting up a local branch of the Green Party. The other main area of participation was in terms of those people who joined the support groups (especially the women), two of the interviewees became school governors and three took part in trade union activities to a much greater extent than they had previously done. One woman admitted to having taken part in hunt saboteur activities. Thus it can clearly be seen that levels of political participation, the first criterion employed in our tripartite definition of politicisation, have increased. Levels of political participation were affected by the role of the police and by the role undertaken by the media. More people were affected by the police than by the media but some did state that it was a cumulative effect. The participation levels of the women is the most striking aspect and here participation took many different forms; going on the picket lines, collecting for strike funds, speaking at rallies and working for the Support Group are a few examples that the women cited.

Political awareness was most notable in terms of changed attitudes in three main areas - towards the media, the police and towards the role of women within society. Many of those who were interviewed, as stated in Chapter Six, claim to have become much more questioning as a direct result of the Strike, they were now less willing to accept information and events at face value. This also meant that many of them developed a much greater interest in political affairs than they had held previously. An interesting point to note is the way that many of the interviewees had to reassess their own attitudes and opinions towards other oppressed groups, such as homosexuals, ethnic minorities and people living in Northern Ireland. Another factor which may indicate heightened political awareness was the by-election which took place in Hemsworth in November 1991. It appears to have affected politicisation because of the controversy which surrounded it. The row over the Labour Party's decision to impose Derek Enright onto the Constituency Labour Party and the subsequent 42 per cent turn-out supports the view that the by-election was part of the political aftermath of the Strike.

So, the second criterion, namely that of political awareness, evidenced the most striking amount of change. It was particularly apparent when the interviewees stated that they had been directly involved in strike activities themselves rather than if they had witnessed events on the television. This was especially the case when they noted discrepancies between their own version of events and that portrayed by the media. Again, the gender dimension needs to be highlighted with respect to this factor in the model of politicisation. Tied in with claiming heightened political awareness, it is worthwhile re-emphasising the increased levels of confidence which many of the female interviewees claimed stemmed from this increased awareness. In addition, they were able to make a direct link between the actions of politicians and those in positions of power and the impact which that had upon their everyday lives. They made a connection between the public sphere, the world of work and the private sphere, the world of the home.

With respect to the third criterion, namely behavioural changes, again these were most evident with regards to the women of the mining community of Hemsworth. The significant factor here was that the traditional dichotomy between the public and private domains[19] and the associated sexual division of labour were called into question. Specific behavioural changes affecting the women, cited earlier in this book, include two divorces, two women who went on to study in further and higher education (one with the Open University) and a few who changed their newspaper partisanship. Other behavioural changes affecting both the male and female interviewees included crossing the street to avoid a police officer, advising their offspring not to ask a police officer for directions when lost, watching Channel Four News as opposed to other coverage of events and sharing in the household chores (the male interviewees). It takes a lot of effort to actually change one's behaviour and, even though the numbers actually doing this were relatively small, this aspect of change is still worthy of emphasis precisely because of the effort involved. As to why behavioural change was so marked amongst the women, the point to note is that, allied with their menfolk, their existence was threatened too. They had to fight for their communities and they found that they had, hitherto hidden, qualitities.

The three criteria which make up the model of politicisation have been examined in detail. It is worthwhile, however, looking in a little more depth at some of the specific findings of this research which were raised in earlier chapters. As stated throughout the thesis, police tactics utilised and put into action for the first time in 1984/5 had an impact upon politicisation. As stated in Chapter Four, the use of the National Reporting Centre, the Police Support Units and the targeting of pickets who were travelling towards Nottinghamshire were measures which affected the political perceptions of many in the mining community of Hemsworth. The style of policing appears to have led to a heightened political awareness. A majority of the interviewees in Hemsworth were deeply affected by the type of and scale of policing employed during the 1984/5 Miners' Strike. One interviewee did express surprise at what he called the sheer 'political will' that had led to police being deployed in such huge numbers. This is an interviewee who picketed at Orgreave and witnessed first-hand the huge numbers who were involved.

Sixty per cent of the interviewees stated that their attitudes towards the police had changed. The remaining 40 per cent had not changed their attitude but one interviewee did claim that, in his opinion, he knew 'what the police were like before' due to his involvement in race relations. An important feature with regards to attitudes towards the policing was that the interviewees tended not to blame the local police. It is worth reiterating, however, that Andrew Taylor of the University of Huddersfield believes this failure to apportion blame to the local constabulary is based upon a fallacy. The Chief Constable of West Yorkshire Police, Keith Hellawell, however, states in Chapter Four that 'we didn't have Metropolitan police officers within this County'.

The women who worked for the Support Group were greatly affected in terms of their attitudes towards the police. Eighty per cent of this sector of the interviewees claim that their attitude towards the police deteriorated as a direct result of the Strike, with only 20 per cent claiming that they had not changed their attitudes. Those who experienced the greatest changes were those who participated directly - be that in the Support Groups or on the picket lines. In some cases this led to increased political participation such as joining the Labour Party or becoming a school governor.

The event or 'riot' which took place in the centre of Hemsworth in July 1984 affected a number of the interviewees. The perceived heavy-handed police tactics led many of the witnesses to reassess their opinions with regards to the police-force and this was as a direct result of this one incident or 'flash-point'. All of those who were actually present were deeply affected and, indeed, the event affected many of those who were not actually present but who had listened to the accounts of friends and relatives. To reiterate, many of the interviewees, due to the police tactics, felt able to empathise with other oppressed groups.

An additional factor to emerge from an examination of the policing of the Strike is that most of the interviewees felt that the police tactics represented a marked departure from that which had gone before and were *not* part of a wider general trend. It needs to be emphasised though that subsequent police tactics - in disputes such as the Wapping dispute - appear to have built upon those deployed in 1984/5.

Of the interviewees who claim that their attitudes towards the police did *not* deteriorate, many believe that the police were just political pawns who were exploited by the Government. Examination of the interviewees who *were* affected by the policing reveals that 89 per cent of these claim to be interested in politics. The remaining 11 per cent expressed no real interest. It could be the case, therefore, that an interest in politics led to an increased awareness of police operations. With regards to those who claim that their attitudes towards the police worsened *and* that they have an interest in politics 33 per cent claim that they became interested in politics *during* the Strike. Of the remainder, 61 per cent say that they were already interested in politics and one person, 6 per cent, claims to have become interested in politics after the Strike. In terms of those who said that their attitudes towards the police did not change, 75 per cent said that they were interested in politics. The remaining 25 per cent expressed no interest. Overall then, those interviewees who criticised the police tactics during the Strike were slightly more likely to express an interest in politics.

From the findings with regards to the mass media, all but five of the interviewees read a newspaper every day. The surprising fact was that none claimed to read the *Sun* newspaper. Given that this is a mass circulation newspaper, it could be that the interviewees were unrepresentative or it could be the opposite, i.e. that they *are* representative but representative of a community which has turned against the *Sun* newspaper due to the politicising effects of the Miners' Strike. An attempt was made via both local retail outlets and a regional distribution centre to ascertain the number of *Sun* newspapers which are delivered on a regular basis to Hemsworth. Only one line of investigation in this area, however, produced a positive response and revealed that there does appear to be a discrepancy between the local circulation figures and the number of interviewees who admitted to reading the *Sun* newspaper. It could be the case that the newsagent business is an extremely competitive area and they do not wish to furnish potential rivals with any advantageous data whatsoever. Another important finding is that many of those questioned noticed a distinct difference between the local and national television coverage of the Strike. Local coverage was felt to be much more impartial and, therefore, trustworthy. A majority of those questioned felt that coverage was biased against the striking miners but the interviewees did not really analyse *why* the media behaved as it did.

In relation to politicisation, the other major finding is the effect of the 1984/5 Miners' Strike upon the women. Of the male interviewees, 30 per cent claim to have become politicised as a direct result of the Strike, 19 per cent claim not to be politicised, 49 per cent say they were politicised before the Strike and one person, 2 per cent, claims to have become politicised after the Strike. With regards to the female respondents, the contrast is as follows; 65 per cent claim to have been politicised as a direct result of the Strike, 13 per cent claim to be non-politicised and 22 per cent say that they were already politicised before the outset of the 1984/5 Miners' Strike. Statistically speaking, therefore, the Strike appears to have had a remarkable effect upon the women.

For many of the women, they were able to see how politics did have an effect upon *their* everyday lives. A connection which they had, hitherto, been unable to make. The most lasting effect in terms of the women appears to be in the area of political awareness. They may have undergone increased political participation and behavioural changes but increased political awareness was, for many of the women, the most lasting feature which the Strike gave to them. Andrew Taylor of Huddersfield cites the changes in the women, the realisation that the personal can be political and the consciousness-raising aspects as very important legacies of the Strike.

To return to the other (potentially) politicising event - the imposition of Derek Enright by the Labour Party's National Executive Committee to fight the Hemsworth by-election in November 1991, of those electors questioned in an EXIT poll, 42 per cent disagreed with the choice of Derek Enright, 44 per cent agreed and 14 per cent neither agreed nor disagreed. The by-election turnout of 42 per cent, low even by by-election standards, illustrates that a significant proportion of the electorate appears to have 'voted with its feet'. Turn-out returned to its usual levels for the 1992 General Election so perhaps electors had forgotton their previous annoyance or possibly they were pleased with Derek Enright's record as a vocal and hard-working Member of Parliament. There is also the most obvious point to be made here that the most likely explanation is that the higher voting levels during the General Election were due to the belief that this was a national event in which their votes could help to change the Government.

It is worthwhile examining the findings of the book in terms of the linkage with the model of politicisation. It is fair to say that the Miners' Strike, when the tripartite definition of politicisation is employed, was a great politicising event. On the basis of the responses given by the sixty interviewees, the majority of them do claim to have become politicised and they make the connection between their heightened levels of politicisation and the events which took place during the course of 1984/5. Interviewees were keen to stress that their heightened levels of politicisation were directly attributable to the 1984/5 Miners' Strike. It was not due to sheer coincidence or to other entirely unrelated factors that they may have participated more in the political arena, become more politically aware or altered their behaviour in some way.

Using the tripartite definition of politicisation, it is necessary to attempt to analyse the relative importance of the forms of politicisation in Hemsworth and the relationship between the various categories in the light of the empirical findings. It is apparent, via an in-depth analysis of the overall findings, that the most obvious change was in terms of the second criterion, namely, political awareness. Obviously, this is a slightly more woolly and ephemeral concept than either political participation or behavioural changes but, on the basis of what the interviewees said, this factor witnessed by far the greatest amount of change. If this attempt to rank the three criteria is continued, it is fair to say that behavioural change is placed second in the hierarchy with political participation at the bottom. Speculation as to why this should be the case leads to the suggestion that political awareness requires less exertion and less of a concerted effort than either of the other two criteria. Continuing this theme, behavioural change such as switching one's allegiance from a tabloid to a broadsheet, requires less effort than, say, attending political party meetings.

In terms of the overall analysis of the results of this book, a degree of reflection is required as to the usefulness of the model and whether or not any changes are required to the model in the light of the empirical analysis. The model of politicisation adds to the debate regarding why some people are interested in politics and others are not. It helps us to analyse what kind of factors and issues galvanise people into political activity. It helps in terms of producing a kind of continuum of political activity and focuses upon highlighting differing degrees of political activity. Some people are obviously more politicised than others and this model helps us to fully appreciate this.

As regards the limitations of the model; on reflection, it is necessary to appreciate that it is unlikely that all three criteria will occur at once. As stated above, there are degrees of politicisation. In addition, political awareness, whilst obviously an extremely important factor in this equation, is very difficult to measure accurately. To a certain extent, you are particularly reliant upon what the interviewees say they feel. Having said this, is this not one of the limitations of qualitative methodology and not necessarily a limitation of this model of politicisation? Likewise, behavioural change may be more difficult to measure than political participation. If an interviewee states that household duties are now performed on a rota basis how do you measure this? Are they telling the truth or not?

As far as any changes to the model are concerned, it is felt that there are no glaringly obvious limitations in the basic design of the tripartite definition of politicisation. During its conceptual stage a great deal of effort and attention to detail went in to the design of the model. Aspects such as political knowledge and class consciousness were eliminated from the equation, for reasons outlined in Chapter Two, and it was felt that a relatively watertight definition was reached. With the benefit of hindsight, however, one possible improvement would have been to follow up those who stated that their level of political participation had increased and to analyse in greater depth the extent of that participation. If, for example, they claimed to have joined the Labour Party then it would have apt to have focused upon the extent of that participation in terms of whether they were just card carrying members. Did they attend Party meetings? Were they active and vocal participants in Party meetings and debates? This approach would have necessitated a significant extension to the qualitative interviews but may possibly have added to the overall analysis. Certainly, it would have sharpened the focus in terms of a continuum of politicisation but whether it would have affected the overall thesis in a significant manner is a debatable point.

The issue of parochialism with respect to this book was broached when the respective roles of the police and the media were assessed. In the case of the police, the issue centres around the apparent failure to apportion blame to the local police and the corresponding willingness to regard the Metropolitan Police Force as the major villains of the piece. Likewise, in the case of the media, the local press and regional television coverage of events was generally felt by the interviewees to have been less biased than that given by the national media. It would appear, therefore, that the interviewees expressed a distinct tendency to blame the outsider. Why should this be the case? Any explanation of this phenomenon is purely conjectural but, nevertheless, it is important to postulate reasons as to why those at local level were regarded in a more favourable light than people and organisations emanating from outside of the immediate vicinity. Presumably, in such a confrontational situation as a major industrial strike, the participants, such as those in this particular mining community, have almost a psychological need to deny that local 'forces' could be anything other than supportive of the 'cause'. Surely, to allow negative thoughts to enter into the equation will undermine the notion of a 'Them and Us' oppositional scenario and may lead to a weakening of the strike effort? Secondly, was it simply that they could not believe that those who live and work in and near mining communities could be anything other than supportive?

Thirdly, is it the case that living in a mining community makes you parochial in outlook; that is to say, the inward-looking, insular, geographically isolated nature of mining communities? The implication being that it would have been surprising had they not been parochial. Whatever the reason, the essentially parochial outlook of many of the interviewees is worthy of emphasis.

In conclusion, the events of 1984/5 have had a significant and, more importantly, an enduring effect upon the inhabitants of the mining community of Hemsworth in West Yorkshire. The tri-partite definition of politicisation has been analysed and employed and, using this approach, it has been shown how the majority of the interviewees were affected in a profound and lasting manner by the events of 1984/5 notably by the actions of the Conservative Government and by the tactics which bodies such as the police and the courts operated and by the way in which these activities and those of the miners, both striking and non-striking were portrayed by the mass media. Certain groups, such as the women, were affected more than others but, nevertheless, it is clear that all groups were profoundly and irrevocably changed by the 1984/5 Miners' Strike.

The Wider Scenario

The findings unearthed by this book are particularly interesting but, in one sense, it is necessary to attempt to move beyond the immediate findings in order to attempt to assess their wider implications. The wider applicability of the book is raised earlier on in this Chapter but it is necessary to go into greater depth at this particular point and to focus more explicitly on the wider scenario. For example, by trying to ascertain whether there is something special about the politicising effect of an industrial dispute as opposed to some other form of direct action. A comparison could be made with the peace movement or with a local dispute in order to see how they differ from industrial disputes. Secondly, it would be worthwhile examining how much of this is special to mining communities and not just industrial communities in general. Thirdly, it would then be beneficial to move on and examine the extent to which the findings are exclusive to Hemsworth. Fourthly, it is pertinent to examine and make comparisons between the 1984/5 Miners' Strike and earlier strikes. Another perspective would be to look at this dispute in relationship to disputes in other nations. Finally, it might also be worth examining the effect which the duration of a dispute has upon politicisation.

It is necessary to examine the first issue, that is to say whether there is something peculiar to industrial disputes *vis-a-vis* other forms of direct action. It is fair to say that industrial disputes are generally able to galvanise people to an extent which goes far beyond the capacities of other disputes. An industrial dispute involves a threat to the workers' livelihood, however great or small that threat may be, it may concern worker demands for increased payments or fears regarding job security. Whatever, the workers perceive a challenge to their lifestyles.

The politicising character of industrial disputes is obviously worthy of emphasis but it would be wrong to give the impression that *all* industrial disputes are politicising. This clearly is not the case. Yet there are features of some industrial disputes which make them more politicising than others. It is necessary to attempt to isolate these characteristics. What makes one industrial dispute more politicising than another?

With regards to the mining industry and using the specific example of Hemsworth, the major factor to stress is the *extent* of employment in the mining industry. The community is predominantly composed of miners. Virtually everyone is involved, is related to or knows someone who works in the mining industry. The mining industry pervades the whole of the community, livelihoods are interconnected. The dispute is not just about individual jobs, it is about whole communities. The actions of both the N.C.B. and the Government were seen as an overt and deliberate threat to their community. Gainful employment is not an option elsewhere due to the dearth of jobs in existence generally.

A second factor which makes an industrial dispute politicising is whether the work-force and those who are closely involved are able to make the connection and blame political forces for events. The link was apparent with the 1984/5 dispute in that communities blamed the Government; the Government was regarded as the root cause of the crisis. This then faciltated the development of a distinct 'them and us' mentality with the Government clearly ranged against the miners. The dispute is seen as a definite class struggle.

A further factor to take into consideration is the extent to which a consensual attitude pervades the community. There exists, in distinctive mining communities, a marked similarity of opinion. Hemsworth, for example, is overwhelmingly a Labour community. It is relatively rare to encounter a Conservative, or for that matter a Liberal Democratic, viewpoint.

A fourth factor which cannot be ignored is related to the first. This concerns the degree of integration of mining communities. The historical perspective is also not to be ignored, as Carolyn Baylies depicts in her text on the history of the Yorkshire miners, 'The community was tied up with the pit in a close and symbiotic manner'[20]. Returning to the present, in some industrial disputes the community is dispersed, the work-place is not quite so integrated with home- life. This is not so with mining communities where the rest of the family, notably the women, are intricately involved. Mining has, throughout the decades, relied upon the unpaid support of the women; preparing the 'snap', washing clothes, etc. Although legislation was passed in 1843 which prohibited women from working down the pit, the contribution which women continue to make to the mining industry is without question. There is the added dimension that people work together *and* they socialise together. The community spirit/bond is without question.

One final factor which may shed light on why some industrial disputes are more politicising than others is bound up with the nature of the job itself. The inherent dangers, the dirt and the ensuant diseases, such as pneumoconiosis, predispose mining communities to politicisation. The life-threatening type of work which those in mining communities undertake has a greater effect upon attitudes than if, for example, the majority was employed in white-collar work.

It is also necessary to attempt to compare the politicising impact of strikes with other forms of direct action (for example, the anti-Vietnam demonstrations, the Campaign for Nuclear Disarmament). How can one compare these forms of direct action? The politicising effect of a dispute such as the 1984/5 Miners' Strike can be clearly identified if the focus is upon the fact that here people are concerned with their livelihoods. It is about survival and, more particularly, about community survival. This is not 'frivolous' post-affluence politics, it is 'bread and butter' politics. If you are concerned about where your next meal is coming from then you will not be quite so interested in human rights, animal rights and other, relatively new, social movements. It is fair to say, however, that given the importance of the police's role in the politicisation process, here is a factor which is common to the Miners' Strike and to some non-industrial movements - the policing, for example, of the anti-Criminal Justice Bill and the recent demonstrations concerning animal welfare does seem to have shocked many of the participants.

It is perhaps the case that an industrial dispute would lead to a greater degree of politicisation because of the collective nature of the workplace environment. A fair assumption can be made that if a people are in contact at least eight hours per day on a regular basis then it is likely that attitudes and opinions will spread and may perhaps permeate the whole of the cohort. In this situation there is likely to be the cross-fertilisation of ideas and it is hardly surprising that politicisation would take place on a higher level than might be expected of other 'types' of dispute. Would a local dispute, such as a planning dispute, affect levels of politicisation to the same extent as a workplace dispute and in particular a dispute which involves workers in heavy industry? The sheer nature of the work involved in a heavy industry would seem to be enough to encourage a collective outlook and to produce and maintain a 'them and us' mentality. The notion of class consciousness, whilst not an essential ingredient of the concept of politicisation used here, is more likely to be fostered in the workplace environment and hence facilitate the politicisation process.

It is also necessary, in our quest to analyse politicisation, to attempt to discover whether there is something specific and unique about mining communities. There are certain elements which we can highlight in respect of this fact. The closed nature of mining communities is definitely one aspect of this; on the whole it is a fair judgement to say that mining communities have tended to be very insular and inward-looking. They tend to be distinct communities and it takes time for newcomers to be assimilated. The fact that mining communities depend almost solely upon the one industry for their very existence is definitely an aspect of this, the reliance upon one major employer is bound to have an impact. Another significant factor is the closeness of home to the working environment. This would seem inevitably to create a specific and definite sense of community. The nature of the work involved in the mining industry also needs to be emphasised. The physical, dirty and, not to mention, downright dangerous work adds to the distinctive qualities of mining communities. These elements probably combine to ensure that mining communities do have a particular impact upon the politicisation process. Or if not have an impact upon the politicisation process, at least have an impact upon the tendency to strike.

The next step in the quest to examine the politicisation processes to focus upon whether the community of Hemsworth is special or different in any way to other mining communities. Various studies, such as Henriques *et al.*[21] and, more recently, Warwick and Littlejohn's[22] work, have investigated aspects of mining communities and their inherent culture. It is, therefore, not an impossible task to attempt to ascertain whether Hemsworth is in fact unique. As stated in previous chapters, Hemsworth is significant because it constitutes a definite geographical entity and because of the high numbers which were, at one time, employed in the mining industry. Along with Bolsover in Derbyshire, Hemsworth stood out due to having, at one time, over 30 per cent of the male work-force employed in the mining industry. Allied to this is the high levels of support for the Labour Party.

A further angle from which to continue the investigation is to look at mining disputes over time. In this respect a perusal and comparison with earlier mining disputes would prove beneficial. Did, for example, the 1972 and 1974 disputes have similar effects to the 1984/5 debacle? Retreating even further back into the annals of time, did the '1926 Lockout' have comparable outcomes in terms of its impact on the politicisation process?

Francis and David in their history of the South Wales miners entitled *The Fed*, focus upon the impact of the 1926 Lockout. They state that 'The nine days of the General Strike and more especially the seven-month lock-out revealed an alternative cultural pattern which had no comparable equivalent in the other British coalfields'[23]. The major similarity, however, with the 1984/5 Miners' Strike was the effect which it had upon the women of the South Wales mining communities. They refer to the disturbances of October and November 1926 and state that 'an edge was provided by the involvement in the disturbances of married women who inevitably felt the hardships most acutely. Women figured prominently in twelve major prosecutions and from the limited evidence available, on each occasion their average age was always considerably greater than the men being prosecuted: a pattern which was to be repeated in the unrest of the 1930s'[24]. The reason why the women were slightly older than the men is because many of the younger women had moved out of the mining communities to work as domestic servants and also many of the younger men were unable to get financial help from the Poor Law Unions and, therefore, it was pragmatic to assume that they would be more likely to resort to direct action.

The role undertaken by the women in 1926 attracted considerable comment. Francis and Smith highlight the fact that the '*Western Mail* considered their involvement "surprising" and "strange" but in essence it was another indication of the totality of involvement of these communities in extra-legal and extra-parliamentary actions'[25]. They continue and cite an extract from the *Western Mail* (5 November 1926), 'A strange feature of the disturbance is the surprisingly prominent part played by the women folk, many of whom loiter persistently in the drizzling rain with babies in arms to witness the wretched spectacle. Their presence considerably hampered the police in their efforts to clear the streets'[26]. The involvement of the women is evident from the details referred to by Francis and Smith and, clearly, parallels can be drawn with the 1984/5 national dispute.

A connection can also be made with another South Wales dispute, the Garw Valley dispute of 1929. This dispute was over the question of non-unionised labour in the mines. On 22 October 1929, the non-unionists are reported as facing a demonstration of approximately 1,000 people as they left the pit. A Cardiff reporter is cited by Francis and Smith thus; 'First it was a dull roar, then a howl, which was followed by a savage hissing. The women seemed possessed by frenzy as they beat a barbaric tattoo with their feet on the corrugated roofs of the garden sheds and poured imprecations on the heads of the workers' ... women at the back of the houses signalled their approach by the 'loud beating of tin cans, kettles and frying-pans, a great deal of booing and jeering'[27]. By way of an aside, these are precisely the kind of tactics which Republican women in Northern Ireland are reputed to utilise even today in an attempt to warn their men folk of the presence of British soldiers in the immediate vicinity. Again the women's involvement in an industrial dispute is highlighted as being of significance. 'Women seem to have taken a prominent part in the demonstrations in this valley, undoubtedly because, with unemployment benefits unavailable and poor law relief exhausted, they felt a special grievance against the small number who had driven 2,500 men to hand in their notices'[28].

The international angle is a further perspective from which to analyse the situation. A cross-national study will undoubtedly shed further light upon the question of politicisation and why some industries have a greater propensity to strike than others. Kerr and Siegel's work[29] which examines the 'Inter-Industry Propensity to Strike' is of value at this particular juncture. Examination of the big unionisation strikes in the United States in 1936/7 is valid. The strikes are not directly comparable to the 1984/5 Miners' Strike because they were not, strictly speaking, defensive strikes attempting to combat government action. They are, nevertheless, relevant because of the way in which they did involve mobilisation on a mass scale in an attempt to extend union membership. Jeremy Brecher's 'Strike'[30] furnishes some useful comparative data.

With reference to Kerr and Siegel, they focus upon why some industries are more strike prone than others and they also look at whether this greater tendency to strike or not to strike can be encouraged or discouraged. The Kerr and Siegel hypothesis is cited by Jonathan Winterton in his review article entitled 'The End of a Way of Life'. Winterton states, 'Certain mining localities, dominated by a single industry and insulated from wider society, have often been held to exemplify communities which exhibit distinctive working class characteristics in their local institutions and patterns of social relations'[31]. This is really the crux of Kerr and Siegel's argument.

Kerr and Siegel examine eleven countries over a period of time. They highlight the 'uniformity in behaviour among coal miners'[32]. The authors attempt to explain 'the high propensity to strike of miners, longshoremen, sailors, and loggers and the low propensity of government employees, grocery clerks, railroad employees, and garment workers'[33]. One of the reasons which they put forward is the actual physical location in society of certain employees. 'The miners, the sailors, the longshoremen, the loggers, and, to a much lesser extent, the textile workers form isolated masses, almost a "race apart". They live in their own separate communities: the coal patch, the ship, the waterfront district, the logging camp, the textile town'[34]. In such communities, the authors believe that there are 'few neutrals in them to mediate the conflicts and dilute the mass'[35].

With specific respect to the mining industry, Kerr and Siegel believe that the communities are distinctive because 'The employees form a largely homogeneous undifferentiated mass - they all do about the same work and have about the same experiences'[36]. They highlight the fact that skills are less transferable and that 'Protest is less likely to take the form of moving to another industry and more the character of a mass walkout'[37]. In mining communities, 'The union becomes a kind of working-class party or even government for these employees, rather than just another association among many'[38].

In industries where there is a low propensity to strike activity, Kerr and Siegel state that this may be due to these industries being better integrated into the general community. It may also be the case that the government is able to assert 'the supremacy of the public interest in continuity of service'[39]. The nature of the job is also examined; 'If the job is physically difficult and unpleasant, unskilled or semiskilled, and casual or seasonal ... it will draw tough, inconstant, combative and virile workers, and they will be inclined to strike'[40]. The attitudes of society at large are also deemed relevant, 'the community is more sympathetic with striking miners coming out of the ground than with school teachers abandoning their desks'[41]. Mention is also made of psychology in that a 'lower middle-class psychology'[42] may make some groups, for example bank clerks, less inclined to strike. Lack of 'face-to-face relations'[43] between employees and employers is also regarded as a contributory factor which makes some industries more strike prone than others. Industries which are more strike prone tend to have more violent origins, according to Kerr and Siegel[44]. Ideology is referred to; 'Communist-led unions probably cause more trouble and tough-minded employers invite more than do non-Communist-led unions and softhearted employers'[45]. An industry which has a 'greater monopoly in the labour market'[46] is regarded as more likely to strike.

The Kerr-Siegel hypothesis is, as Winterton highlights[47], challenged by Rimlinger. Gaston Rimlinger undertakes a comparative study of the strike propensity of coal miners in the United States, Great Britain, France and Germany. He argues, firstly that there are 'substantial differences in strike behaviour between Anglo-American and continental miners'[48] and that there is also an indication that 'mining can be rather a peaceful industry'[49]. He questions whether, in view of international differences, it can really be claimed that mining represents a strike-prone industry. He goes on to argue that 'It is quite possible ... for a socially distinct group like the miners to be well integrated into society'[50] and that 'so long as the group as a whole interprets acceptance of managerial authority as proper conduct, deviators will be exposed to strong pressures to comply'[51]. He has 'no doubt about the miners' sense of separateness but does not support the Kerr-Siegel arguments concerning the formation of the 'isolated mass', which is an entirely different phenomenon'[52]. Rimlinger prefers to replace the notion of an 'isolated mass' with 'some notion of a 'separatist group' which may or may not be socially integrated, and may or may not be strike prone, depending on the historical situation'[53]. As his concluding remark aptly illustrates, 'miners in a given country may have either very many strikes or practically none at all'[54].

A final angle from which to approach this question of whether or not the 1984/5 Miners' Strike was unique is to examine the impact, if any, which the length of industrial disputes has upon the politicisation process. It appears to be a fair assertion to state that the longer a dispute lasts the greater the conviction must be of the participants in the dispute. One strike which lasted for a significant period of time was that at the Grunwick Photographic Processing Company in North London. This dispute lasted from 1976 to 1978 and was due to the management refusing to recognise and give bargaining rights to the trade union APEX (Association of Professional, Executive, Clerical and Computer Staffs). Ward's text, *Fort Grunwick*[55] and Dromey and Taylor's book, *Grunwick: the workers' story*[56], give both sides of the debate. As Dromey and Taylor state, 'Grunwick was a defeat for the immediate objectives of the trade union movement but a dispute like that at Grunwick is never lost. The strike bulletins often spoke of 'from Tolpuddle to Tonypandy, from the Matchgirls to the Miners', placing Grunwick in the best traditions of the British trade union movement'[57]. In certain respects, there are parallels between the Grunwick Strike and the 1984/5 Miners' Strike. The literature does not make explicit reference to it but it would be interesting to ascertain whether politicisation occurred to the same extent as it did during the Miners' Strike.

A year's duration undoubtedly signifies that a substantial proportion of those involved must genuinely believe in the 'cause'. In addition, the longer a strike lasts the more likely it is that strikers will become politicised along the way. The length of a strike no doubt contibutes to a hardening of attitudes but it is necessary to pursue in a little greater depth why this should lead to changes in political attitudes. The length of the Strike indicates the depth of feeling of the inhabitants and it also, as time went on, illustrates the extent of the Government's determination to see the Strike through to the bitter end. It is inevitable that, due to this overtly 'political' connection, politicisation took place. The time factor cannot, therefore, be ignored. Whether the same level of politicisation would have taken place after say, a period of two months, three months or even six months is open to debate. The question of whether there is almost a cut-off point for politicisation is worthy of further discussion and is perhaps outside the remit of this particular research and, indeed, it may be very difficult to give a definite answer to it anyway. Suffice to say it remains a further issue which is worthy of being flagged up as a debatable concept.

The relevance of the mass strike is perhaps worthy of further investigation. Brecher, in his text *Strike*, cites Rosa Luxemburg who earlier this century has written on the concept of the mass strike: 'Its uses, its effects, its reasons for coming about are in a constant state of flux ... political and economic strikes, united and partial strikes, defensive and combat strikes, general strikes of individual sections of industry and general strikes of entire cities, peaceful wage strikes and street battles, uprisings with barricades - all run together and run along-side each other, get in each other's way, overlap each other; a perpetually moving and changing sea of phenomena'[58]. From Luxemburg's account then it appears to be difficult to be able to make generalisations regarding strike action.

Brecher goes on to say that 'Strikes during depressions are often extremely bitter, but they are difficult to win because employers have little margin of profit from which to grant wage increases or improvements in working conditions, and little to lose by closing down'[59]. This point about closing down remains apt in contemporary times, reference need only be made to the 1992/3 Timex dispute in Dundee. Timex is the biggest lockout since Wapping. *The Guardian*[60] called it 'an epic drama of industrial bad relations'. Timex has had a base in Dundee since 1946. The dispute began at Christmas 1992 with talk of layoffs. The plan was that half of the workforce would work for six months and then the remainder would work for the final six months of the year. The Union, the Amalgamated Engineering and Electrical Union (A.E.E.U.), wanted rotation with everyone being allowed to work alternate weeks. Peter Hall, the President of Timex, refused this preferring instead for the management to decide which workers would 'take a sabbatical in giroland'[61]. When workers refused to accept the management's conditions Timex locked them out and hired a non-union workforce. To quote the *Sunday Times*; 'Positions became entrenched with scenes reminiscent of Grunwick, Wapping and the miners'[62]. Gavin Laird, the A.E.E.U. general secretary 'blamed the dispute on "brutal" anti-union legislation which had been exploited by the company'[63]. Parallels can be drawn with the miners to the extent that many of those who were striking were galvanised into political activity. 'The fun factor in withdrawing your labour is often overlooked. People get tired and broke, but many lives are energised'[64]. For many of the, predominantly female, workforce the dispute provided them with opportunities to become involved in political activity on a scale which they had never before encountered. Similarities exist between the Timex dispute and the Miners' Strike in terms of the way in which both were policed. Mention has been made of the heavy-handed police tactics employed in both instances. Is this what the future holds with respect to the policing of industrial disputes? The case of Timex suggests that politicising strikes do not have to involve the government as an employer. But maybe the police is an important common factor, especially if cases such as Grunwick, the miners, Timex, etc. are all taken into consideration.

To return to the Brecher statement that 'employers [have] little to lose by closing down'[65], the upshot of the Timex dispute is that Peter Hall resigned in June 1993 and Timex's only European site, at Dundee, closed at Christmas 1993.

Another dispute was at Burnsall, Ltd., a metal finishing company in Smethwick. Here the predominantly female, Asian workforce was in dispute over low wages, unequal wages for women, compulsory overtime and issues of health and safety. The dispute went on for more than twelve months and it is interesting to note that the *Guardian*[66] described a group of Sikh Pujabi women as 'The most assiduous pickets'. So, here again parallels can be drawn with both the women of Timex and the women of the miners' strike.

Another support group which has echoes of the Women Against Pit Closure campaign is the Women of the Waterfront. This group of dockers' wives acts in support of the sacked Liverpool dockers. These dockers have been on strike for more than eighteen months. As Millar states, 'The circumstances surrounding the dispute - perhaps the most vociferous since Timex in Dundee in the early 1990s - are complex. The men were sacked after a strike which took place without a ballot. The company line is that the dockers sacked themselves, with the result that the union movement cannot support them'. With respect to the female supporters, he goes on to state that the 'transition from apolitical Merseyside housewives to sophisticated campaigners has not been easy'. He proceeds to cite Sue, one of the campaigners, who states 'I'm proud that my husband refused to cross a picket. We're not just doing it for their jobs, but for the future of Graeme and the other children who will need jobs when they grow up'[67]. Clearly, the similarities with the 1984/5 coal dispute are marked.

Conclusion

To summarise then, an attempt has been made to ascertain the precise impact of the 1984/5 Miners' Strike. Quoting Coates and Topham, 'This strike was clearly much more than an 'absence'; the miners imposed a debate upon society which it would otherwise have passed by'[68]. A contrast is highlighted, firstly between political disputes and industrial disputes. Secondly, between industrial disputes and mining disputes. Thirdly, between mining communities in general and Hemsworth in particular, and finally between mining disputes over time and between industrial disputes on an international basis. The difference in terms of the duration of disputes is also mentioned.

To reiterate, evidence revealed by the in-depth interviews illustrates that the Miners' Strike of 1984/5 was a significant politicising experience in that, (according to the three criteria already mentioned), a majority of those interviewed seem to have been politicised on the three levels in varying degrees.

To sum up, this book has discovered that a significant degree of politicisation occurred in Hemsworth, a large proportion of which is directly related to the events of 1984/5. One thing is certain, the community of Hemsworth continues to be affected by the events of 1984/5. At the time of the 1996 by-election, instigated by the death of the sitting Member of

Parliament, Derek Enright, the *New Statesman and Society* produced a snap-shot picture of this former mining community. It described Hemsworth as a 'classic example of Britain's bleak, de-industrialised landscape. Once the archetypal mining area, as late as 1985 the constituency could boast six pits. There are none left now - and it shows'. The article proceeds to paint a picture of a community with high unemployent, 'a survey carried out by Leeds Metropolitan University recently revealed hidden unemployment on such a scale that 44 per cent of men of working age were without jobs'; rising crime, 'Burglary in Hemsworth town, for example, has risen by 468 per cent since the 1984/5 miners' strike. Car thefts were up by 520 per cent over the same period' and societal break-down, 'The strong working-class moral code of mining areas, and the social cohesion that spawned it, is breaking down. But in contrast to inner-city riots, this sort of social break-down goes almost unnoticed by the outside world. The victims of economic dislocation here are almost invisible, more likely to seek solace in anti-depressants than to set the streets on fire'. The theme of an 'absence of hope' is a strong one. The demise of the coal industry is blamed for Hemsworth's ills, 'The de-industrialisation that has so damaged Hemsworth, like so many other parts of Britain, has involved a forcible divorce from the past without the provision of mechanism to enter the future ... Destruction of the coal industry, in just a few years, has brought the social pathologies normally associated with inner cities - crime, family instability, drug abuse - to communities where previously they had no purchase'[69]. Hemsworth is not alone in terms of this bleak scenario, nearby Grimethorpe appears to have similar problems. The drugs issue was highlighted in the *Observer*, 'The children of those Harold Macmillan called "the best men in the world who beat the Kaiser's army and never gave in' are hooked on heroin"[70]. This pattern of post-industrial decay is repeated throughout former mining communities. A comparative study of four communities by Waddington, Dicks and Critcher found that 'Drug abuse, petty theft, vandalism and "joy riding" were proliferating among local youths in each of our four communities'[71]. Their research examined the economic, political, psychological and cultural implications of pit closure. They state that their 'study and related research on economic policy in other British mining regions indicates that regenerative activity has been primarily regressive in form and done little to stimulate the long-term development of mining communities affected by pit closure'. There is little to be positive about because even 'the new industries are locally unaccountable, and have been developed on a platform of routine, low-paid and low-skilled work'[72]. The immediate prospects make depressing news. Who knows, therefore, what long-term impact the recent coal dispute will have upon these communities?

Given that the research for this book is based upon sixty in-depth interviews, it is appropriate to end with a comment from one of the interviewees regarding their interpretation of politics; 'Politics to me is the root of the family. It's Labour politics. I like to talk about politics and I get into an awful lot of political arguments. What annoys me about a lot of politicians is they get all these policies, they bring all these policies out but they don't actually come down to grass-roots. They don't actually ask the individual what they think ... for example, this Bill about the Wildlife and Countryside Act. They don't ask you, they just vote on it, like the poll tax. But I write letters, I'm always writing letters. I think that if you believe something then don't sit back *do something about it!*'

Notes:

---

[1] *The Guardian*, 14th October 1992.

[2] Ibid.

[3] James, S. (1997) *British Government: a reader in policy making*, (London: Routledge), p. 187.

[4] *The Times Higher Educational Supplement*, 23rd October 1993.

[5] *The Times Higher Educational Supplement*, 13th November 1992.

[6] Source: British Coal Headquarters, 8th September 1994.

[7] *The Observer*, 28th March 1993.

[8] *The Guardian*, 13th February 1993.

[9] *The Observer*, 28th March 1993.

[10] *The Guardian*, 30th March 1993.

[11] *The Observer*, 28th March 1993.

[12] Ibid.

[13] *The Guardian*, Letters' Page, 15th October 1993.

[14] *The Guardian*, 10th April 1993.

[15] Warwick, D. and Littlejohn, G. (1992) *Coal, Capital and Culture - a sociological analysis of mining communities in West Yorkshire*, (London: Routledge), p. 1.

[16] Ibid., p. 17.

[17] See Inglehart, R. (1977) *The Silent Revolution: Changing Values and Political Styles Among Western Publics*, (Princeton: Princeton University Press) for further details regarding the post-affluence theory.

[18] See Richardson, J.J. and Jordan, A.G. (1979) *Governing Under Pressure*, (Oxford: Martin Robertson), p. 90 for further discussion of Anthony Downs' 'Issue Attention Cycle'.

[19] See Siltanen, J. and Stanworth, M. (Eds.) (1984) *Women and the Public Sphere*, (London: Hutchinson), esp. Chapter 18, for further details regarding the public/private dichotomy.

[20] Baylies, C. (1993) *The History of the Yorkshire Miners, Volume 2, 1881-1918*, (London: Routledge), p. 30.

[21] Dennis, N., Henriques, F. and Slaughter, C. (1956) *Coal is our Life*, (London: Tavistock Publications Limited).

[22] Warwick and Littlejohn, *Op. Cit.*

[23] Francis, H. and Smith, D. (1980) *'The Fed' - a history of the South Wales Miners in the twentieth century*, (London: Lawrence and Wishart), pp. 54/5.

[24] Ibid., p. 65.

[25] Ibid.

[26] Ibid.

[27] Ibid., pp. 135/6.

[28] Ibid., p. 136.

[29] Kerr, C. and Siegel, A. (1954) 'The Interindustry Propensity to Strike - An International Comparison', in *Industrial Conflict*, Edited by Arthur Kornhauser, Robert Dubin and Arthur M. Ross, (New York: McGraw-Hill), pp. 189-212.

[30] Brecher, J. (1972) *Strike*, (San Francisco: Straight Arrow Books).

[31] Winterton, J. (1993) 'The End of a Way of Life: Coal Communities Since the 1984/5 Miners' Strike', *Work, Employment and Society*, (Volume 7, part 1, pp. 135-46), p. 137.

[32] Kerr and Siegel, *Op. Cit.*, p. 191.

[33] Ibid.

[34] Ibid.

[35] Ibid.

[36] Ibid., p. 192.

[37] Ibid.

[38] Ibid., p. 193.

[39] Ibid., p. 198.

[40] Ibid., p. 195.

[41] Ibid.

[42] Ibid., p. 196.

[43] Ibid., p. 199.

[44] Ibid., p. 200.

[45] Ibid., p. 201.

[46] Ibid., p. 202.

[47] Winterton, *Op. Cit.*, p. 138.

[48] Rimlinger, G.V. (1959) 'International Differences in the Strike Propensity of Coal Miners', *Industrial and Labour Relations Review*, Ithaca, New York, (Volume 12, part 3, pp. 389-405), p. 390.

[49] Ibid.

[50] Ibid., p. 395.

[51] Ibid.

[52] Ibid.

[53] Ibid., p. 405.

[54] Ibid.

[55] Ward, G. (1977) *Fort Grunwick*, (London: Temple Smith).

[56] Dromey, J. and Taylor, G. (1978) *Grunwick: the workers' story*, (London: Lawrence and Wishart).

[57] Ibid., p. 199.

[58] Brecher, *Op. Cit.*, p. 22.

[59] Ibid., p. 244.

[60] *The Guardian*, 29th May 1993.

[61] Ibid.

[62] *The Sunday Times*, 20th June 1993.

[63] *The Guardian*, 16th June 1993.

[64] *The Guardian*, 29th June 1993.

[65] Brecher, *Op. Cit.*, p. 244.

[66] *The Guardian*, 16th June 1993.

[67] Millar, S. 'Reminder of old fashioned struggle', *The Guardian*, 10th September 1996.

[68] Coates, K. and Topham, T. (1986) *Trade Unions and Politics*, (Oxford: Blackwell), p. 222.

[69] *New Statesman and Society*, 'New Labour, Old Capitalism', editorial, 2nd February 1996, p. 5.

[70] Sweeney, J. 'Miners' children in the pits of heroin', *The Observer*, 6th October 1996, p. 5.

[71] Waddington, D., Dicks, B. and Critcher, C. (1994) 'Community Responses to Pit Closure in the Post-strike Era', *Community Development Journal*, Volume 29, Number 2, p. 144.

[72] Ibid., p. 149.

Bibliography

Adeney, M. and Lloyd, J. (1986) *The Miners' Strike 1984-85 Loss Without Limit*, (London: Routledge and Kegan Paul).

Allen, V.L. (1981) *The Militancy of British Miners*, (Shipley: Moor Press).

Banner Film Production (1984) *Coal Not Dole - Miners United,* (Channel Four, VIDEO).

Banner Film Production (1985) *Here We Go,* (Channel Four, VIDEO).

Barnsley Metropolitan Borough Council, (1984) *Coal Mining and Barnsley -a study of employment prospects*, (Barnsley: Barnsley Metropolitan Borough Council).

Baylies, C. (1993) *The History of the Yorkshire Miners, Volume 2, 1881-1918*, (London: Routledge).

Bell, C. and Newby, H. (1977) *Doing Sociological Research*, (London: George Allen and Unwin).

Beynon, H. (Ed.) (1985) *Digging Deeper - issues in the miners' strike*, (London: Verso).

Beynon, H. (1984) *Working For Ford*, (London: Penguin) second edition.

Bottomore, T. (1979) *Political Sociology*, (London: Hutchinson).

Brammah, F. and Brammah, A. (1985) *Margarella, The Moles and the Money Tree*, (Pontefract: Yorkshire Art Circus).

Brecher, J. (1972) *Strike*, (San Francisco: Straight Arrow Books).

Brooks, R. (1990) 'Coal Chief: Let them have coke', *The Observer*, (Sunday 21 January).

Brown, A. 'Hemsworth's Pigs', *The Spectator*, (21 July 1984, pp. 15-16).

_____ 'Return to Hemsworth', *The Spectator*, (9 February 1985, p. 15).

_____ 'Back to What?', *The Spectator*, (9 March 1985, pp. 11-12).

Bulmer, M.I.A. (1975) 'Sociological Models of the Mining Community', *Sociological Review*, Vol. 23, pp. 61-92.

Bulmer, M. (Ed.) (1975) *Working Class Images of Society*, (London: Routledge and Kegan Paul).

Bulmer, M. (Ed.) (1978) *Mining and Social Change*, (London: Croom Helm).

Bulmer, M. (Ed.) (1984) *Sociological Research Methods*, (London: Macmillan), second edition.

Bulley, J. (1957) *Hemsworth in History,* (Hemsworth: Bulley).

Butler, D. and Butler, G. (1986) *British Political Facts: 1900-1985*, (London: Macmillan).

Butler, D. and Kavanagh, D. (1988) *The British General Election of 1987*, (London: Macmillan).

_____ (1992) *The British General Election of 1992*, (London: Macmillan).

Callinicos, A. and Simons, M. (1985) *The Great Strike*, (London: Socialist Worker).

Campbell, B. 'The Other Miners' Strike', *The New Statesman*, (27 July 1984).

Charlesworth, A. *et al.* (1996) *An Atlas of Industrial Protest in Britain: 1750-1990*, (Basingstoke: Macmillan).

Charlesworth, J. (Ed.) (1926) *Hemsworth Parish Registers 1654-1812*, (Issued to subscribers for the Yorkshire Parish Register Society).

Coates, K. and Topham, T. (1986) *Trade Unions and Politics*, (Oxford: Blackwell).

Cockburn, C. (1983) *Brothers - Male Dominance and Technological Change*, (London: Pluto Press).

Cocker, P.G. (1986) *Government and Politics*, (London: Edward Arnold).

Connolly, W. (1983) *The Terms of Political Discourse*, (Oxford: Martin Robertson), second edition, esp. pp. 10-41.

Conservative Research Department, 'The Coal Industry', in *Politics Today*, (London: Conservative Central Office, No. 19, 5 November 1984).

Coulter, J., Miller, S. and Walker, M. (1984) *State of Siege*, (London: Canary Press).

Coxall, B. and Robins, L. (1989) *Contemporary British Politics*, (London: Macmillan).

Craig, F.W.S. (1977) *British Parliamentary Election Results, 1918-1949*, (London: Macmillan), second edition.

Craig, F.W.S. (1983) *British Parliamentary Election Results, 1950-1973*, (Chichester, Parliamentary Research Services) second edition.

Craig, F.W.S. (1984) *British Parliamentary Election Results, 1974-1983*, (London, Parliamentary Research Services).

Craig, F.W.S. (1987) *Chronology of British Parliamentary By-Elections, 1833-1987*, (Chichester, Parliamentary Research Services).

Crewe, I. (1984) *British Parliamentary Constituencies - a statistical compendium*, (London: Faber and Faber).

Crick, B. and Crick, T. (1987) *What is Politics?*, (London: Edward Arnold).

Cumberpatch, G. 'Bias that lies in the eye of the beholder', *The Guardian*, (19 May 1986).

Cumberpatch, G., McGregor, R. and Brown, J. (1986) *Television and the Miners' Strike*, (London, Broadcasting Research Unit).

Dennis, N., Henriques, F. and Slaughter, C. (1956) *Coal is our Life*. (London: Tavistock Publications Limited).

Denver, D. and Hands, G. (1992) *Issues and Controversies in British Electoral Behaviour*, (London: Harvester Wheatsheaf).

Denver, D. *et al.* (Eds) (1993) *British Elections and Parties Yearbook 1993*, (Hemel Hempstead: Harvester Wheatsheaf), esp. pp. 205-215 article by Webber, R. 'The 1992 General Election. Constituency results and local patterns of national newspaper readership'.

Denver, D. and Bochel, H. (1994) 'Merger or Bust: Whatever Happened to Members of the S.D.P.?', *British Journal of Political Science*, Vol. 24, pp. 403-417, (Cambridge: Cambridge University Press).

Devine, F. (1992) *Affluent Workers Revisited*, (Edinburgh: Edinburgh University Press.

Dicks, B., Waddington, D. and Critcher, C. 'The quiet disintegration of closure communities', *Town and Country Planning*, (July 1993, pp. 174-176).

Douglass, D. (1987) *Tell Us Lies About the Miners*, (London: A.S.P.) second edition.

Dowse, R.E. and Hughes, J.A. (1972) *Political Sociology*, (London: John Wiley and Sons).

Dromey, J. and Taylor, G. (1978) *Grunwick: the workers' story*, (London: Lawrence and Wishart).

Dunleavy, P. and Husbands, C.T. (1985) *British Democracy at the Crossroads*, (London: Allen and Unwin).

The Economist, 'Appomattox or civil war?' (27 May 1978, pp. 21-22).

Eder, K. (1993) *The New Politics of Class*, (London: Sage).

Edgell, S. (1993) *Class*, (London: Routledge).

Evans, E.J. (1983) *The Forging of the Modern State 1783-1870*, (Harlow: Longman).

Field, J. 'Labour's Dunkirk', *New Socialist*, (April 1985).

Fine, B. and Millar, R. (Eds) (1985) *Policing the Miners' Strike*, (London: Lawrence and Wishart).

Francis, H. and Smith, D. (1980) *'The Fed' - a history of the South Wales Miners in the twentieth century*, (London: Lawrence and Wishart).

Francis, H. and Rees, D. (1987) *Class, Community and Miners: The British Coalfields and the 1984/5 Strike*, (London: Lawrence and Wishart).

Franzosi, R. (1995) *The Puzzle of Strikes: Class and State Strategies in Postwar Italy*, (Cambridge: Cambridge University Press).

Gallie, D. (1978) *In Search of the New Working Class*, (Cambridge: Cambridge University Press).

Gallie, D. (1983) *Social Inequality and Class Radicalism in France and Britain*, (Cambridge: Cambridge University Press).

German, L. (1989) *Sex, Class and Socialism*, (London: Bookmarks).

Gibbon, P. 'Analysing the British miners' strike of 1984-5', *Economy and Society*, (Volume 17, Number 2, May 1988, pp. 139-194).

Giddens, A. (1973) *The Class Structure of the Advanced Societies*, (London: Hutchinson).

Giddens, A. and Held, D. (Eds.) (1982) *Class, Power and Conflict*, (Los Angeles: University of California Press), pp. 353-416.

Giddens, A. (Ed.) (1987) *Introductory Sociology*, (London: Macmillan).

Glyn, A. (1985) *The Economic Case Against Pit Closures*, (Sheffield: National Union of Mineworkers).

Goldthorpe, J.H. *et al.* (1968a) *The Affluent Worker: Industrial Attitudes and Behaviour*, (Cambridge: Cambridge University Press).

Goldthorpe, J.H. *et al.* (1968b) *The Affluent Worker. Political Attitudes and Behaviour*, (Cambridge: Cambridge University Press).

Goldthorpe, J.H. (1969) *The Affluent Worker in the Class Structure*, (Cambridge: Cambridge University Press).

Goodman, G. (1985) *The Miners' Strike*, (London: Pluto Press).

Gosling, M. (1990) 'Let Scargill Reply', in *Free Press*, (London: Campaign for Press and Broadcasting Freedom, Sept/Oct. 1990, p. 3).

Green, P. (1990) *The Enemy Without - Policing and Class Consciousness in the Miners' Strike*, (Milton Keynes: Open University Press).

Greenberg, E. (1986) *Workplace Democracy. The Political Effects of Participation*, (Ithaca: Cornell University Press).

Hague, H. 'Village Haunted by Enemy Within', *The Independent on Sunday*, (2 December 1990).

Hain, P. and McCrindle, J. 'One and All: Labour's Response to the Miners', *New Socialist*, (October 1984, Number 20, pp. 44-46).

Hain, P. (1986) *Political Strikes*, (Harmondsworth: Penguin).

Hancock, H. 'Grimethorpe', *London Review of Books*, (15 November-6 December 1984, Volume 6, Number 21, p. 5).

Haralambos, M. and Holborn, M. (1990) *Sociology: Themes and Perspectives*, (London: Unwin Hyman) third edition.

Harrison, R. (Ed.) (1978) *The Independent Collier*, (Hassocks: Harvester Press).

Harrop, M. and Millar, W.L. (1987) *Elections and Voters: A Comparative Introduction*, (London: Macmillan).

Head, J., Watson, M. and Webb, T. (1986) *Striking Figures*, (Halifax: Artivan and Striking Figures).

Hindess, B. (1971) *The Decline of Working-Class Politics*, (London: MacGibbon and Kee).

Holdsworth, G. (1982) *Hemsworth High Hall - a Georgian Country House*, (Wakefield: Wakefield Historical Publications).

Hood, M. and Woods, R. (1994) 'Women and Participation', in *Housing Women*, edited by Gilroy, R. and Woods, R. (London: Routledge), pp. 58-74.

Howell, D. (1983) *British Workers and the Independent Labour Party 1888-1906*, (Manchester: Manchester University Press).

Howell, D. (1989) *The Politics of the N.U.M.: A Lancashire View*, (Manchester: Manchester University Press).

Huddle, R., Phillips, A., Simons, M. and Sturrock, J. (1985) *Blood, Sweat and Tears - Photographs from the Great Miners' Strike 1984-5*, (London: Artworker Books).

Ignatieff, M. 'Strangers and Comrades' in *New Statesman*, 14 December 1984, pp. 25-27.

Inglehart, R. (1977) *The Silent Revolution: Changing Values and Political Styles Among Western Publics*, (Princeton: Princeton University Press).

Jackson, B. (1968) *Working Class Community*, (London: Routledge and Kegan Paul).

Jackson, M.P. (1987) *Strikes. Industrial Conflict in Britain, U.S.A. and Australia*, (Brighton: Wheatsheaf).

James, S. (1997) *British Government: a reader in policy making*, (London: Routledge), pp. 186-194.

Jedrzejczyk, I. *et al.* (1986) *Striking Women*, photographs, (London: Pluto Press).

Jenner, B. (1986) *The Coal Strike - Christian Reflections on the Miners' Struggle*, (Sheffield: Urban Theology Unit).

Jones, D. *et al.* (1985) *Media Hits the Pits*, (London: Campaign for Press and Broadcasting Freedom).

Jones, M. (1985) *The Story of David Gareth Jones*, (London: New Park Publications Ltd.).

Jones, N. (1986) *Strikes and the Media*, (Oxford: Basil Blackwell).

Jowell, R. and Airey, C. (Eds.) (1984) *British Social Attitudes - the 1984 Report*, (Aldershot: Gower). Esp. Chapter Two 'Political Attitudes' by Ken Young, pp. 11-45.

Keniston, K. (1968) *Young Radicals*, (New York: Harcourt, Brace and World, Inc.).

Kerr, C. and Siegel, A. (1954) 'The Interindustry Propensity to Strike - An International Comparison', in *Industrial Conflict* Edited by Kornhauser, A., Dubin, R. and Ross, A. M., (New York: McGraw-Hill), pp. 189-212.

Killip, C. (1988) *In Flagrante*, (London: Secker and Warburg).

King, A. (1976) (Ed.), *Why is Britain becoming harder to govern?*, (London: British Broadcasting Corporation).

King, A. *et al.* (1993) *Britain at the Polls, 1992*, (New Jersey: Chatham).

Kirkpatrick, S.A. (1974) *Qualitative Analysis of Political Data*, (Ohio: Merrill Publishing Company).

Labour Research Department, *The Miners' Case*, (pp. 1-20). ISBN 0900508728

Labour Research, 'Miners' Strike. Picketing against the law', (May 1984).

Lane, R.E. (1962) *Political Ideology*, (New York: The Free Press of Glencoe).

Lane, T. and Roberts, K. (1971) *Strike at Pilkingtons*, (London: Fontana).

Laybourn, K. (1993) *The General Strike of 1926*, (Manchester: Manchester University Press).

Lloyd, J. (1985) *Understanding the Miners' Strike*, (London: Fabian Society No. 504).

Lockwood, D. (1966) 'Sources of Variation in Working-Class Images of Society', *Sociological Review*, (Volume 14, pp. 249-67).

Lockwood, D. (1988) 'The Weakest Link in the Chain: Some Comments on the Marxist Theory of Action', *Research in the Sociology of Work 1*, pp. 435-81, reprinted in Rose, D.'s 1988 text.

Lovenduski, J. and Randall, V. (1993) *Contemporary Feminist Politics*, (Oxford: Oxford University Press).

MacGregor, I. (1986) *The Enemies Within - the story of the Miners' Strike 1984-5*, (London: Collins).

Madgwick, P.J. (1984) *Introduction to Politics*, (London: Hutchinson, third edition).

Mann, M. (1973) *Consciousness and Action Among the Western Working Class*, (London: Macmillan).

Marshall, G. (1988) 'Some Remarks on the Study of Working Class Consciousness', in Rose, D. (ed), *Social Stratification and Economic Change*, (London: Unwin Hyman).

Millett, K. (1977) *Sexual Politics*, (London: Virago).

Milne, S. 'In the Hall of the Miners' King', *The Guardian*, (Friday 31 August 1990).

'Mining the Meaning: Keywords in the Miners' Strike', *New Socialist*, (March 1985).

Morgan, J. (1987) *Conflict and Order. The Police and Labour Disputes in England and Wales 1900-1939*, (Oxford: Clarendon Press).

Morgan, W.J. (1990) *The Nottinghamshire Coalfield and the British Miners' Strike of 1984-85*, (Nottingham: University of Nottingham Department of Adult Education).

Murphy, R. (1988) *Social Closure*, (Oxford: Clarendon Press).

Newsline, (1985) *The Miners' Strike 1984-5: in pictures*, (London: New Park Publications).

Newton, G. (1985) *We are Women: We are Strong. The Story of the Northumberland Miners' Wives 1984-85,* (Northumberland: Published by the People Themselves).

Newton, K. (1969) *The Sociology of British Communism*, (London: Penguin).

N.C.C.L., (1984) *Civil Liberties and the Miners' Dispute*, (London: N.C.C.L.).

North Yorkshire Women Against Pit Closures, (1985) *Strike 84-85*, (Leeds: North Yorkshire Women Against Pit Closures).

O'Donnell, K. (1988) *The Impact of Colliery Closures on Wakefield M.D.C. 1985-88*, (University of Leeds: School of Economic Studies).

O'Donnell, K. 'Pit Closures in the British Coal Industry: a Comparison of the 1960s and 1980s', *International Review of Applied Economics*, (Edward Arnold, pp. 62-77). ISSN 0269 2171.

Pahl, R. E. (1989) 'Is the Emperor Naked? - Sociological Theory in Urban and Regional Research', *International Journal of Urban and Regional Research*, (Volume 13, part 4, pp. 709-20).

Parker, T. (1986) *Red Hill. A Mining Community*, (London: Hodder and Stoughton).

Parkin, F. (1972) *Class Inequality and Political Order*, (St. Albans: Paladin).

Parkin, F. (1979) *Marxism and Class Theory: A Bourgeois Critique*, (London: Tavistock).

Parry, G., Moyser, G. and Day, N. (1992) *Political Participation and Democracy in Britain*, (Cambridge: Cambridge University Press).

Pateman, C. (1970) *Participation and Democratic Theory*, (Cambridge: Cambridge University Press).

Percy, S. 'Gnome Truths. Is there life after coalmining?' *New Statesman and Society*, (27 April 1990).

Ray, G. 'British Coal', *National Institute Economic Review*, (November, 1989) pp. 75-84.

Reed, D. and Adamson, O. (1985) *Miners' Strike 1984-5. People versus State*, (London: Larkin Publications).

Rees, G. (1985) 'Regional restructuring, class change, and political action: preliminary comments on the 1984-1985 miners' strike in South Wales', *Society and Space*, (Vol. 3, pp. 389-406).

Rees, G. (1993) 'Class, Community and the Miners: The 1984-85 Miners' Strike and Its Aftermath', *Sociology*, (Vol. 27, part 2, pp. 307-12).

Rimlinger, G.V. (1959) 'International Differences in the Strike Propensity of Coal Miners', *Industrial and Labour Relations Review*, Ithaca, New York, (Volume 12, part 3, pp. 389-405).

Tolleson Rinehart, S. (1992) *Gender Consciousness and Politics*, (London: Routledge).

Roberts, E. 'Hart of the Coal Strike', *Yorkshire Evening Post*, (23 February 1990).

Rogers, M. 'Miner Discrepancies', *The Listener*, (22 February 1990).

Rose, D. (1988) *Social Stratification and Economic Change*, (London: Hutchinson).

Rose, R. 'Ungovernability; is there fire behind the smoke?' *Political Studies* Vol. XXVII, Number 3, (pp. 351-370).

Rowbotham, S. 'More than Just a Memory: Some Political Implications of Women's Involvement in the Miners' Strike, 1984-1985', *Feminist Review*, 23 (Spring 1986).

Routledge, P. (1993) *Scargill: The Unauthorized Biography*, (London: Harper Collins).

Rush, M. (1992) *Politics and Society*, (London: Prentice Hall).

Samuel, R., Bloomfield, B. and Boanas, G. (Eds.) (1986) *The Enemy Within. Pit Villages and the miners' strike of 1984-5*, (London: Routledge and Kegan Paul).

Sanders, D. 'Voting Behaviour in Britain', *Contemporary Record*, (February 1991, pp. 2-6).

Saunders, J. (1989) *Across Frontiers (International Support for the Miners' Strike)*, (London: Canary Press).

Saunders, L. 'Striking a blow for unity', *The Guardian*, (7 March 1990).

Saville, J. (1988) *The Labour Movement in Britain*, (London: Faber, 1988), esp. the Epilogue 'The Labour Movement and the miners' strike 1984-5', pp. 144-150.

Scargill, A. (1990) *Response to the Lightman Inquiry*, (Barnsley: Campaign to Defend Scargill and Heathfield).

Scase, R. (1992) *Class*, (Buckingham: Open University Press).

Schwarzmantel, J. (1987) *Structures of Power*, (London: Wheatsheaf).

Seddon, V. (Ed.) (1986) *The Cutting Edge: Women and the Pit Strike*, (London: Lawrence and Wishart).

Siltanen, J. and Stanworth, M. (Eds.) (1984), *Women and the Public Sphere*, (London: Hutchinson), esp. Chapter 18.

Spencer, S. (1985) *Police Authorities During the Miners' Strike*, (London: The Cobden Trust).

Stead, J. (1987) *Never the Same Again*, (London: The Women's Press).

Stradling, R. (1977) *A Programme for Political Education. The Political Awareness of the School Leaver*, (London: Hansard Society).

Sutcliffe, L. and Hill, B. (1985) *Let Them Eat Coal. The Political Use of Social Security During The Miners' Strike*, (London: Canary Press).

Taylor, A. (1984) *The Politics Of the Yorkshire Miners*, (London: Croom

Helm, 1984).

Taylor, A. (1985) 'The Politics of Coal: Some Aspects of the Miners' Strike', *Politics*, Volume 5, Part 1, pp. 3-9.

Taylor, A. 'Terrible Nemesis? The Miners, the N.U.M. and Thatcherism' in *Teaching Politics*, (London: The Politics Association, May 1986), Volume 15, number 2, pp. 293-314.

Taylor, B. (1983) *Eve and The New Jerusalem*, (London: Virago).

Thatcher, M. (1993) *The Downing Street Years*, (New York: Harper Collins), chapter XIII, pp. 339-378.

Thornton, J. (1987) *All the Fun of the Fight*, (Doncaster: Doncaster Library Service).

Turabian, K. (1982) *A Manual for Writers of Research Papers, Theses and Dissertations*, (London: Heinemann).

Turner, H.A. (1969) *Is Britain Really Strike Prone?*, (Cambridge: Cambridge University Press).

Turner, J.E. (1978) *Labour's Doorstep Politics in London*, (London: Macmillan).

Waddington, D., Jones, K. and Critcher, C. (1989) *Flashpoints. Studies in Public Disorder*, (London: Routledge).

Waddington, D. and Wykes, M. (1989) 'Voting with their Feet', *New Statesman and Society*, (6 January 1989).

Waddington, D., Wykes, M. and Critcher, C. (1991) *Split at the Seams? - community, continuity and change after the 1984-5 coal dispute*, (Milton Keynes: Oxford University Press).

Waddington, D., Dicks, B. and Critcher, C. (1994) 'Community Responses to Pit Closure in the Post-strike Era', *Community Development Journal*, Volume 29, Number 2, pp.141-150.

Wajcman, J. (1983) *Women in Control*, (Milton Keynes: Oxford University Press).

Ward, G. (1977) *Fort Grunwick*, (London: Temple Smith).

Warwick, D., Allen, S. and Littlejohn, G. (1986) *Some implications of the Coal Miners' Strike of 1984/5*, (Leeds and Bradford Universities).

Warwick, D. and Littlejohn, G. (1992) *Coal, Capital and Culture - a sociological analysis of mining communities in West Yorkshire*, (London: Routledge).

Wass, V. 'Life After Redundancy', *The South Wales Miner*, (Autumn 1988).

Wass, V. (1988) *Redundancy and Re-employment: Effects and Prospects following Colliery Closure*, (Cardiff: University of Wales).

Weir, D. (Ed) (1973) *Men and Work in Modern Britain*, (London: Fontana), esp. pp. 169-80, D.T.H. Weir, 'The Wall of Darkness'.

Welsh Campaign for Civil and Political Liberties and N.U.M. (South Wales Area) (1985) *Striking Back*, (Cardiff: W.C.C.P.L.).

Wilsher, P. *et al. Strike*, (Sunday Times Insight Team, Andre Deutsch, 1985).

Winterton, J. 'Coal Board's computerised threat to jobs', *Socialist Viewpoint*, (February 1985) No. 3.

Winterton, J. (1987) 'The Miners' Strike: Lessons From the Literature', *Industrial Tutor*, (Vol. 4, part 4/5, pp. 92-106).

Winterton, J. and Winterton, R. (1989) *Coal, Crisis and Conflict*, (Manchester: Manchester University Press).

Winterton, J. 'All Gone Up in Smoke', *The Times Higher Education Supplement*, 11.1.91.

Winterton, J. (1993) 'The End of a Way of Life: Coal Communities Since the 1984/5 Miners' Strike', *Work, Employment and Society*, (Volume 7, part 1, pp. 135-46).

Women Against Pit Closures, (1985) *Deep Digs (cartoons of the miners' strike)*, (London: Pluto Press).

Worborough Community Group, (1985) *The Heart and Soul of It*, (Worsborough: Worsborough Community Group and Bannerworks).

Yates, I. (1960) 'Power in the Labour Party', *Political Quarterly*, (Vol. 31, part 3, pp. 300-11).

Yorkshire Art Circus, (1988) *Privy to Privatisation. Communities under the Hammer*, (Castleford: Yorkshire Art Circus).

Appendix 1: 1991 CENSUS - AREA PROFILE

	HEMSWORTH WARD (PRE 1983)	WAKEFIELD M.D.	GREAT BRITAIN
Population			
Residents	14,063	310,915	54,888,844
Total Males	6,935	151,772	26,574,954
Total Females	7,128	159,143	28,313,890
Males 0 to 15	1,608	32,533	5,646,659
Females 0 to 15	1,435	31,061	5,377,064
Males 16 to Retirement Age	4,421	100,543	17,392,621
Females 16 to Retirement Age	4,097	93,029	16,196,875
Males Retirement Age & Over	905	18,696	3,535,674
Females Retirement Age & Over	1,607	35,053	6,739,951
Ethnic Groups			
% Resident Population - White	99.5	98.5	94.5
% Resident Population - Black Groups	0.1	0.2	1.6
% Resident Population - Indian, Pakistani, etc.	0.2	1.0	2.7
% Resident Population - Chinese & Other	0.2	0.3	1.2
Migration			
Number of Migrants into Area	1,096	24,367	336,656
Limiting Long-Term Illness			
% Residents With Limiting Long-Term Illness	19.9	15.3	13.1
Households			
Number of Households	5,424	123,478	21,897,322
Car Ownership			
% Households With No Car	47.4	38.2	33.4
% Households With 1 Car	40.8	43.6	43.5
% Households With 2 or More Cars	11.8	18.1	23.1
Household Composition			
Number of Households with Pensioner(s)	1,761	39,194	7,331,317
Number of Lone Pensioners	793	18,236	3,302,289
Number of Households with Children	1,801	39,090	6,574,431
Number of Lone Parents	266	4,619	825,238
Dwellings			
Number of Dwellings	5,583	127,325	23,000,473
% Detached	12.0	16.2	20.2
% Semi-Detached	52.1	46.2	29.1
% Terraced	28.9	27.1	29.2
% Flats. Bedsits etc.	6.9	10.5	21.5
Number of Vacant Dwellings	166	4,043	1,066,508
Housing Tenure			
% Owner Occupied	52.7	61.0	66.7
% Rented - Private	6.9	4.2	6.6
% Rented - Housing Association	2.2	1.7	3.1
% Rented - Local Authority	36.9	31.7	21.6
% Rented - Other	1.3	1.3	1.9

	HEMSWORTH WARD (PRE 1983)	WAKEFIELD M.D.	GREAT BRITAIN
Household Amenities			
% Households with No Bath, WC etc.	0.6	0.5	1.3
% Households with No Central Heating	15.5	16.1	18.9
% Households with Over 1 Person per Room	1.7	1.7	2.2
Communal Establishments			
Number of Communal Establishments	11	149	55,984
Residents (including Staff) in Communal Establishments	211	3,152	833.151
Economic Establishments			
% Males Economically Active	66.4	71.6	73.3
% Females Economically Active	44.1	49.3	49.9
% Unemployment - Males	17.4	12.4	11.2
% Unemployment - Females	10.0	6.5	6.8
% Households With 1 Employee	25.7	23.5	28.7
% Households With 2 or More Employees	31.0	35.9	35.7
% Households With No Employees	43.4	37.6	35.6
Social Class*			
% Professional/Managerial/Technical	9.7	16.6	23.0
% Skilled Non-Manual	4.1	6.9	8.3
% Skilled Manual	19.2	20.9	16.4
% Partly & Unskilled/Govt. Scheme/Not Stated	17.9	14.0	12.9
% Retired & Economically Inactive	47.9	40.6	38.3
Working Hours			
% Females 15hrs & Under	20.0	16.9	15.4
% Females 16 to 40hrs	75.2	76.0	75.2
% Females 41+hrs	1.0	4.5	6.6
% Males 15hrs & Under	0.4	1.2	1.7
% Males 16 to 40hrs	77.4	73.4	69.7
% Males 41+hrs	20.5	22.2	25.0
% Persons Hours Not Stated	2.6	2.9	3.3
Means of Travel to Work			
% Public Transport	18.7	14.7	15.7
% Car/Motor Cycle	57.6	64.2	62.2
% Pedal Cycle/Foot	18.9	16.2	14.8
% Work at Home	2.8	3.3	5.0
% Not Stated/Other	2.0	1.7	2.4
Qualifications			
% Persons with a Higher Qualification	4.3	9.1	13.4
Industry of Employment			
% Agriculture	3.2	0.9	1.9
% Energy (inc. Coal Mining)	8.7	6.9	1.9
% Minerals & Chemicals	2.6	4.0	2.8
% Manufacturing	15.0	19.1	17.8
% Construction	11.2	8.0	7.4
% Distribution/Transport	30.4	27.8	26.9
% Banking & Finance/Other Services	28.8	33.4	41.3

* Individuals assigned to Social Class based on the Occupation of the Household Head.

Appendix 2: TABLE 1.1: PARLIAMENTARY ELECTION RESULTS FOR THE HEMSWORTH CONSTITUENCY SINCE 1950

PERCENTAGE OF VOTE

YEAR	TURNOUT %	LABOUR %	CONSERVATIVE %	LIBERAL %	MAJORITY %
1950	88.2	82.4	17.6*	-	64.8
1951	85.1	82.7	17.3	-	65.4
1955	79.9	83.3	16.7	-	66.6
1959	83.6	82.2	17.8	-	64.4
1964	78.8	83.1	16.9	-	66.2
1966	76.0	85.4	14.6	-	70.8
1970	71.8	80.8	19.2	-	61.6
1974(Feb)	77.1	82.8	17.2	-	65.6
1974(Oct)	70.2	76.5	12.0	11.5	64.5
1979	73.3	69.9	19.7	10.5	50.2
1983	68.6	59.3	19.6	21.2	38.1
1987	75.7	67.0	17.2	15.8	49.8
**1991(Nov)	42.8	66.3	10.5	20.1	46.2
1992	75.9	70.8	18.6	10.5	52.2
***1996(Feb)	39.5	71.9	8.8	6.9	63.1
1997	67.9	70.6	17.8	8.9	52.8

* Candidate stood as a joint candidate of the Conservative Party and the National Liberal Organisation.

** By-election caused by the death of George Buckley.

*** By-election caused by the death of Derek Enright. The Socialist Labour Party obtained 5.4 per cent of the vote in this by-election.

Appendix 3: INTERVIEW QUESTIONS

Begin with 'personal' questions:

   - name
   - present occupation
   - biographical details

How clearly do you remember the Miners' Strike?

Do you think the experience changed you in any way? Please explain.

POLITICS
Would you say you were interested in politics?

How interested?

What does politics mean to you?

What do you understand by the term 'political'?

How often do you discuss politics?

Do you read a newspaper every day?
Which ones?

Do you regularly watch the news programmes on T.V.?
Which ones/channels?

Do you watch other current affairs programmes?
Which ones?

Have you changed any of your views/opinions as a result of the Strike?

Would you say that your friends are interested in politics?

Do you always vote?
(European elections, National, Local, By-elections)

Have you become more/less active in politics as a result of the Miners' Strike? Explain how.

Has your level of political participation increased/decreased?

COMMUNITY
Do you have a strong sense of community?

Do you believe that a mining community is, in any way different, to other types of community?
Explain how.

Is it just a matter of living in a certain area or do you have to be born into a mining community to really 'belong'?

What are the key features of a mining community?

How long has this sense of community existed?

Has it changed in any way over the past few years/decades?

Did you notice any specific changes as a result of the 1984/5 Miners' Strike?

THE POLICE
What are your opinions with regard to the police force?

Have your opinions changed in any way due to the Miners' Strike?

DURING THE STRIKE

What was your own personal experience during the Strike?

Is there any one (or series of) specific events which fundamentally affected your political opinions? Explain.

LOOKING BACK

When you remember the events of 84/5 have your views become tempered?

In what ways has time modified the feelings you had?

THE GOVERNMENT

What are your opinions regarding the Government's actions during the Strike?

Have those views changed?

What are your opinions regarding the Opposition?

What do you think of the Government's plans to privatise the coal industry?

The proposals for the privatisation of Electricity suggested massive redundancies for miners, do you think that this may have been part of the Government's thinking back in 1984/85?

Appendix 4: NOTES OF THE EIGHTH AND SPECIAL MEETING OF THE PONTEFRACT POLICE COMMUNITY FORUM HELD AT THE HIGH SCHOOL, HEMSWORTH ON 19 JULY 1984 AT 7.30PM CONCLUDING AT 9.50PM

Present:-

County Councillor J D Alexander (Chairman)
Mrs T Horvath (Vice-Chairman) - Pontefract CVS
County Councillor H Best - Vice-Chairman, WY Police Authority
Ch Supt E P McQuoid - Police
Supt N Thornton - Police
Supt A Charlesworth - Police
Inspector J T Coates - Police
Inspector J Jones - Police
PC Womersley - Police
PC Pinder - Police
PC Watson - Police
County Councillor F I Pennington - WYMCC
County Councillor W Jenkins - WYMCC
County Councillor J Schofield - WYMCC
County Councillor W Sykes - WYMCC
Mr A Warden - CEC's Department, WYMCC
Mr R Woodlock - CEC's Department, WYMCC
Councillor Mrs M Brown, JP - Upton and North Elmsall PC
Mr A E Winter - South Kirkby and Moorthorpe Town Council
Councillor K Millett - Wakefield MDC
Mr P Andrews - Nostell Parish Council
M Jolly - Carnegie Centre
Mrs G Brown - Pontefract AHA
Mr T Ballance - Probation
W Stones - South Elmsall Town Council
M Pepper - Thorpe Audlin Parish Council
Police Sergeant Robinson - Police Federation
Mrs E Goodwin - South Elmsall CAB
T Watson - Featherstone High School
J R Ellis - Badsworth Parish Council

R T Lagden - East Hardwick Parish Council
K Kerslake - Cobblers Lane Community Association
Mr F Young - TGWU
Mr R Hirst
Mr D Cawdron
Mrs Enright
(together with 6 representatives of the media and 8 members of the public).

1. The Chairman welcomed all representatives to the special meeting and outlined the reason why it was convened. He referred to the Terms of Reference of the Forum which empowered him to convene a special meeting in circumstances which warranted it. He explained that Police Community Forums had been established throughout the country following the problems at Brixton and Chapeltown as referred to in the Scarman Report. With that in mind and in view of the tension and unrest within the Hemsworth area over recent weeks he considered it was essential that members should have an opportunity of discussing the issues involved with the Police.

2. Apologies were received from Mr A Woodall MP, Mr G Lofthouse MP, Mr M Calvert, Area Youth Service and Mrs J Megson, Carleton High School.

3. At the invitation of the Chairman, Ch Supt McQuoid explained the Police role both prior to, during, and after the recent disturbances and pointed out that the Chief Constable had discussed the problems in the Hemsworth area with the Chairman and Vice-Chairman of the West Yorkshire Police Authority and also with Mr Alec Woodall MP and Councillor Gerald Andrews of Fitzwilliam. The Chief Constable had walked the streets of Hemsworth from 11pm to 1am on Saturday night and had spent some time talking about the problems with local residents. A meeting had been held on Sunday afternoon between the Police and a wide cross-section of the public and their representatives. The Chief Constable intended to have further meetings and discussions and the whole matter would be reported to the Police Authority on the 25 July. If complaints were made about Police Officers these would be dealt with in accordance with the Police Act 1964. In the meantime, the

Chief Constable had asked that everyone should be prepared to work together and co-operate in restoring normality to the area.

4. The Chief Constable's policing strategy was referred to and in particular the objective to police local communities with local officers with a policy of 'see and be seen'. This involved improved crime prevention, attempts to reduce burglary and street offences by an increased foot patrol police presence. He explained further that in the event of serious crime and outbreaks of disorder the Chief Constable had to vary his policing methods by way of response. Reference was made to the miners' dispute and the successful approach which had been adopted by low-key policing methods brought about by a policy of consultation and dialogue.

5. Ch Supt McQuoid pointed out that the situation in West Yorkshire was different from that of other areas. In this area there were no miners crossing miners' picket lines. The following incidents were identified where this low-key approach had proved successful:- 23 March - South Kirkby - Funeral of David Jones - 5000 mourners; 14 Police officers used for traffic control; 2 April - picket of Wakefield Power Station. Chief Constable attended personally and discussed matters with pickets; 9 May - picket at Horbury - 5 police officers attended; 16 June - Wakefield Miners Gala - 30,000/35,000 people: 70 PCs in two shifts; 27 June - Funeral of Joseph Green - 10,000 mourners: 6 Police women and traffic wardens used for traffic control; 4 July - Incident at South Kirkby Colliery - defused by Divisional officer; 9 July - picket at South Kirkby and Frickley Collieries defused by ACC Operations.

6. He explained that other incidents had heightened the tension in the area and he drew certain conclusions from the following incidents e.g. the reaction following the fatal accident involving Joseph Green at Ferrybridge Power Station; windows of a Police Station in the South Yorkshire area broken and similar damage caused the following day; on the 17 June an incident at Fitzwilliam involving a crowd of 30-40 persons when local police had to withdraw; on the 18 June anti-Police slogans found painted at three locations in Featherstone; 23, 29 and 31 June - further incidents at Police Stations in South Yorkshire; On the 1 July an attack on a Police Constable's house at Fitzwilliam; on 4 July

an incident at Kinsley drift mine; on 5 July a Police house damaged at Wakefield; on 9 July an incident involving the besieging of Rossington pit.

7. Ch Supt McQuoid pointed out that arrests had been made arising from the incidents in the Fitzwilliam and Hemsworth areas and explained that he was unable to comment on them because of the sub-judice rule and the contempt of court legislation as the cases were set down for hearing at court. He commented on the conflicting views arising from these incidents and pointed out that the task for this evening's meeting should be one of trying to ensure there was no repetition. He then introduced Inspector Jones as the Inspector for the Hemsworth area and Constables Womersley, Pinder and Watson.

8. The Chairman thanked Ch Supt McQuoid for his introduction and asked the meeting if they had any points to raise or questions to ask.

9. Mr Winter said that the meeting could sit and talk about the problems all night but if the Police were constrained by the sub-judice rule then nothing much could be done. He had visited the Fitzwilliam area and talked to the public. There were conflicting reports and the incidents would take a long time to settle down. Replying, the Chairman explained the object of the meeting was to look to the future; any looking back should be in general terms of why the happenings took place.

10. Councillor Millett pointed out that all the information he had received was second hand but asked if it was normal practice for the Police to enter a pub in the way recently reported in the press, and were the incidents dealt with at local level?

11. Ch Supt McQuoid stated that on the 9 July there were four separate incidents:- at Hemsworth Police Station, Fitzwilliam Hotel, and Kinsley Drift Mine (twice). Only West Yorkshire Police were involved; at no time were officers outside West Yorkshire involved. He said that if anyone had any information about these incidents he would be pleased if they would make that information available as potential witnesses.

12. Mr Evans asked why Fitzwilliam was surrounded by Police vans on Monday afternoon and Police vehicles with tannoys driving around the area and taunting people?

13. Ch Supt McQuoid answered and said that vans had not surrounded Fitzwilliam as stated and there were no public address equipment fitted to police transit vans.

    Note At this point in the meeting a photograph was taken by a press representative from 'Mail on Sunday'. County Councillor Sykes commented on the harm which could ensue from bad press publicity. The Chairman censured the photographer and although a vote was requested as to the taking of photographs during the meeting, it was not proceeded with on an undertaking given by the photographer not to take any more.

14. Roy Hirst asked what the Police priorities were - dealing with pickets or fighting crime?

15. Ch Supt McQuoid stated that the Police were in a 'Catch 22' situation. The Chief Constable was charged with maintaining law and order, whether it was on the picket line or in the streets. So far as the mineworkers' strike was concerned, this had been policed in this Force area by consultation and co-operation as he had explained earlier.

16. Roy Hirst commented that in the past there was a good relationship with the local Police but that this wasn't evident at present. Ch Supt McQuoid said the increase in staff for the area might now resolve this.

17. County Councillor Jenkins said that as a community representative he had never been invited to consultations with the Police over these issues. He said he was saddened that Hemsworth had been drawn into violence. Rumour and frustration was now rife. He outlined social and environmental problems of the area, the effects of the miners' strike, and described the result as a time-bomb waiting to go off. He said violence could never be condoned and he felt the events of Tuesday 10th and Friday 13th had been created by opportunists. He concluded by saying the Forum was no substitute for a fully frank and fearless

discussion involving an independent body. He was concerned the Police would be judge, jury and witnesses to events. He then posed a number of questions:- e.g.

(a) Why was Police presence heightened throughout 9 July?

(b) Why was an undertaking given to a certain individual then withdrawn - and on whose orders?

(c) Why were there Police taunts from vans indicating the Police were going to get that individual?

(d) How many Police entered Fitzwilliam Hotel - on whose orders?

(e) Why did those officers wear 'riot gear'?

(f) Was it usual for Police to inflict violence and damage in public houses?

(g) Was it usual for the Police to surround the houses of old aged people?

(h) Was it usual for Police to use 8 officers for the arrest of 2 people?

(i) Was it usual for the Police to use foul language? (he had personal knowledge of such an incident).

(j) Why were elected members told on Friday 13th that operations would be low-key and yet virtually every road contained Police officers that evening and press representatives were stopped on their way into Hemsworth?

(k) Why did Police chase a group of youths along Barnsley Road?

He maintained that errors of judgement had been made and the Chief Constable's policing policy was open to question. In saying this, however, Councillor Jenkins paid tribute to the sterling work and efforts of PC Womersley.

18. Ch Supt McQuoid stated that an inquiry was being undertaken into all aspects of the incidents, asked Councillor Jenkins to supply names and addresses of witnesses; and reminded him of opportunities afforded to make complaints about the actions of specific Police officers.

19. County Councillor Best asked County Councillor Jenkins to let him have a copy of his statement at the meeting (and his questions) for consideration by the Police Authority.

20. Mrs W Goodwin said that 8 Officers were alleged to have been sent to arrest a man at Fitzwilliam where rowdy scenes had developed and asked if this could have been the spark which had triggered off the incidents? She stated that provocation by the present Government made the future appear bleak - the Police were in a cleft stick and civil strife was in the air.

21. Gwyneth Brown agreed that the Police were being used as scapegoats.

22. Mrs Brown was concerned at the relatively few people present at the meeting and stressed the need for publicity.

23. The Chairman commented on his right to convene a special meeting for a special purpose. This meeting had been called, albeit at short notice, for the reasons which were self-evident and he wanted it before the Police Authority meeting on 25 July 1984.

24. Councillor Andrews expressed sympathy with genuine miners but pointed out the trouble was being caused by young and left-wing miners. He said that 'Arthur's mob' should be removed and that respect for law and order was needed. The Chairman ruled out of order any reference to Arthur Scargill.

25. Bill Stones said that the Police were not angels. Young people from this area had been at Orgreave - how could they return here and have respect for the Police when they had witnessed the events at Orgreave? There should be more understanding and less force on the part of the

Police. The Chairman agreed with these sentiments but stated he could not comment on policing in other Force areas.

26. Dave Cawdron, as a general observation, said that the concern should not be with the past but, where should we go from here with young people? The youngsters were enjoying the recent outbreaks of trouble. Their Youth Club was now the Blue Bell. Public and Police must work hand in hand to achieve reconciliation. The Chairman looked earnestly towards getting back to normality.

27. Michael Jolly supported the comments of Dave Cawdron. He envisaged an increase in minority activities, more vandalism etc. as a result of closing youth clubs.

28. Ch Supt McQuoid said that the West Yorkshire Police prided themselves on community relationships. There must be dialogue about the future - links needed cementing and community leaders must do their bit to help reconciliation.

29. Councillor Millett pointed out that strikes were not new. In the strikes of 1972 and 1974 friendships had been formed. The situation in 1984 was very different, particularly in the attitudes of policing. He pointed out that he was Chairman of the District Council Planning Committee and was concerned about the high unemployment situation in Hemsworth. He pointed out, however, that 3 local areas had been granted enterprise zone status and that further improvements were planned in the area. He was concerned however, that because of the recent problems this could be seen as a deterrent to developers. Allegations made during the meeting would have to be investigated. He asked where do we go from here and is the tension receding?

30. Ch Supt McQuoid said that there was indeed an element of tension on Saturday night but that the discussions held on the Sunday and Monday had helped considerably in easing it. However, he was still of the opinion that there were some people intent on causing trouble and he appealed to all members to dispel rumour and speculation.

31. One member expressed his sorrow for the Community Constables. He said that the Police brought in from outside the Hemsworth area had made it difficult for them. These outsiders would not always be in the area and the Community Constables would have to bear the brunt of any acrimony.

32. Ch Supt McQuoid referred again to Hemsworth Police Station being under siege and the incidents at Kinsley drift mine. The Chairman commented that if people were sufficiently incensed about Police behaviour then they should certainly complain.

33. County Councillor Best gave a resume of the Police complaints procedure and the role of the Police Authority's Complaints Sub-Committee which was totally honest and able to scrutinise and consider in depth any complaint.

34. Ch Supt McQuoid said that rumour and speculation created tension and that people with definite information should be encouraged to provide it.

35. Mrs Brown asked how the police were covering the rest of the community and was crime increasing? The Chairman pointed out that policing was being carried out with a degree of difficulty because of several factors including the Government cut-backs.

36. Ch Supt McQuoid said that there was indeed an increase in crime though this was not peculiar to the Hemsworth area - this was over the country as a whole. He also pointed out that the Chief Constable was in the process of reviewing the whole of the future needs of West Yorkshire with the Police Authority and that an analysis would be completed within 12 months.

37. Councillor Sykes referred to the outstanding qualities of the Chief Constable and said we should appreciate what he is doing for the community. He was sure that he would be as much distressed by the troubles in Hemsworth as anyone else. He felt that as responsible citizens everyone should try to defuse the present situation. He highlighted one particular problem at Frickley Colliery which had been

satisfactorily defused by the Police with the use of tact and diplomacy. He pointed out that it was not the man in the street who had created the incident at Frickley but management who had over-reacted to a situation. It was for us all to work together to defuse the present situation with the new Inspector appointed for the area.

38. The Chairman said that he would give serious thought to the holding of another special meeting to follow up this one.

39. Councillor Best referred to problems which had occurred in the Chapeltown area of Leeds in 1981, following which Leeds City Council had set up a community based committee to discuss local problems e.g. social, educational, housing, environmental, community need, etc.

40. Mrs Brown asked if the Chief Constable's report would be made public and Councillor Best said that it was likely that it would be heard by the Police Authority in private but assured her that it would be considered in depth.

41. Mrs Enright said that Councillor Best's suggestion for a community based committee could, perhaps, be more appropriately dealt with by the Hemsworth Town Council and Councillor Jenkins undertook to refer the matter to that Council.

42. The Chairman, in concluding, thanked everyone for attending the meeting and echoed the sentiments for a return to normality and a speedy end to the miners' strike.

Appendix 5: MAIN SUCCESSOR COMPANIES OF BRITISH COAL

RJB Mining
Harworth Park,
Blyth Road,
Harworth,
Doncaster,
DN11 8DB

Celtic Energy Limited,
Farm Road,
Aberamen,
Aberdare,
Mid Glamorgan,
CF44 6LX.

The Scottish Coal Company,
160, Glasgow Road,
Corstorphine,
Edinburgh,
EH12 8LT.

Coal Investments plc,
2, Savoy Court,
Strand,
London,
WC2R OEZ.

Licensing Authority:

The Coal Authority,
200, Lichfield Lane,
Mansfield,
Nottinghamshire,
NG18 4RG.

(Source: British Coal Headquarters).

Appendix 6: INCIDENCE OF DIVORCE: STATISTICS RELATE TO PONTEFRACT COUNTY COURT

	1987	1988	1989	1990	1991	1992	1993	1994 JAN-MAY
DIVORCE								
PET. FILED	780	764	750	725	702	768	739	302
DEC.NIS	695	657	635	631	568	608	639	299
DEC.ABS	692	638	632	611	625	553	625	249
NULLITY								
PET.FILED	4		1		1	1		1
DEC.NIS	1				1		1	
DEC.ABS	2	1	1	1			1	
J/SEPARATION								
PET.FILED	23	14	8	10	10	16	14	6
DEC.NIS	9	8	3	4	1	14	9	3

SOURCE: THE LORD CHANCELLOR'S DEPARTMENT